CREATING A STORM:
JEWISH WOMEN IN THE ARTS

To my husband Ivor Seddon for his overwhelming love, kindness and support and to my daughters Sophia and Anya Broido who have followed their passions and are determined and independent women.

Creating A Storm:
Jewish Women In The Arts

Dr ISABELLE SEDDON

With Editorial Additions By
Jennifer Craig-Norton

VALLENTINE MITCHELL
LONDON · CHICAGO

First published in 2025 by Vallentine Mitchell

<table>
<tr><td>Catalyst House,
720 Centennial Court,
Centennial Park, Elstree WD6 3SY, UK</td><td>814 N. Franklin Street,
Chicago, Illinois,
IL 60610 USA</td></tr>
</table>

www.vmbooks.com

British Library Cataloguing in Publication Data:
An entry can be found on request

ISBN 978 1 80371 068 6 (Paperback)
ISBN 978 1 80371 069 3 (Ebook)
ISBN 978 1 80371 070 9 (Kindle)

Library of Congress Cataloging in Publication Data:
An entry can be found on request

Contents

Acknowledgements

With utmost gratitude to Professor Tony Kushner for his unbelievable encouragement, support and tremendous patience. He is truly inspirational.

My appreciation goes to Jennifer Craig-Norton for her invaluable and generous input.

My thanks also to Toby Harris, Sue Garfield and Jenni Tinson at Vallentine Mitchell for their guidance.

Foreword

By Dame Maureen Lipman DBE

This fascinating book is a companion piece to Isabelle Seddon's well received book, Intrepid Pioneers, in which we learned about Jewish women in the public arena. Women who have given so much of their skill and erudition to the worlds of science, medicine and political life.

In this book she has unearthed, as Mel Brooks once, memorably, said - 'the great and the near great.' I count myself in the second category but have been thrilled and delighted to discover brilliant women whose achievements I hadn't known about and to read fresh details about women I thought I knew.

Seddon divides her book into tranches, representing the Arts, Sport, Music and the written word. The latter has of course always been open to the 'housewife and mother at home. One fitted it in between pie making, scrubbing't' front steps or supervising servants, didn't one?

In the Arts section we learn much about the chauvinism and misogyny of the male dominated world of Art, where - *'After much debate and petitioning the Royal Academy agreed to provide life classes for "the study of the partially draped figure" to female students. Even then it was ten years before women were actually admitted to these classes.'*

Small wonder that a number of female artists dressed as men, smoked cigars like men and painted and partied with the boldness of their male contemporaries. Women like "Gluck", (no prefix, no suffix, or quotes) the alias of Hannah Gluckstein, the daughter of one of the founders of Lyons Corner House, who was as notorious for her affair with flower arranging expert Constance Spry and various actresses as she was for her painting.

The section on cookery writers is resplendent with female stars from nineteenth century Judith Montefiore, wife of Moses, and Florence Greenberg, whose much spattered pages are still yanked out by me every Passover, to check for the sixtieth time how to make Charoseth, through to the innovative Evelyn Rose and all the way to our very own and golden

Nigella, who was also a Gluckstein descendant. Combining family, tradition, love of eating, a businesswoman's brain and fluid prose seems almost inevitable to our ethnic evolution.

I particularly enjoyed the singers and musicians, from Myra Hess to Amy Winehouse. Both had a ribald sense of humour and the devil in their make-up, Hess once playing Chopin at an Embassy party with an orange in the palm of her hand. Amy's sardonic take on life and her bittersweet minor chord music stemmed from a fairly traditional, London Jewish upbringing. Alma Cogan, who died at the height of her fame, and was a national treasure beloved by Jews and non-Jews alike and Helen Shapiro, whose faith rebounded her into a fervent belief in a Messianic prophet which she believes, Judaism has failed to recognise.

I also learned, with some glee, that when Queen Mary met concert pianist Marion Stein, who would shortly marry her son the Earl of Harewood, she cried; *"Not only Jewish … she doesn't hunt."*

You perhaps wouldn't think the chapter on Jewish sportswomen would yield such splendid nuggets but that was almost my favourite chapter and source of revelations. Dorothy Levitt, sponsored and encouraged by her lover, raced cars at 80 miles per hour in the nineteen twenties wearing eye-catching motoring outfits and clutching her Pomeranian dog Dodo which yapped ferociously at all the other competitors.

Sheila van Damm was a familiar name to me as the owner of the fabled Windmill Theatre, but I needed reminding that she was also a dare devil behind the wheel of a racing car. In another era her logo could have read - "they're naked and she moves!"

Much admiration goes to the tennis player Angela Buxton (Bakstansky) 1934-2020, although I may take issue with the phrase - *"One of the greatest Jewish tennis players of all time,"* on the grounds that it is rather like saying 'one of the greatest Seventh Day Adventist Roman blind-makers of all time. Angela was the child of a stereotypical Jewish businessman who evacuated his family to South Africa at the start of the war. This is where she encountered prejudice and developed the fervent anti-racism which coloured – no pun intended- her professional life. She befriended and supported the black tennis player Althea Gibson with whom she won the women's doubles at Wimbledon in 1956, when both were shunned by the All-England Lawn Tennis Association. She seems to me to personify the best of our defiance in the face of the prejudice which has dogged, repressed and perhaps seeded our creativity for four thousand years.

In my own category I would have given a massive space to Tracey Ullman as the most successful international actress of us all. And a devastating actress. Oddly she is less recognised in her own country than the controversial Miriam Margolyes.

What fascinates is how much or how little the cast of creative Jewish women acknowledge or ignore the value of their race and nurture on their work. From that point of view alone this compilation is a delight.

Jewish women weigh-in hard when we have to and frequently **punch** well above our weight and that is my **punch**-line for this book.

Introduction

Overall the twentieth century was a time of great change for women in Britain. Through education, job opportunities and in personal relationships, new possibilities emerged in the nineteenth century, and the twentieth century saw extraordinary progress. But against that backdrop was their struggle to challenge the conventions imposed upon them by a patriarchal society. Within this restraining context, Jewish women faced particular problems – and opportunities. How they performed their 'Jewishness' in the public sphere is the question that this book will confront, exploring a wide range of cultural outputs and expression.

It was in the arts and performance especially that women made great strides, including those of a variety of Jewish backgrounds. This introduction focuses on the world of Jewish women's self-representation. A brief coverage of Jewish women in theatre and literature in the Victorian era will introduce this book's wider analysis of British Jewish women in the worlds of writing, music, drama, art and leisure. The following chapters will highlight their achievements in the cultural world and look at how their Jewish history and background impacted and contributed to their success.

The first chapter focuses on Jewish actresses and profiles their careers over a century from the days of the Yiddish theatre and explores their roles on stage and screen and the challenges they faced as Jewish women in this world. In the Victorian era, theatre was largely a male domain. The few exceptional women who managed to break through on and off stage held a unique position within society. At a time when women were barred from pursuing an education or occupation, being a performer offered a change to carve out independence and power. And, despite being denied the same rights and status given to men, those that were successful were able to use the position earned through their talents to challenge traditional Victorian perceptions of femininity and bring about social and political change.

Victorian theatre stars found their voices and artistic freedom through acting, creating bold female characters on stage. Outside the theatre, in the music halls, female performers from the working classes played up to the male gaze but also subverted it, overcoming misogyny and sexism to advocate for women's rights. They engaged in industrial action, contributing to the wider fight for women's equality and freedom.[1]

Beginning in the nineteenth century, acting provided independent women a space in the public sphere, and Jewish women were among those who chose to pursue this profession as a career. For the first generation of aspiring Jewish actresses, the Yiddish theatre provided an acceptable venue for their ambitions, and they were wholly embraced by audiences, playing both Jewish and non-Jewish roles. Unlike French actor Sarah Bernhardt (1844-1923)[2] who became one of the best known figures in the history of the stage and was applauded throughout Europe and America, none of these earlier actresses achieved widespread fame nor did they cross over to the English stage, but as the Yiddish theatre scene declined after the interwar period, subsequent generations of Jewish actresses were able to establish successful careers in mainstream theatre, films and television. Several generations of actors are featured in this volume beginning with those born in the interwar and early Second World War period - - Miriam Karlin, Fenella Fielding, Claire Bloom, Eleanor Bron and Miriam Margolyes – all of whom contended with the gendered stereotype of the 'English Rose' which sharply curtailed the range of roles offered to those with unconventional looks and with few exceptions tended to limit their roles to comedic and Jewish ones. The issue of Jewishness also affected the careers of those born after the Second World War – Maureen Lipman, Tracy-Ann Oberman and Sophie Okonedo – though in different ways than the previous generation had dealt with. For all these women, looking or being 'too Jewish' (or not Jewish enough) was a key factor in their acting careers.

It was during the Victorian period that British Jewish women began to enter the field of writing. They became the first Jewish women in the world to publish novels, histories, periodicals, theological tracts and conduct manuals. Their romances, some of them which sold as well as novels by Dickens, argued for the emancipation of Jews in Britain and women's emancipation in the Jewish world. 'These texts served as emblems of Jews' desire to become acculturated to modern English life while simultaneously maintaining a distinct collective identity'.[3]

Stories about Jewesses proliferated in nineteenth century Britain as debates about the place of the Jews in the nation took place. Nadia Valman's *The Jewess in Nineteenth-Century British Literary Culture* presents a reassessment of this literature with a focus on Jewish women's role in a wide range of literary texts. It engages with the figure of the Jewess as the embodiment of virtue and sacrifice and reveals how hostility towards Jews was accompanied by pity, identification and desire.[4] Valman's argument is that British writers regarded Jews with 'desire and pity' as well as 'fear and loathing' and that the splitting of Jew into masculine and feminine types enabled them to express ambivalent and even contradictory sentiments that reviled but also redeemed the Jew.[5]

Valman looks at the way in which cultural shifts over the century altered the woman's question, the Jewish question and their relation to one another. She begins by pointing out traditional approaches to the figure of 'the Jew' have taken for granted the masculinity of their subject. In contrast, her study places the gendered subject at the centre of discussions of Jewish ambivalence. She shows that the texts in this period emphasised on the one hand, the dangerous carnality of the Jewish woman, and on the other her exceptional spirituality and amenability to restoration, conversion or radical assimilation. She exposes the rich interplay between the woman question and the Jewish question. Jewish questions were discursively intertwined with, or echoed, woman questions. She shows two dominant examples for the nineteenth century's figure of the Jewess. The first focuses on Walter Scott's *Ivanhoe* (1819) which Valman considers the century's most influential novel about a Jewess.[6] Valman argues that the Jewess herself could embody conflicting themes of purity and carnality and she gives as evidence the eroticization of Rebecca. She is 'endowed with knowledge as with beauty' and generous and good to the poor and 'loyal to the faith of her fathers'.[7]

The book influenced two Victorian texts: Augustin Daly's melodrama *Leah, the Forsaken* (1862)[8] and Anthony Trollope's *Nina Balatka* (1867).[9] Valman maintains that in these works the figure of the Jewess was a symbol for the Jews' potential for virtue, which could be released and harnessed by the modern state if only it and its citizens were freed from outdated prejudice. At the same time, however, the Jewess is imagined to be thoroughly embodied, the 'carnal Jewess', who stands for 'the peril of uncontrolled passion'.[10] Thus in this first example of the Jewess, Valman shows how the figure of the Jewess 'both embodied the liberal case with her pathos and undermined it with her passion'.[11]

Valman also examines popular Evangelical writing from the 1820s-1840s by women who wrote for a predominantly female Christian audience and focused on Jewesses who, unlike Ivanhoe's Rebecca, are depicted as wanting to convert to Christianity. Valman argues that many women readers were swayed by the Evangelical rhetoric that called for action to protect the moral wellbeing of other women, understood to be their sisters. Jewish women were therefore represented as needed to be saved from their 'uncivilized' Jewish community by their Evangelical sisters.[12] In contrast Valman illustrates how the first generation of Jewish women writers in England countered their Evangelical sister authors with anti-conversion rhetoric. Published against the background of the political debates about Jewish emancipation, these writers used the form of and language of popular non-Jewish women's fiction in their demand for Jewish equality. For Grace Aguilar, domestic fiction provided the moral language and narrative framework into which Jews could be inserted. Her vision of the Jewish woman as a pious Bible reading martyr could speak powerfully to Protestant woman readers. Her work was seen as evidence of the Jews increasing refinement and acculturation. In contrast Celia and Marion Moss engaged with the political debate by invoking a Jewish history of persecution and linking the demand for contemporary Jewish civil rights with the campaign to abolish slavery. All these novelists' writings were ways to lay claim to an identity as English that was compatible with Jewish rights.[13]

These earlier writers laid a foundation for the seven women writers included in this volume. Though they hailed from across the UK, varied in their educational and religious backgrounds, and wrote in a variety of genres, they share much in common. Writing across the twentieth and twenty-first centuries, their novels vary widely in settings and plot and include both explicitly Jewish and entirely non-Jewish characters and themes. Yet a number of common themes predominate in their work, especially those that focus on problematic identities and difficulties with belonging – all tied to their own identities as Jewish women born and growing up in Great Britain.

Beginning with the late Victorian era novelist Naomi Jacob, the daughter of a mixed marriage who embraced the Jewish identity of her father and wrote extensively on Jewish subjects, though through the lens of Jewish stereotypes of her day, the chapter continues with Gerda Charles, Bernice Rubens and Anita Brookner, all born prior to the Second World War and who explored themes of Jewish 'otherness'. The post-war writers featured herein – Linda Grant, Naomi Alderman and Charlotte Mendelson – felt liberated from the immigrant and outsider themes their predecessors dwelt on and focused their gazes on sexuality, gender and Jewish life in a post-Holocaust world.

The next two chapters focus on music. The changing entertainment tastes of the post-Second World War era and the exchange of new musical influences between Britain and the United States heralded a wave of female singing stars, among whom were a notable number of British Jewish women. Although the six vocal artists profiled in this chapter span almost eight decades and represent a wide range of musical styles and genres, they share some striking similarities in background, connections to their religious heritage, pioneering musical careers and personal and professional challenges. Alma Cogan, who was born before the Second World War, rose to a pinnacle of fame in the 1950s before her untimely death in 1966, while the musical careers of Helen Shapiro, Elkie Brooks, and Pauline Black, all born in the post-war period, were deeply influenced by the explosion of new musical genres of the 1960s and 1970s. Amy Winehouse and Jessie Ware came to prominence in the twenty-first century, pioneering new musical forms and mastering fame in the era of the internet and social media.

In the world of classical music prior to the twentieth century, female classical musicians had a struggle to be accepted in a professional capacity as it was considered immodest for women to perform music in public. The private sphere of the home allowed women to perform as singers and pianists and British Jewish women conformed to that pattern, especially as they linked the piano as a totally respectable piece of Victorian and later domestic furniture. It is therefore not surprising that the two pianists featured in this book, Myra Hess and Fanny Waterman, born in the late nineteenth and early twentieth centuries respectively, became icons in the musical world. The third musician, Natalie Clein, came of age in the late twentieth century and benefitted from the expansion of women's roles in public and artistic spheres, becoming a renowned cellist. These musicians' careers were deeply impacted by the Second World War, which affected their roles as professional musicians, and the Holocaust provided inspiration and meaning to their post-war musical undertakings.

The final section will look at the success achieved in the fields of art and leisure. Western art before the twentieth century was dominated by male artists. Women artists have historically struggled to have their work recognised and they were often hampered by societal expectation, a difficulty accessing artistic training and a lack of financial independence. Jewish women artists faced all these obstacles, but the three profiled in this book each overcame them in her own way. Victorian era artist Rebecca Solomon found some success with the Pre-Raphaelites, whose artistic styles and interests in social reform corresponded with hers. Hannah Gluckstein reaped the benefits of greater freedoms for women and enjoyed a brief period of artistic success in the 1920s and 1930s, while pursuing an unconventional private life, dressing androgynously and taking a series of female lovers. Jewish life and history has animated Rachel Lichtenstein, a contemporary artist, sculptor, teacher and historian whose work focuses on Jewish place, identity and memory.

Like art, an area of British life not usually associated with the Jewish community is sports. It is therefore impressive that the three Jewish women featured in this chapter made headline news in their sporting fields: Dorothy Levitt and Sheila van Damm, who were pioneers in female motor racing and Angela Buxton in the world of tennis.

The chapter on cookery demonstrates how Jewish cooks helped bring Jewish cuisine and Jewish cultural approaches to meals and the sharing of food to wider audiences in Britain and beyond. The first Anglo-Jewish cookery book *The Jewish Manual,* attributed to Judith Montefiore, was published in 1846 and fused Jewish cookery with the sensibilities of upper middle class Victorian dining. In the 1930s and 1940s, Florence Greenberg brought Jewish cookery to the masses through her cookbooks, newspaper columns and BBC programmes. After the Second World War, Jewish food writers such as Evelyn Rose brought Jewish food to the wider British public and Jewish food, both Ashkenazi[14] eastern- and Sephardi[15] entered the mainstream. It paved the way for Nigella Lawson to emerge as a global food personality.

The issue of gender links the experiences of all of the women featured in this volume, across their varied cultural outputs and contributions from acting to musicianship, writing to art, sport to cookery. In addition, themes related to Jewishness, social status, education and cross-cultural heritages unite these women's lives and careers. Historical Jewish persecution, including the Holocaust, is one of the factors that ties many of these highly accomplished women together, which, along with the legacies of immigrant and refugee backgrounds, motivated and inspired them to make their mark in British culture.

1

Theatre

Beginning in the nineteenth century, acting provided independent women a space in the public sphere, and Jewish women were among those who chose to pursue acting as a career. For the first generation of aspiring Jewish actresses, the Yiddish theatre provided an acceptable venue for their ambitions, and they were wholly embraced by audiences, playing both Jewish and non-Jewish roles. Unlike Sarah Bernhardt, none of these earlier actresses achieved widespread fame nor did they cross over to the English stage, but as the Yiddish theatre scene declined after the interwar period, subsequent generations of Jewish actresses were able to establish successful careers in British theatre, films and television.

This chapter profiles over a century of Jewish actresses, exploring their roles on stage and screen, the part that Jewishness played in their private and public lives, their political involvement with left-wing and Jewish causes, and the challenges they faced as Jewish women in the cultural milieu of British theatre, film and television. Many of these women felt they were typecast into distinctly Jewish and/or comic roles, or as character actors who were rarely offered meatier roles. Perceptions about their appearance and their Jewish identity also affected their careers and the roles they were offered.

That Jewish actresses have long confronted such prejudices is evidenced by the career of Sarah Bernhardt (1844-1923), known as 'The Divine Sarah', who dominated the theatrical scenes of both Europe and America for over half a century. Although not British, any study of Jewish women and theatre must begin with Bernhardt, who became one of the first great 'stars' of the world stage. Considered one of the greatest actors of all time, she overcame vicious antisemitism early in her career, achieving worldwide celebrity based not only on her talent, but her larger-than-life personality and extravagant lifestyle.

Sarah Bernhardt was born Henriette-Rosine Bernard to the Dutch Jewish courtesan Julie Bernard, daughter of oculist and small-time crook Maurice Bernard and Jeannette Hart. Bernhardt did not know her father, a Parisian who never married her mother, a woman who had little time or inclination to raise a child in the social whirl of the Paris salon set. She was sent to an Augustine convent near Versailles and then studied acting in the Paris Conservatoire. At the Conservatoire she learnt about the acting tradition of an earlier student, the French Jewish actress Rachel Felix, known by her first name Rachel, who became a celebrity in Paris and London.[1] Bernhardt kept a portrait of Rachel in her drawing room and chose to adopt the stage name Sarah.

Bernhardt debuted professionally in 1862 and built a reputation as a versatile actress with an expressive voice and poetic gestures. She used to sleep in a coffin because it helped her to prepare for tragic roles. Throughout the 1880s and 1890s she bought a series of French theatres to produce modern experimental plays while touring Europe, the United States, Latin America and Canada. She reinvented herself as a public icon, allowing the romances and tragedies of her stage heroines to reflect her own life. She intrigued and scandalized society. She became a household name for her femme-fatale roles such as Cleopatra, as well as for her overall unsurpassed talent. She inspired much commentary in the media – from positive coverage to criticism and caricature, some of it racist, sexist and antisemitic. These developments converged to make Bernhardt a pioneer of modern celebrity.

Professor Sharon Marcus comments that Bernhardt was able to select her own roles. 'A type of persona, a femme fatale, that was very strong willed, very sexual, filled with desire, determined to have her own way'. Marcus points out that what comes through is her incredible technical control, her facial expressions, her voice, the full range of her body. As a lot of male and female actors were quite stiff in Bernhardt's day, people who saw her on stage were hypnotized and mesmerized by her.[2]

Bernhardt never tried to conceal or deny her Jewish origins, despite being baptized as a Catholic just before her twelfth birthday. Yet she not only considered herself Jewish but asserted her pride in her Jewishness, despite the difficulties it created. Formal religion was more an afterthought in her life than a central concern. Jewishness was a matter of race, not belief.[3] In 1880 when Bernhardt was a superstar there was a notable increase in antisemitism in France. There were concerns that her mother was Jewish. Caricaturists exaggerated her curly hair, her profile, her nose, claiming that she was venal, greedy and cared just about money. Marcus says that there was a relentless need to belittle her fame. There were also negative comments about her thin appearance and that she had a child out of wedlock.[4] When after the Franco-Prussian war she was accused of being German and Jewish in the press, she was reported to have responded 'Jewish most certainly, but German, no. If I have a foreign accent – which I much regret – it is cosmopolitan, but not Teutonic. I am a daughter of the great Jewish race, and my somewhat uncultivated language is the outcome of our enforced wanderings'.[5] Although publicly identified, and maligned, as a Jew through the first decades of her career, she eventually escaped the specifics of her personal history to become an icon so that by the 1890s the public apparently didn't find it anomalous or blasphemous that this scandalous 'Jewess' was impersonating Joan of Arc.[6]

Bernhardt played at least 70 roles in 125 plays over the course of her career, both female and male and played 19-year-old Joan of Arc when she was 46. Most popular were her dramatic death scenes. She continued to tour the world late in life. After an accident, which resulted in her right leg being amputated, she still performed on stage as well as for the troops on the battlefront during the First World War. She did not use a prosthetic limb, instead relying upon strategically placed set pieces as she moved across the stage or was carried on a satin sedan chair. Many consider her the most famous actress the world has ever known. When she died, a million people lined the streets of Paris as her coffin made its way to the cemetery.[7] Bernhardt was one of the earliest celebrities.

There was no equivalent to Sarah Bernhardt in the British theatre scene of the late nineteenth and early twentieth centuries. Instead, Jewish women who aspired to careers on stage were primarily involved in the Yiddish theatre. The Yiddish theatre in London was a theatre created by and for the Jewish immigrants from Eastern Europe who crowded into the narrow streets of London's East End. A rich Yiddish cultural life blossomed together with an increasingly enthusiastic audience for Yiddish theatre, the main form of entertainment for the immigrant working-class. Yiddish was the mother tongue of the vast majority of Eastern European Jewry and was the language spoken in the home and the workplace in contrast to Hebrew, the language of prayer. It is a richly expressive language based on medieval German but interspersed with Hebrew, Russian and Polish words and was a medium for a rich and varied folk culture.

The first professional Yiddish actors, Jacob Adler and his company, arrived in London in 1883 from Riga. They performed lightweight musical comedies, folk operas of Goldfaden[8], melodramas of Shomer[9] and nineteenth century dramas in translation. They opened a theatre in Princes Street and young men and women vied for places in the chorus, attracted by the glamour of the theatre. The early decades of the twentieth century were the heyday of the Yiddish theatre in London. During this period there was hardly a large room or hall in the East End which was not used at some point as a venue for Yiddish plays. Plays ranged from provocative and political new writing to folkloric tales and Yiddish translations of classics including Shakespeare, Strindberg, Ibsen and Gorky.[10]

Immigrant women played a role in the development of the Yiddish theatre in the East End and were a key part of the Yiddish theatre's appeal, whether as chorus girls, music hall singers, actresses or running their own theatre companies. Talented, independent and unconventional, their personal lives and relationships were followed as closely as their stage careers.[11] Yiddish theatre presented a safe area, offering women the protection of their own community. There were also many roles for female performers in the Yiddish music halls. Women had a rare opportunity to gain some financial independence, with the additional potential to cross-dress and subvert the norms around gender roles. Yiddish song content included marriage, lodgers, rabbis, immigration and pogroms, work and London. They exaggerated class differences, immigrant woes and family relationships.[12]

Theatre director Alice Malin maintains that Yiddish theatre is a genre that is surprisingly feminist. It embraced women's rights and sexual freedom and was full of examples of bold, combative women who refused to accept the path that convention had laid out for them. She cites Sholom Asch's *God of Vengeance*, written in 1918, that tells the story of the daughter of a brothel owner who falls in love with one of her father's prostitutes. They kiss passionately on stage and elope together. This show toured without comment around Eastern Europe for several years but the first night it was put on in Broadway in 1923 the entire company of actors was arrested the next day and the show lambasted for its immoral content. There was also Jacob Gordin's family saga *Mirele Efros*, often called the Jewish Queen Lear, in which a powerful matriarch's authority is challenged by her daughter-in-law. The title character has not inherited her empire, as Shakespeare's Lear does, but has built it herself through hard graft. When she is ousted, she puts up a raw, savage fight, reasoning, shouting and cursing at full throttle. Even in plays which, more conventionally, have male storylines at their heart, the female characters do not give the male protagonists an easy ride.

Radical politics underpinned many Yiddish plays. Although Jewish people were suffering dreadful persecution in Russia in the early 1900s, Yiddish drama was in the curious position of being able to challenge the status quo and explore radical ideas because it was in Yiddish: it was protected by its language. The authorities were less likely to pick up on politically inflammatory content in a Yiddish play than they were in plays performed in Russian, a language they could understand. In David Pinski's tragicomedy *Treasure* (1906), the Marxist anger at the bourgeoisie that was bubbling under the surface of Russian society at the time, catalyses the plot. The protagonist Tillie is the mouthpiece for the working-class' frustration with their position: to struggle 'in the snow, in the rain, all for a pittance', she repeatedly asks of her family who have been beaten into submission to servitude and serfdom, 'you think that's right?'[13]

Yiddish theatre continued to give enormous pleasure in the interwar period but the enthusiastic faithful diminished yearly. Demographic and social trends were the main cause: there was no significant immigration of Yiddish speaking Jews and inevitably there was a decline in spoken Yiddish as the children of the immigrant generation became increasingly anglicised. The population of the East End was falling at a rapid rate as more people moved into the suburbs.[14] The last Yiddish theatre, the Grand Palais, closed its doors in 1970; an end of an era. Yet its feminism, radical politics and strong women's roles illuminated the path for Jewish actresses in subsequent decades.

While a career in the Yiddish theatre had been considered acceptable for immigrant women that settled in the East End and was easy for them to access, the next generation of Jewish actors, growing up in the London suburbs or the provinces, had to take different routes to have a career on the English stage. In the first half of the twentieth century in Britain, an expanding market of film, an enhanced repertoire of plays, popular variety and revue all offered an extended range of opportunities for professional engagement. Access to the professional labour market and to professional status was still a relatively new development for women in this period. The theatre industry was becoming more consciously professionalised as it moved into the mid-century and to some extent this was one of the few professions in which women were able to progress.

There were a variety of ways of entering the profession and an assortment of means through which to manage one's professional career as an actress, in a vocational setting that was becoming more acceptable to the middle-classes. Theatre had become a more respectable calling by the opening decades of the twentieth century. Theatre and film offered women a social status which, even by the middle of the twentieth century was difficult to find in other professions. Many actresses continued their working lives after marriage; there was no legislation that impacted on their vocation in the same way as the teaching professions.[15]

As careers on the stage became more respectable, the floodgates opened and there was a host of Jewish names in the post-war generation. Charles

Landstone points out that Jewish names became more prominent among the artists. 'These young actors and actresses whose reputation stood high in the world of British entertainment were not ashamed to let the world know their Jewish origins'. For many of these aspiring actors, attendance at drama school was now the starting point. The first two London drama schools, RADA and Central School of Speech and Drama attracted a significant majority of female and became a recognised route into the profession. As students had to find their fees, at least until local authorities provided a limited amount of funding for drama schools in the late 1950s, this meant there was a continuing reliance upon personal affluence and family support.[16] Among these young artists was Miriam Karlin, whose family were able to support her wish to become an actress and supported her through drama school. Landstone cites

Karlin as part of this new group of Jewish actors who appeared in Jewish plays as well as flourishing in the wider field of the theatre.[17]

Miriam Karlin (1925-2011)

Miriam Karlin (Samuels) was born in Hampstead, London in 1925 and brought up in an Orthodox Jewish family. She was the daughter of Celine (Aronowitz) and Harry Samuels, a barrister who specialised in industrial action and trade union law, stood as a Labour candidate and campaigned on health, education and housing. When Karlin appeared in the 1950s radio play *Top of the Town*, she based some of the zany characters she invented on people who had appeared before the rent tribunal chaired by her father.[18] He founded, together with Emanuel Snowman (later Mayor of Hampstead) the North West London Jewish Day School which Miriam attended. Her elder brother Michael was a historical linguist responsible for the *Historical Thesaurus of the Oxford English Dictionary.*

Her father believed in education for his daughter and encouraged her socialism. Miriam's life was indelibly marked by an early incident on Hampstead Heath when her father was called 'a dirty Jew'. She became fiercely involved in politics, battling against racism and inequality and better conditions for actors. Her career stretched from the early days of television and film to cabaret and stage.[19] After training at RADA, Karlin made her stage debut for the Entertainments National Service Association for entertaining troops. She took her stage name from her mother's maternal grandfather Elias Karlin who had been a court jeweller in St Petersburg.[20]

Karlin showed aptitude for performing at an early age when she learnt that impersonation would make her parents laugh. She began imitating foreign accents at the age of six when German refugee children came to her school in Hampstead before the war. She spoke German, Dutch and French due to her Continental background. Her mother was born in Amsterdam to Russian parents and her father's family were from Poland. Rabbi Julia Neuberger considers that there is a tradition of funny Jewish women. Some come from the Yiddish jokes about mothers and mothers-in-law, where the strong figure in the home, the chicken soup, perhaps the *sheitl*,[21] the iron rod in the velvet glove, are all features of the caricature. Others derive from a more obviously sentimental streak in Jewish, particularly, East European tradition. This is behind the mixture of humour and tugging at the heart strings in Sophie Tucker's *My Yiddishe Mama* or at some points in Barbara Streisand's portrayal of Fanny Brice in *Funny Girl*. Humour prevents the over-sentimentalisation of the *shtetl* (the small Jewish towns and villages in Eastern Europe), the golden tradition of Eastern Europe, since its forte is self-depreciation, the hands held out to either side. Things are dreadful but they could be worse.[22]

Jews through the ages have been able to laugh at themselves. Playwright Arnold Wesker believed that Jewish humour was rooted in the sufferings of the past; without humour the Jews would never have survived.[23] Comedy is where Jews have excelled and in the 1950s and 1960s they dominated the film and television screens – Bernard Bresslaw, Alfie Bass and Sid James as the lynchpin of the *Carry On* films. Right behind them came Marty Feldman, Mike and Bernie Winters, Fenella Fielding and Eleanor Bron and following with their special brands of subversive humour were Stephen Fry, Ben Elton, David Baddiel, Matt Lucas and Sasha Baron Cohen. In between these two great waves of talent were Warren Mitchell in *Till Death Us Do Part*. Many of Britain's greatest Jewish talents have been able to play it straight as well as for laughs, particularly the women like Miriam Karlin.[24]

It was Karlin's aptitude for comedy and her appearance in revues that launched her career. This type of entertainment first appeared in the Royal Court Theatre *(Under the Clock*, 1893) and the public demand for revue continued with the belief that practically any production with a reasonable standard of invention and scope would attract large audiences. It was notable for bringing new young artists to the fore.[25] Her early appearances included *Made to Measure* at The Lyceum, Edinburgh where she was congratulated on her clever character studies[26] and *Private View* at the Theatre Window Club where it was noted that she had a warm friendly personality with an eagle eye for characterisation. Her golden moment was an impersonation of a Wardour Street salesperson luring an unwilling customer into her shop.[27]

As a result of her revues and private party skits, it was suggested that she audition for the BBC Light Programme's *Variety Bandbox*.[28] She joined the show in 1950 and together with Peter Sellers they appeared in a sketch about a hotel Blessem Hall where they played all the guests and put on a cabaret, again playing all the parts. *Variety Bandbox* was the first time she was heard on radio as a comedienne and she became a big radio name. *The Sunday Empire News* gave the verdict that 'they think we have found one of the best new comediennes for years'.[29]

Throughout the 1950s she was applauded for her revue work and comic roles. 'Watching her revue at the Park Lane Theatre Club I was struck once more by this brilliant girl's immense vitality, warmth and sharp sense of comedy. Miriam has something more precious than beauty – a personality that tingles'.[30] 'A gal with a pronounced flair for comedy'.[31] A reviewer commented on her cabaret at The Arts Theatre: 'Brilliant is the only word that describes Miriam Karlin. An actress of striking qualities who has a warmth of personality and a sense of incisive wit that are seen to best advantage in revue and cabaret'. Further comments were that her intimate appeal was immediate, for she had the knack of making each member of the audience feel that she was sharing her jokes with that person alone and the secret of her success lay in a brand of humour that was both sophisticated and broad.[32] It was considered that she was 'a woman of forceful character, wit and originality that brings a refreshing zest and colour to all her work'.[33]

She was best known for her portrayal of the bolshie shop steward in the 1960s BBC sitcom *The Rag Trade* (1961-63). *The Rag Trade* chronicled the trials and tribulations of Mr Fenner, the owner of a small clothing company Fenner Fashions who had incessant battles with his workforce, particularly with the shop steward, Miriam Karlin's Paddy, who called a strike at the slightest whiff of unfair treatment of workers. Paddy's battle cry of 'Everybody Out' became a national catch phrase.[34] *The Rag Trade* caught the imagination of a nation that was putting the austerity of the war years behind it and beginning to question the establishment.[35] Paddy was abrasive, confrontational and difficult. To the unruly character Karlin brought a vulnerable and humane side which endeared her to the public and she became one of the most popular actresses on television in the 1960s.[36] The series was written by Harvey Wolfe of East End Jewish stock and Ronald Chesney. It was noteworthy for the salience it gave to female characters and for their gentle and at the same time courageous treatment of issues related to industrial relations.[37] Karlin recalled that many trade unionist and other women told her that she had been their role model.[38]

In a remake of *The Rag Trade* for LWT (1977-1978) Karlin was a shop steward in a store where the girl employees were rather terrified of her but would come out on strike at a nod of her head. James Thomas commented that Karlin could not be considered a sympathetic character but she is, if a hard lady, one who was certain to raise a good laugh and one who never lost the chance of making the most of a good comedy line. 'Miss Karlin could carry off anything with that voice and that face which says as much as any script writer could say in words. She has always seemed to me to be a little neglected and too often type cast by television. She is, without doubt, one of the best comedy actresses in the business'.[39] Karlin was typecast; predominantly in Jewish roles as well as that of the prostitute/good time girl and 'the wife'.

Karlin appeared in Jewish roles throughout her career. One of her first stage appearances was in 1949 in *It's Hard to be a Jew* by Sholem Aleichem at The Embassy Theatre and The Whitehall Theatre, London. Set in a university town of Tsarist Russia at the beginning of the twentieth century, the play was centred around two young students, a Jew and a Gentile who exchange identity for a year so that the Gentile could learn from practical experience how hard it is to become a Jew. He has to secure permission to reside in the town and then suffers from restrictions imposed by one decree after another until he is finally selected by the authorities to pay the price of a blood libel. Comic confusion ensues as he masquerades as a Jew. 'As his landlady with a consuming sense of curiosity, Karlin enriched her part with her colourful gesture, warm humour and a keen observation of the daughters of Israel'.[40]

Other Jewish theatre roles, usually as a Jewish mother, continued in the following decades. These included: *My Friend the Enemy* by Sheila Hodgson at the Boltons Theatre Club in 1952, a domestic drama dealing with a Christian and Jewish family sharing the same house. The play broached subjects such as antisemitism, the housing shortage and general post-war frustration. The Harper family, living in the suburbs, had let their upstairs flat to a foreign Jewish family, the Freshmans. When Elizabeth Harper wanted to marry a Fascist thug, she had her eyes on the flat for herself but was unable to get the Freshmans out legally. A feud grew, with petty blows, such as turning off the gas and hiding mice behind the radiator. 'The best acting comes from Miriam Karlin as the Jewish mother'.[41] *Spring Song*, by Bella and Samuel Spewack, at The Embassy Theatre, London in 1953, centred on Jewish family life on New York's Lower East Side. 'Karlin as the Yiddish mama, torn between the love of her daughters and her faith in orthodoxy is very moving. She plays the hardworking stall keeper with remarkable technique and exquisite feeling'.[42] Also at the Embassy Theatre in 1955 was *The World of Sholem Aleichem* (three one act plays). In *The High School,* which told of the efforts of a Jewish couple to get their son into a high school during a period of antisemitic discrimination, Karlin was 'an admirably contrasting mixture of soberness and tenderness as the mother'.[43]

In 1956 she appeared in the first London production of *The Diary of Anne Frank* at the Phoenix Theatre, London where she played the part of Mrs. Van Daan, the mother of Anne's boyfriend. *The Jewish Chronicle* commented that in her comparatively short stage career she had specialised in mature Jewish parts, both comic and tragic. The part resonated with her. 'But for the grace of God, this story instead of being the Diary of Anne Frank might have been the story of Miriam Karlin', as her mother and all her family came from Amsterdam. She left Holland when she was a young girl and settled in England.[44] *The Stage and Television Today* commented that Karlin 'has probably never given a better performance. She gives another of her able studies of the coarser aspect of the Jewish race'.[45]

The Stage and Television Today gave another review tinged with antisemitism when they commented on *Three One Act Plays* by Saul Bellow at the Fortune Theatre in 1966. The critic reacted against the writing and called Bellow yet another of those American Yiddish writers whose prose glories in all those foibles and defects of his race. 'If he writes about a blue rinse matron she's not just a grotesque American matron but she's also a grotesque Jewish-American matron. The Jewishness does of course enhance the writer and actor to incorporate into the play accents and gestures which otherwise would not be needed'. He nevertheless played tribute to Karlin's performance as a middle-aged woman who dresses as a teenager and her veritable bundle of gestures and nutty kosher accents.[46]

The Secret of the World (Ted Allan) at Theatre Royal Stratford East in 1962 was set in Montreal at the time of Khrushchev's 1956 speech attacking the record of Stalin. The hero of the play, a Canadian Jew who for 15 years has been president of his trade union is spiritually shattered by the expose of communism's infallibility and disintegrates physically and mentally. 'Karlin playing a Jewish middle-aged wife has plenty of opportunity to shine in the line of sharp character comedy in which she excels'.[47]

Karlin was Golde in *Fiddler on the Roof* that opened at Her Majesty's Theatre, London in 1967 for which she received critical acclaim. 'Karlin deepens with every fresh part she undertakes. The harassed mother and housewife, seeking to hide her natural love behind a sharp tongue is resented with an effortless perfection'.[48] Sadie Levine wrote that there was an astounding moment when actor and 'character' are in such total sympathy that fantasy is suspended and real life seems to take over. Golde, wife of Tevye, lights the Sabbath candles. 'There is in her face a radiance and repose which is devoutly and distinctly Jewish'. Regarding her role in the production, Karlin remarked that it was something that came from within.[49]

Other Jewish theatre roles included *Torch Song Trilogy* (1985) where she was cast as an archetypal American Jewish mother; the Jewess Ruth in *Down Every Street* (1989) at the Theatre Royal Stratford East concerning the lives of four East End women; a Polish Jewish grandmother in *Tongue of the Bird* at the Almeida (1997); an elderly resident in a Jewish care home who shared make up and millinery tips with her Muslim nurse in *Many Roads to Paradise* at the Finborough Theatre (2008) and a Jewish grandmother in the film *Suzie Gold* (2004).

Karlin's success in sitcoms was repeated in *So Haunt Me* (1992-1994) where she played a Jewish ghost Yetta Feldman. The programme topped BBC TV comedy ratings, netting over 10 million viewers. The family of a newly redundant advertising executive has just moved into a house in Willesden. One night the wife wakes up to the smell of chicken soup and Yetta enters. The woman grabs a couple of candlesticks and makes the sign of the cross. 'If you'd do the Star of David, then I'd be impressed', retorts the Yiddishe mama from beyond the grave. Yetta has been on the haunt for 20 years, driving successive occupants from her home while she awaits the return of daughter Carole who walked out after a row. 'When I can meet my Carole then I can rest in peace', Yetta explains. She keeps the pot of chicken soup simmering all the time because she was cooking some on the night that she left.[50]

Simon Rocker writes that the maternal phantom was the latest Jewish character to appear in a small screen series. Jews used to be few and far between but since writers Marks and Gran[51] opened the gates there has been no stopping them. Their Jewish characters included Dorien (Lesley Josephs) in *Birds of a Feather* and Ivan Fox (Warren Mitchell) in *So You Think You've Got Troubles*. Sitcom writer Paul Mendelson believes that Maureen Lipman's Beattie ads for British Telecom may have helped people realise that Jewish humour is more universal than they thought. He had first submitted the idea for *So Haunt Me* eight years before it was aired but it was rejected then as too 'offbeat and weird'. While Yetta must be identifiably Jewish, Miriam Karlin is concerned not to exaggerate the ethnic mannerisms. 'I'm using my own voice, with a little Jewish intonation but not this kind of "oi oi" voice. Without being frightened of who we are, we've got to be careful not to allow ourselves to be caricatured'.[52] She was adamant that, despite her stance on integrated casting (she was an active member of the Afro-Asian committee in Equity, the theatre trade union) her role of Mrs Berkoff in Torch Song Trilogy, could not be played by anyone who was not Jewish. 'You see there are certain gestures. I don't know that I am doing them—certainly my parents never did — but they come naturally to me. It's deep inside – after 2,000 years of tradition. A non-Jewish actress doing it would turn out a caricature'.[53]

Karlin believed that Jewish actors fell into three main groups: those who were wholly Yiddish like Meier Tzelniker, those who were Jewish and happen to be on the stage like herself and those who were Jewish but did not want to be generally known as such.[54] Karlin was Jewish to all. Noel Coward called her 'that very clever Jewish girl'[55] and throughout her career she played Jewish roles.

'When I was about 21 and terribly fat I was already playing Jewish mommas'. Sam Wanamaker directed her in production of *The World of Sholem Aleichem* (1954) at the Embassy Theatre, London where she played a mother. Wanamaker told her he did not want to see any mama walk or mama gestures. He wanted to see a beautiful upstanding model of Jewish womanhood. 'It was a tough experience for me but he gave me the freedom to find Jewish characters not based on any kind of stereotype'.[56]

Karlin said it was impossible for her to divorce the fact that she was Jewish from the rest of her life. 'It wouldn't be me. It was an integral part of her personality and make up'.[57] Nevertheless she had an experience early in her career which convinced her to be careful about audiences. She used to do what she called 'kosher concerts' at the London Palladium on Sundays, where her impersonations included shoe sellers at Berwick Street market or a German-Jewish refugee. These concerts were for a Jewish audience, telling very Jewish jokes and playing very Jewish characters. She was then asked to repeat her act in Brighton to a mixed audience and it did not go down well. 'What you can do when it is 100% your own is quite different'.[58] Karlin was a strong, tough personality and this was reflected in other strong female characters that she was chosen to portray, such as the prostitute and 'the wife'.

In total contrast to being the Jewish mother were her prostitute roles. *Women of Twilight* by Sylvia Rahman was performed at the Embassy and Vaudeville Theatres, London (1951-52). The play was set in a home for unmarried mothers who lived in a horrible communal home run by a sinister female with criminal instincts. 'Karlin gives a full-blooded performance as a woman of the world with no illusions about it'.[59] A strong forceful drama about the plight of unmarried mothers, Karlin is Olga, 'an unrepentant tramp. A brazen Jewess'.[60]

In *Rain* (based on Somerset Maugham's story *Miss Thompson)* at The Embassy Theatre in 1953, Karlin played the prostitute Sadie Thompson. The story was set on a Pacific island where a missionary's determination to reform a prostitute leads to tragedy. 'Karlin is steadily becoming an actress to note. Here as Sadie Thompson, she shows she is capable of considerable pathos; a wide variety of emotions come at will'.[61] *All Kinds of Men* by Alex Samuels (Arts Theatre, London, 1957) was set in a city in mid-west America and concerned a couple whose marriage disintegrated after their child was killed in a motoring accident. The man turned to a prostitute for comfort in a cheap saloon and he brought her to his home where he accidentally throttles her. 'Karlin gives an excellent study in colourful coarseness as the prostitute'.[62] In *'Fings Ain't Wot They Used T'Be* (Theatre Royal Stratford East and Garrick Theatres 1959-1960), she played the prostitute Lilly Smith. 'Karlin's warm and gorgeous personality is ideally suited to the girl who has been twelve and a half years "on the game" without a penny to show for it. Never has this fine actress been more relaxed, as she peers through the haze of her own cigarette smoke to speak volumes in sentences of no more than three or four words'.[63]

One of her first appearances as 'the wife' was in a 1954 provincial tour of *No Escape* by Rhys Davies. A woman who was jilted 12 years previously finally gets her revenge by killing the man when he turns up at her house and she disposes of his body in the rose garden. She is later visited by his wife (Karlin). 'The brassy, cockney, wise cracking but philosophical Miss Myers scenting that her husband has met a sticky end, she tries a little blackmail. She cunningly cornered her enemy and extorted the truth'.[64]

During the 1970s Karlin appeared in *Story*, a tale of a marriage in suburbia that breaks down as the social climbing husband finds his wife's earthy ways a hindrance. 'Karlin as the wife revelled in shuffling her way through the part, throwing off rude remarks about the snobby neighbours and relishing her social gaffes'.[65] In *Who's Afraid of Virginia Woolf*, Karlin plays the wife Martha. As the evening progresses and Martha drinks more and more alcohol, she wages total war against her husband for whom she has lost all respect, 'Karlin becomes so utterly identified with the character that she is playing she transfigures herself into a totally different being. Never in 50 years of playgoing have I seen an actress submerge herself so completely'.[66] In *The Undertaking* , a play about a family funeral service at which doubt is raised as to the identity of the deceased who turns out not to have died at all, Karlin was the wife whose spouse had sacrificed his lover for the sake of a career in the foreign office.

During the later years of her career she appeared in a mixture of roles such as the witch in the Jacobean drama *The Witch of Edmonton* at The Other Place, Stratford where she caught 'the impotent, bitter frustration of an old woman's anger',[67] Mistress Quickly in *Henry IV Parts One and Two* at The Barbican in 1982 and a variety of Chaucer women in the Chaucer Festival, Canterbury in 1986. In *84 Charing Cross Road* (Richmond Theatre), the autobiographical story of authoress Helene Hanff who corresponds with the owner of a London bookstore specialising in rare editions, Karlin gave 'a marvellously warm and true characterisation which grips the audience from the word go and and builds a conclusion as deeply moving as it is inevitable'.[68] She was the lead in Brecht's *Mother Courage* (Nottingham Playhouse) where it was noted that she was an 'eponymous businesswoman bringing a totally appropriate wryness (and East End drawl) to the part'.[69] In the 1989 production of *Arsenic and Old Lace* (Derby Playhouse), Karlin was one of the two old ladies who as a Christian duty ease off lonely old gentlemen into the next world and bury their bodies in the cellar.

In addition to her theatre roles, she made her film debut in *Down Along the Z Men* (1952) as well as featuring in *A Touch of the* Sun (1956), *Room at the Top* (1959) and *The Millionairess* (1960). She appeared opposite Sir Laurence Olivier in the film adaption of John Osborne's *The Entertainer* (1960) and as a shrewish Jewish housewife in *The Small World of Sammy Lee* (1963), *Ladies Who Do* (1963) and *Just Like a Woman* (1967). In 1971 she made a brief but memorable appearance in *A Clockwork Orange* as Catlady, who is attacked by the delinquent Alex with a phallic sculpture. In 1975 she was appointed OBE and she continued to play on stage in her 70s and appeared in TV series such as *Casualty, The Bill* and *Holby City* and in the films *Children of Men* (2006) and *Flashbacks of a Fool* (2008).

Despite such versatility and range of roles, Karlin, although appreciated in reviews, did not achieve great fame as a theatre actor. At the start of her career it was noted that 'Miss Karlin's emotional power, talent for characterisation and expressive style hold promise of an exceptionally interesting progress to the top of the ladder'.[70] This did not happen. Her notoriety was always as the shop steward Paddy in the television sitcom *The Rag Trade*. Yet Paddy's militancy and confronting people was mirrored in Karlin's personal life.

She was an activist since childhood when she wore stickers proclaiming Boycott German goods in the 1930s.[71] 'My father was a socialist and I was brought up with a tremendous social commitment, a kind of militancy, and I have followed in his footsteps'.[72] Karlin admitted that her politics were known to be quite radical even though she was working in the West End. 'My political involvement became all-encompassing during the 1960s and 70s; this was the period that I began to really take part and speak publicly on platforms of all kinds'. Some of her mother's family were murdered at Auschwitz, a fact that encouraged her to become a militant member of the Anti-Nazi League (ANL).[73] Razor blades concealed in the envelope of a letter were sent to Karlin as a result of her activities. It steeled her resolve to continue the fight against extremist groups.[74] She was on the steering committee of the ANL when it was reformed in the 1990s. The ANL was boycotted by the Jewish Board of Deputies in the 1970s because of its links with the anti-Zionist Socialist Workers Party. She regarded the attacks on the ANL as a 'ridiculous diversion from the main business which is stopping racism in its tracks'.[75] She considered Jews in Britain were tremendous as far as investigation is concerned but ghetto minded when it came to action.[76]

She became so involved in politics that at one point she was phoned by the Labour Party in Mitcham and Morden and asked if she would consider standing in the forthcoming by-election there. Through *The Rag Trade* she was perceived to be an activist and got invited to a Labour Party meeting where she met Harold Wilson. 'I had a pretty extraordinary relationship with him'.[77] She supported the miners' strike and spoke out at a rally in an impassioned speech about what Margaret Thatcher was doing to the miners. She became close friends with Neil Kinnock[78] and joined his wife Glenys when she was president of One World Action which was formed in response to the idea of transforming communities in Africa, Asia and Central America whereby the organisation, rather than donating to the governments of those countries, seek partners in these communities who work on specific projects.[79] Always an active Labour supporter, she renounced her membership when Tony Blair was in power as she could never forgive him for Britain's involvement in the Iraq war but signed up again when Gordon Brown became prime minister.[80]

An active campaigner for the actors' union Equity, she took up the women's struggle as they were being paid less than men and was involved in setting up the first monthly branch meetings to deal with regulated entry. She saw over the years the results of the work that she did whilst on the Equity Council Afro Asian Committee (the token white Jewish woman) when there were no black or Asian actors in leading roles and she worked with writers to persuade them that this could be otherwise.[81] Theatre critic Michael Billington remembered her for her passionate political convictions. 'She didn't just talk a good political game, she was also fervently active'.[82]She considered that people concerned her most, supporting 'the suppressed – those minority groups who flee from home and country because they can't live with prejudice'. She was unflagging in her work for such causes.[83] At the same time she did not forget her Jewish background.

For most of her life, Karlin identified strongly with her Jewishness and was a committed Zionist. As a child she enjoyed Jewish rituals. Her grandfather, who was president of the Jewish National Fund in Holland, Belgium and then England, was a passionate Zionist and had attended the first Zionist conference with Theodor Herzl in 1897. On Karlin's 10th birthday, trees were planted in Israel in her name.[84] Her upbringing was Orthodox and she considered she received the best of Judaism as a child as she was brought up with a conscience.[85] Addressing the Hampstead Synagogue where she had attended in her youth, she emphasised the lasting value of a background of Yiddishkeit and pleaded with parents to lavish this on their children instead of expensive toys.[86] She always identified herself with the plight of Soviet Jewry and during the 1970s she campaigned outside the Soviet Embassy in London demanding freedom for Soviet Jewry and an end to antisemitism in the Soviet Union.[87]

Her visits to Israel began in the 1950s and she worked on a kibbutz. 'It was exhilarating to see at that time real socialism in action'.[88] In 1968 she took part in the 20th anniversary concert commemorating the creation the state of Israel at the Albert Hall.[89] In later years she changed her views about Israel and became more comfortable speaking out for Jews for Justice for Palestinians. 'I think I was beginning to lose a bit of faith and the thing that finally finished me was when Rabin was murdered by an ultra-Orthodox Jew. It probably killed my Judaism and my Zionism both together in a way'. She wanted to see Israel back as it was 'when there were no class distinctions. As soon as they got into bed with apartheid South Africa it was very difficult to get out'.[90] She subsequently renounced her Judaism and became a member of the British Humanist Association.[91]

Karlin died of cancer in 2011. Her role of Paddy in *The Rag Trade* had been watched by millions and quoted by millions. Yet neither that success, nor her more serious roles on stage, removed the growing dissatisfaction she felt at not achieving something more serious.[92] Sydney Tafler[93] when paying tribute to the Jewish contribution to theatre and cinema said that Jews had produced superb writers like Pinter, Wesker and Rosenthal, impresarios such as Lord Grade and Lord Delfont and leading directors such as John Schlesinger but Jewish actors had not reached 'dizzy heights'. He considered that once a Jewish actor had played Jewish parts it was difficult to escape from being labelled with them. It was also a problem for the Jew when he was asked to play a role that showed the Jew in an unpleasant light. Karlin said she was hypertensive about what she played in front of a mixed audience. She had been asked to play the part of a property developer and had turned it down.[94]

Nevertheless, Karlin considered that she had been lucky to have been offered such a range of work and could see that whatever you can learn in one field could be directly transferred to another discipline and the experience becomes accumulative.[95] Yet it was as a comedienne that she had first come to notice in satirical revue and this is how she will be remembered. Playing Yiddisher mommas or Jewish satirists, back-chatting Cockneys or brash Americans, Karlin could be tigerish or kittenish, leaving her comic mark on scores of comedies, dramas, musical comedies and revues.[96]

Miriam Karlin's contemporary, Fenella Fielding, was another Jewish actress who came from a fairly affluent background, had a strong Jewish identity, attended drama school, started her career in revues and excelled in comedic roles, though her path to an acting career was rockier than Karlin's. Fielding also shared with Karlin the disappointment that despite a long career and wide range of roles, she was never offered the serious roles she craved nor was able to achieve the kind of success she had hoped for when she began her theatrical career.

Fenella Fielding (1927-2018)

Fenella Fielding's fame was based on two physical attributes. Her remarkable husky voice and her enormous eyes, much enhanced by false lashes and a great deal of make-up. Overall her appeal might be called 'camp vamp'. She rose to fame in the 1960s, notably for her appearances in the *Carry On* films.[97]

Fenella Fielding (Fenella Feldman) was born in London on 17 November 1927. She and her brother Basil Feldman[98] lived comfortably in an apartment in an Edwardian mansion block in Clapton before moving to Edgware in 1940. Her mother Tilly Katz was from a small town in Rumania and had come to England in her mid-teens. Her spoken English was quite fluent but she was unable to read or write. Her father Philip Feldman came from Lithuania when he was a baby but had to leave school at 12 to help in his father's butcher shop. He subsequently did well and managed a cinema in Silvertown, east London.

Fielding, like Karlin, came from a relatively affluent background, and the family were able to employ a nanny who would take her to dance classes and where she got her first urge to be on the stage. She performed a popular pantomime number 'Nobody Loves a Fairy When She's Forty' which many years later she repeated to great acclaim in a gay club.[99] Her sister-in-law Gita Feldman commented 'The gay community loved her. She was a bit of a queen'.[100]

She was educated at North London Collegiate School and then won a two-year scholarship at RADA but this lasted only a year due to her parents' intervention. At first they were pleased that she had won a scholarship as 'a scholarship is a scholarship whatever it's for' but then it dawned on them that she was set on becoming an actress. Her mother would arrive at lunchtimes, calling the people she was with 'common' and often dragging her away from the premises. The principal eventually told Fielding to leave.

Fielding described her home life as 'horrid', saying that her father used to beat her with his fists and her mother would egg him on. She referred to her father as a 'street angel, house devil'. He would hit her at home and be charming in public. Her father did not have patience for her and kept telling her what sacrifices he had made on her behalf. He was resentful that she had had more opportunities than him. When she announced that she might want to go to university he said that he would rather see her dead at his feet.[101]

Gita Feldman takes a slightly different perspective about Fielding's upbringing. She recalled that she was brought up by adoring parents. 'Her father was like her in many ways. He was difficult and prejudiced and pretended not to like women'. She was brought up in a very Jewish household. They attended synagogue and ate kosher food. 'Her parents brought her up as a star. She was always a star. If people came round, they would say "show them what you can do". However, when it came to going on the stage, the answer was no. They just wanted her to get married. In the end they did accept her choice to appear on stage and were proud of her success'.[102]

A single-minded girl she shocked her Orthodox parents by winning her way into drama school. Eventually she did it the hard way as a 'student' in a fringe theatre and doing everything including understudy to everybody. Between jobs she tried being a secretary, a beautician, a market researcher and a door-to-door salesperson.[103] Before she started appearing professionally she took part in shows at the St John's Wood Jewish Youth Club and the Maccabi Association. 'It was at Maccabi that I first tripped inexpertly and confidently on to a stage. The audience were wonderful. If it hadn't been for that I don't think I would have had the nerve to become an actress'.[104]

Similarly to Miriam Karlin she started her career in revues. There were shows at the Churchill Nightclub where Danny La Rue, who was still unknown, performed and at the Washington Hotel, Mayfair and the Mayfair Hotel.[105] She was starting to attract attention. In *Heaven Sent* (Park Lane Theatre Club) where artistes in the revue made their witty unkind comments on subjects such as British sport and American films, it was noted that Fielding was a 'palpable hit' as a penpal bride.[106] Her first West End show was *Cockles and Champagne*(1954) together with Miriam Karlin.

Her big breakthrough was in 1958 where she played Lady Parvula De Panzoust in Sandy Wilson's legendary Firbank musical *Valmouth*. She was given point numbers which were principally to make people laugh. The story centred around three old ladies living in Valmouth, a magical spa town where people went to take the waters to make them feel young again. Fielding was the youngest of the three old aristocratic ladies. She felt there were two ways to become a star: 'One is to play a part that many people would be successful in if they had a chance to play it and the other is to do a part that very few people would suited for. That was the kind of success I had in *Valmouth*'.[107] Due to *Valmouth's* success, she began to appear regularly on television.

She went on to gain critical acclaim in 1959 for her role in the revue *Pieces of Eight* by Peter Cook and Harold Pinter (which ran for 429 performances). Starring in that production made her more marketable but she wanted to be considered for more serious roles. She decided to take a small part as Phoebe in Shakespeare's *As You Like It* followed by Sheridan's *The Rivals* (1961, Pembroke Theatre, Croydon).

She became part of the 1960s scene when she ran around Soho with the great hell raisers of the era, frequenting the Colony Club with Jeffrey Bernard[108] and spending time there with artist Francis Bacon. Vidal Sassoon did her hair personally and she was often referred to as 'England's first lady of double entendre'. Then came the role which made her a legend, *Carry on Screaming* (1966). A total of 29 *Carry On* films were made from 1958-78 and their popularity also inspired a television series. Fielding considered that nearly everyone loved the *Carry On* films due to their sauciness, the double entendres delivered so innocently. 'You're socially safe with innuendo because you can choose which meaning you prefer'. The films were successful from the word go. The critics were scathing but the public loved them. 'You can't keep real comedy down, not comedies like these that are larky and daring and full of cheek and make your blood run faster'.[109] She starred in *Carry on Regardless* (1961) where she played the bosom heaving Penny Panting before taking on the unforgettable role of the seductive vamp Valeria in *Carry On Screaming* (1966). Detective Sergeant Bung accompanied by his assistant Slobotham are investigating the sudden disappearance of Doris and come face to face with the bloodcurdling experiments organised by the mysterious Dr Watt and his siren sister Valeria who are vitrifying young women to sell to local stores as shop window dummies.[110] Reclining on a chaise longue, in a figure hugging red dress, Fielding fluttered her heavy lashes and purred huskily 'Do You Mind If I Smoke?' But rather than light up a cigarette, she famously began emitting plumes of smoke as a sexy vampire Valeria, the ultimate 1960s femme fatale.[111]

The 1960s saw her become increasingly acknowledged and praised for her comic roles. So *Much To Remember* at the Vaudeville Theatre marked a turning point in Fielding's career. 'In a sizzling two hour performance in which she hardly ever leaves the stage, this effervescent artist with the deliciously hoarse voice shares rare talent and firmly establishes herself as one of our best musical comedy actresses. As Maudie Marlow she skips lightly down memory lane, recalling highlights in her very varied career – from Brixton to Broadway, her brief encounters with the top set, her weakness for the opposite sex'.[112] She was referred to as a comedienne when it was announced that she was to play Cleopatra in BBC2's presentation of the *Ides of March*, Thornton Wilder's story of the events leading up to Caesar's assassination.[113] She was again referred to as a comedienne in a report on her rehearsals for *High Spirits*, the musical comedy based on Noel Coward's *Blithe Spirit*.[114]

Let's Get A Divorce (Mermaid Theatre, 1966), a romantic comedy and nineteenth century period piece was another success. Its fun depends on the situation that only by pretending to be lovers can husband and wife find marital bliss. 'The delight of the evening is Fenella Fielding. She has pushed to one side the mannerisms and affectations which in the past have made her comedy border on burlesque and for the first time she manages to combine a high sense of fun with a rare expression of feeling. She is now in the forefront of contemporary comedy actresses'.[115] Theatre critic Charles Landstone found himself excitedly applauding at *High Bid* (Mermaid Theatre, 1967) as a result of the joy he derived from the glittering performance of Fielding. She played Mrs Gracedew, a transatlantic widow imbued with the moneyed-American early twentieth century adoration of British antiquity. She falls in love with a 600-year-old house and the impoverished last descendant of the family falls in love with her. Together they save the house from the clutches of a newly rich upstart. 'Miss Fielding's style brings tenderness, humility and infectious delight to the part'[116] and he considered her comedy performance placed her in the front rank of English comediennes.[117]

Although known predominantly as a comedienne, Fielding was always eager to take on serious roles. She played Hedda in *Hedda Gabler* alongside Ian McKellen (BBC Radio, 1966) and at the Phoenix Theatre, Leicester (1969). She always acknowledged her Jewish background and took part in various Jewish roles, including a reading of Anthony Horowitz's play *The Picnic* to commemorate the 40th anniversary of the liberation of the Concentration Camps (Savoy Theatre, 14 April, 1985). The play was based on a true episode which took place in 1981 when members of Moscow's Jewish community were arrested as they picnicked in a forest outside the city.[118] She starred, together with David Kossoff and Warren Mitchell, in *The Jericho Players* by Bernard Kops (BBC Radio 4, 1966). The play centred around a troupe of Yiddish Shakespearean actors who performed their way across antisemitic Tsarist Russia driven by ambition and the will to survive whatever the cost.[119]

Gita Feldman remarked that Fielding 'felt very Jewish. So many of her friends were Jewish. She had a Jewish sense of humour'. She came to all the Jewish festival meals at her brother's home where she would sit at the table and parody everything. 'She did not hide her Jewishness in the early years but didn't push it too hard'. She was good friends with other Jewish artists, such as Miriam Karlin and Lionel Bart.[120] Gita and Fielding had been friends since their teens and had been part of the same Jewish crowd. After Gita married Fielding's brother Basil, the relationship changed. Gita became the 'good daughter' to her in-laws and Fielding became jealous. Basil often supported Fielding. He bought her an apartment and she was always ringing his office for assistance. He tried to help her financially as well as with contacts to help further her career.

Gita acknowledges Fielding's talent and her difficulties. 'The ambition in her was very strong. If she came into a room, the room changed. She was a star. She had a beautiful speaking voice. She spoke slowly and dominated the conversation. She was very glamorous but very contrived. She was lovely to be around. At the seder table, she was wonderful. As if she was on stage. She was always on stage and carried on in an affected way. A born talent. A prima donna'. She never married although for years she had two lovers in tandem who did not know about each other. 'She had some nice offers, for example playwright Anthony Shaffer but both realised they were too similar. She also realised she did not want to look after anyone; she would have been a terrible mother'.[121]

Despite the talent, she did not, as was the case with Miriam Karlin, do as well as expected. Serious roles were few and far between. There were professional regrets. She turned down film director Federico Fellini who wanted her to play seven different incarnations of a sex symbol because she was committed to a theatre season at Chichester. She regretted that the critical praise she reaped playing Ibsen and Chekhov in the provinces never led to a West End run which might have cemented her reputation as a serious actress.[122] Gita considered that her personality was another contributing factor. 'A lot of people would not work with her. She would argue and storm out. She could not work as part of a team. She was very difficult'.[123]

In the late 1970s Fielding fell out of fashion. After being swindled by an agent, she ended up broke and had to sell her home. She gradually clawed her way back. She starred in a one woman show at the Lyric Hammersmith and toured in a production of *Lady Windemere's Fan.* Perhaps because no one vamped it up better and because her legendary reputation as a comedienne remains undimmed. Nobody was as provocative and funny as Fielding which is why she was a favourite on television with Morecombe and Wise. All her life she was an independent woman, writing and injecting her own material into shows before it became fashionable for women to do so. Later in life she became a minor cult. She was resurrected by an unlikely succession of modern performers such as Rick Mayall and Ade Edmondson and starred in their film *Guesthouse Paradiso* (1999) and film critic Mark Kermode with whom she reviewed new releases.[124] Rock star Jarvis Cocker included her in the South Bank Meltdown Festival alongside Grace Jones but compared with other brilliant actresses of her generation she was undervalued. She was a one-off and an OBE, which she received at the age of 90 for services to drama and charity.[125]

Fielding died on 11 September 2018 and her funeral held at Mortlake Crematorium. In the programme for Order of the Service Tony Hall, BBC director general, acknowledged that Fielding brought tremendous style to every role she played and did much for the BBC and highlighted the Morecombe and Wise Christmas specials.[126] Her memorial service, attended by around 600 people, was held at St Paul's, Covent Garden. St Paul's is widely known as the Actors' Church. The connection with the theatre began as early as 1662 with the establishment of the Theatre Royal, Drury Lane. Memorials in the church are dedicated to many theatrical personalities, including Charlie Chaplin, Noel Coward and Vivien Leigh. Amongst those giving tributes were actors Gyles Brandeth, Dame Sian Phillips and entertainer Anita Harris. Students from LAMDA performed the opening number from *Valmouth* and Dame Cleo Laine sang 'I Will Miss You' from the same musical. Those attending included Sir Derek Jacobi,

Miss Jennifer Saunders, Lynda la Plante, Amanda Barrie, Timothy West and Prunella Scales. The music included songs by Gershwin and Irving Berlin.[127] They came to celebrate a woman ahead of her time. 'All her life she was an independent woman, injecting her own material into shows before women did that kind of thing'.[128] Fielding, like Karlin, was the antithesis of the Jewish girl next door but like many Jewish artistes in the entertainment world, both showed a great talent for comedy and humour. They excelled in comic roles for which they will be remembered rather than their more serious work.

The actresses of the interwar generation, including Fenella Fielding, Miriam Karlin and their contemporary Claire Bloom all shared similar backgrounds as the children and grandchildren of East European Jewish immigrants who had moved from the East End to London's northern, middle-class suburbs, though still maintaining a strong Jewish identity. All three evinced an early aptitude for entertaining audiences and pursued acting through drama school, but while the bulk of Karlin and Fielding's roles were confined to a narrow range of Jewish characters, Claire Bloom, who had the looks and persona of an 'English rose', was able to transcend the typecasting that often accompanied an openly Jewish identification and enjoyed a rich and full career in serious roles on both stage and screen working (and often entering into relationships) with some of the most famous actors, writers and directors of her generation.

Claire Bloom (1931 –)

Claire Bloom is one of the biggest stars to have emerged from the Anglo-Jewish community. In 1952 Bloom was discovered by Charlie Chaplin to co-star alongside him in the film *Limelight*. Almost overnight she rose from middle-class obscurity in Finchley to international stardom. During her theatre and film career she has played alongside a host of stars that included Richard Burton, Laurence Olivier, John Gielgud, Paul Scofield, Ralph Richardson, James Mason, Paul Newman and Rod Steiger. Her elegant beauty was celebrated in the pages of *Vogue* and *Time* and her acting talent was praised by theatre critic Kenneth Tynan as 'pure gold'.[129]

Patricia Claire Blume was born in Moreland Court, Finchley Road, Childs Hill, London on 15 February 1931 to Elizabeth Grew and Edward Max Blume (originally Blumenthal). Edward's family name Blume was modified to Bloom by his wife at some point in the 1930s; his father had emigrated from Russia and apparently borrowed the name Blumenthal from a fellow passenger's passport. Both sets of grandparents had come to

England at the beginning of the twentieth century. Bloom's maternal grandmother Pauline, the daughter of the Chief Rabbi of Frankfurt, came from Riga together with her husband Henry, who was born in Russia.[130]

Henry Grewski was a cabinetmaker who started off with a modest workshop in London's East End but later on manufactured furniture and wooden mouldings. Bloom's mother was born in the East End and her father in Liverpool. Bloom's early childhood was peripatetic in the extreme and was disrupted both by the war and her father's erratic fortunes as a travelling salesman and gambler. He had a succession of jobs that he lost and with each job the family went up and down the social scale accordingly and moved from town to town.[131] In the years before the Second World War the family moved from Cardiff to Bristol, then Cornwall to New Milton. As a result her schooling was somewhat erratic. She was sent to Badminton, a private girls' school, but soon afterwards her father's fortunes having declined, the family, including her young brother John, moved to Cornwall and she was sent to the local village school before moving to the next location. After the war broke out the family went back to London.[132]

In 1941 Edward's brother David and his wife invited Elizabeth, Claire and her brother to live with them in Fort Lauderdale, Florida while her father stayed in England. As to why he would not join them, Bloom explained that a man would not leave his country in time of war. Although the time spent with her uncle and family was not a happy one, it was when Bloom discovered her love of performing. During her year stay in Florida she was asked by the British War Relief Society to help raise money by entertaining at various benefits at Miami hotels and this was how she broke into show business. After a year her mother persuaded her uncle to give them $50 dollars a month and she moved with her mother and brother to Forest Hills, New York where she attended a dancing school in Manhattan and performed in her first radio play.[133]

Bloom wanted to be an actress at an early age. She was inspired by the films *Romeo and Juliet* (1936) starring Leslie Howard and *Snow White* (1937). She wanted to bring to life the dramatic stories she read. 'I was hooked. I was in there'. She recalled how her mother always read Shakespeare to her and she loved the cadence of the words. 'I was a shy child socially but if I could do a poem or dance around I was completely confident. I was ambitious and probably arrogant'. She wanted to be a serious actress at a young age and it happened quickly and easily. 'My mother always instilled in me "only work with the best" even if it was a small part'.[134] Her eureka moment came after seeing Chekhov's play *The*

Three Sisters on her twelfth birthday. 'From then on I thought only of going into the theatre and playing in Chekhov. Chekhov was moving. That's what I was looking for – something more moving even than my own plight as a little English girl driven from my home by the gods of war'.[135]

In 1943 the family returned to London and as Edward's fortunes had improved, they moved into a large apartment in Curzon Street, Mayfair. Bloom received a scholarship to the Guildhall School of Music and Drama at the age of 13 and a year later to the Central School of Speech and Drama where she was noticed by an agent. She made her professional debut on BBC Radio and then with Oxford Repertory Theatre in 1946. She debuted aged 16 at the Royal Shakespeare Theatre as Orphelia to Paul Scofield's Hamlet. Her London stage debut was in 1947 in Christopher Fry's play *The Lady's Not for Burning* which starred John Gielgud and featured a young Richard Burton. It was during rehearsals for the play that Burton and Bloom began a love affair. Bloom said of Burton 'he had all the intelligence, physical beauty, an incredible voice. There was no one else like him. He proved that a working-class actor could make it and I was proud of him'.[136] It was also around this time that her parents divorced and for many years she had no relationship with her father.[137]

Bloom made her screen debut with a small role in Gainsborough Pictures 1948 film *The Blind Goddess*. Soon after she enrolled – like Dirk Bogarde, Petula Clark and Diana Dors – in J. Arthur Rank's 'charm school' set up to manufacture British film stars along Hollywood lines.[138] It was her second film *Limelight* (1952) in which Charlie Chaplin selected her to be the leading lady that propelled her to stardom. American playwright Arthur Laurents saw her acting as a ballet dancer on the London stage and told Chaplin about her. She sailed to New York and they tested her with three scenes from the film. Three months later, at the age of 20, she had the part.[139] Limelight was a prophetic title. She says 'it was her great moment'. Chaplin famously dictated every move that she made in the film.[140]

In *Limelight,* set in London in 1914 on the eve of World War One, Calvero (Chaplin), an ageing music hall comedian and a washed up drunk, saves a despairing young girl dancer Terry (Bloom) from suicide and imbues her with the will to live and to become a successful prima ballerina. Nursing her back to health, Calvero helps Terry regain her self-esteem and resume her dancing career. In doing so he regains his own self confidence but an attempt to make a comeback is met with failure. Terry wants to marry Calvero despite their age difference although she has befriended a young composer. In order to give them a chance Calvero leaves home and becomes a street entertainer. Terry, now starring in her own show, eventually finds Calvero and persuades him to return to the stage for a benefit concert. He gives a triumphant comeback performance but suffers a heart attack during a routine and dies. Rave reviews included 'Bloom measures fully up to the complexities her part demands of her'[141] and that she was 'beautifully sensitive and expressive of a youngster's complete idolatry'.[142] She won her first BAFTA as that year's most promising newcomer to film. To have had the chance to appear with Chaplin was to her a complete miracle as she was an unknown. Chaplin was looking for someone who was small and who could give the impression of being a dancer. She did not realise at the time that she bore a striking resemblance to his wife Oona.[143] She worshipped Chaplin and thought of him as the father she never had as a child.[144]

Bloom developed a flourishing film career. Laurence Olivier invited her to co-star with him in his film of *Richard III* (1956). She had just appeared on the cover of *Life* magazine and found that playing opposite Olivier was 'like being caught in an electric current'.[145] She continued working with Burton in *Alexander the Great* (1956), *Look Back in Anger* (1959) and *The Spy Who came in from the Cold* (1965). She appeared with Yul Brunner in *The Brothers Karamazov* (1958) and Charlton Heston in *The Buccaneer* (1958). In *The Haunting* (1963), one of the world's most acclaimed horror films voted by the *Guardian* as one of the top 200 horror films ever made, she is one of two women who help a paranormal investigator to explore the haunting of a sinister house. She plays Theo, a hip young woman with psychic ability.[146] In 2009 she played Dr Who's mother in David Tennant's final episode as the Time Lord and she was Queen Mary in *The King's Speech* (2010). Bloom won two BAFTA Best Actress Awards for the television adaptations of *Brideshead Revisited* (1981) and *Shadowlands* (1985). Still performing in her 80s, her most recent work was in television, in the medical drama series *Doc Martin* (2013) and Stephen Poliakoff's *Summer of Rockets* (2019), a drama set in England during the Cold War period and following a Russian Jewish inventor and his family living in Britain.[147] It is ironic that she played an aristocratic role rather than being part of the Jewish family who are the 'outsiders'.

Notwithstanding an impressive film record, Bloom had a strong and significant presence on both the London and New York stages. When *Limelight* was premiered in London, Bloom was performing Juliet in *Romeo and Juliet* at the Old Vic theatre. Theatre critic Kenneth Tynan described her performance as the best that he had ever seen.[148] She joined the Old Vic Company between 1952-54 where she played leading female Shakespearean roles. 'Shakespeare was the basis of my career'.[149]

It has been in the theatre that Bloom has scored her most satisfying triumphs and where, in comparison to the cinema, she feels 'happier and better'. Powerful performances came with *The Trojan Woman, Vivat! Vivat! Regina!* and *Hedda Gabler* In the 1970s her award-winning portrayal of Blanche du Bois in Tennessee Williams' *A Streetcar Named Desire* was a high peak and her favourite role.[150] 'The play is infallibly perfect, line by line, moment by moment, and Blanche is an extraordinary character. I've never known anything so exhausting but it was totally satisfying in that I'd created someone so completely different to myself'.[151] Another significant role was *The Doll's House,* which allowed Bloom to 'fuse two conflicting sides of my nature – spoiled child wife and the determinedly independent woman'. She, like Nora in *The Doll's House* had to slam a door on a husband but in this case it happened three times.[152]

Bloom received considerable media attention regarding her personal life that included three turbulent marriages. She had her first real love affair with Burton and another with Yul Brynner when they filmed *The Brothers Karamazov* (1958). She met Rod Steiger when they appeared together in the Broadway production of *Rashomon*. They married in 1959 and her only child Anna was born in 1960. Bloom and Steiger remained in America, moving to California where Steiger pursued a film career. Steiger was a chronic depressive who took his violent screen roles, that included Al Capone and Benito Mussolini, home to his wife.[153] They divorced in 1969.

Soon afterwards Bloom married Broadway theatre producer Hillard Elkins, who produced Ibsen's *A Doll's House* and *Hedda Gabler*, with Bloom in the leading roles. These productions together with *Streetcar Named Desire* served to consolidate Bloom's reputation as one of the finest actors of her generation.[154] The marriage to Elkins was short lived and Bloom regarded it as 'an enormous mistake'. It was said that Elkins pocketed most of his wife's star salary while he 'owned more shoes than Imelda Marcos and more suits than Liberace'.[155]

Bloom returned to London but on a stopover in New York, a chance encounter brought her together with one of America's greatest novelists Philip Roth. Drawn to Roth's fierce intelligence, she split her time between her home in London and his farmhouse in rural Connecticut. Roth decided that her daughter Anna bored and irritated him and in a letter demanded that Anna move out of Bloom's London home where Roth lived part time. Terrified of losing him, Bloom complied, sending Anna to a nearby student hostel, a decision she rues yet defends. After 15 years of living together, she proposed marriage in 1990 and Roth presented her with a draconian prenuptial agreement that ensured she would receive nothing if they divorced. Against her better judgment she signed. During a mental breakdown for which he was hospitalised in 1993 Roth sued her for divorce.[156]

After Bloom's memoir *Leaving A Doll's House* was published in 1996, Roth threatened legal action if she continued to give interviews to promote the book in which he is portrayed as a brilliant monster, cruel and manipulative. He exacted a literary revenge by pillorying her as a bitch in a novel *I Married A Communist* in which he created the character of Eve Frame, a spoiled social climbing antisemitic Jewish actress who ruins her husband's life and is considered to be a barely disguised riposte to Bloom.[157] Bloom believes that her emotional disasters had their origin in the defection of her father, the itinerant salesman and gambler. 'He had wit and charm and I loved him very much but he was unreliable'. She never got over his divorce from her mother. Her strong yearning for a 'protective male presence' dates from her childhood. [158]

Bloom was very devoted to the women in her family. Her mother was a close and lifelong companion and encouraged her early interest in the stage. She recalls her maternal grandmother Pauline, the family anchor, and her aunt Mary (Mary Grew), a leading stage actress of the Twenties and Thirties with great affection and who became a mentor to her when she was young.[159] Her grandmother Pauline, the daughter of a leading Frankfurt rabbi, underpinned the family's Jewish identity and made sure that Jewish festivals were celebrated and Friday nights enjoyed.[160] 'My mother's family was my family'.[161] She also reflects that her grandmother Grew was the only one of the family in England to practise Judaism.[162] It would appear that they were established in Anglo-Jewish circles as the *Jewish Chronicle* acknowledge that 'Bloom's mother was the daughter of Mr and Mrs Henry Grew, members of a well-known London Jewish family. Mrs Grew was an active social worker for Jewish causes and sister of Mrs Henrietta Diamond, the founder of the Zebulun Seafaring Society[163] and mother of well-known barrister A. S. Diamond'.[164] Pauline Grew was also an avid theatregoer who used to entertain the whole family on Friday night dinners. Bloom remembers these occasions fondly for the food but with resentment towards 'extreme female submissiveness'.[165]

When asked how important her Jewish background is to her, she says 'It's what I am. It's part of my life and I'm Jewish. It makes you who you are, what you are'.[166] She remembers when she lived in Florida as a young girl that she would see signs outside fashionable hotels where she was appearing in a show which informed potential guests that the management welcomed 'restricted' patrons only. She instinctively sensed who would and would not be honoured and if she had not been a performer she would not have been included. 'The presence of racial hatred played a great part in my desire to succeed professionally in later years, to feel myself on a firm footing that nothing could ever wound me or my family. My mother was a product of first-generation Jews transplanted to England. Much was expected of my generation although this was normally applied to the sons rather than the daughters who were expected to be content with marriage'. She added that she felt 'profoundly Jewish ethnically and historically, but religion holds absolutely no attraction for me. Unlike many Jewish actresses of my generation I never made any attempt to hide my origins or to change my name'.[167] Nevertheless the British press would insist on calling her 'the English rose'. 'My family would comment, in strong Yiddish accents, on my English rosiness and we always found it a great source of amusement and wonder'.[168] As a result of her classic English beauty she was not chosen for Jewish stereotypical roles but rather aristocratic ones.

In *Brideshead Revisited* (1981), a television adaptation of the novel by Evelyn Waugh which shows a bygone era of English high living from the 1920s to the early 1940s, Bloom plays the part of Lady Marchmain, the Marchioness of Brideshead. She is a devout Catholic who is publicly known as an extremely virtuous woman whose estranged husband had treated her cruelly. Abandoned by her husband Lady Marchmain rules over her household, enforcing her Roman Catholic morality on her children. Bloom felt sympathy with Lady Marchmain's sense of being an outsider, a Catholic in Protestant England. 'Not such a leap from being a Jew in Protestant England as one would imagine'.[169]. She recalls how she was once presented to Queen Mary and remembered her stance.[170]

Reflecting on her career, during which Bloom worked with the biggest stars of their time, she considers her highlights to be appearing in the film *Limelight* and her roles in *The Doll's House* and the 1974 West End production of *Streetcar Named Desire*. 'It was such a glorious play. I'm so pleased to have been part of such a masterpiece'.[171] She was drawn to playing complicated and destructive characters. 'I was very close to the edge of the character and understood it internally'. She did not do 'fluffy' roles. Although she would have liked to have appeared in a romantic comedy, she did not consider that she had the gift for such a role. 'I find it difficult to do something that doesn't have an echo in me. I was high minded and wanted to do interesting things'.[172] Bloom was awarded the CBE for services to drama in 2013 which she considered to be 'the icing on the cake. It is a very nice thing to be recognised. I have worked hard and tried to do good things'.[173]

A fourth Jewish actress of the interwar generation, Eleanor Bron, was able, like Claire Bloom, to avoid being type cast into traditionally Jewish roles despite a beauty that distinctly reflected her immigrant Jewish heritage. Bron did not follow a conventional drama school path to acting, but slightly younger than her contemporaries Karlin, Fielding and Bloom, she benefited from entering the profession in the 'Swinging Sixties', and she enjoyed early success in political satire and popular films. Despite this, Eleanor Bron, like her predecessors Miriam Karlin and Fenella Fielding, never felt she had reached the heights of acting achievement, held back, she believed, by her early work in revues and comedic satire, which made it difficult to cross over into serious acting roles.

Eleanor Bron (1938 –)

Possessed of a quirky wit and striking Eastern European looks, Eleanor Bron was one of the few women to take a leading role in the male dominated 'satire boom' of the early 1960s. She exploded into this male party with the good manners of a middle-class Jewish girl from north London.[174] She read French and German at Cambridge University and it was there she was 'spotted' by satirist John Bird and invited to join The Establishment, a collective of satirical comedians led by Peter Cook. The Establishment was involved in the pilot for the BBC's fabled satirical revue *That Was The Week That Was.* This launched her career and theatre and film roles followed, including seminal 1960s films *Alfie* (1966) and the Beatles' *Help!* (1965). She was also seen nationwide when she appeared in the BBC comedy *Absolutely Fabulous.*

Bron was brought up in a moderately observant Jewish family. Before her birth her father legally changed his name from Bronstein, in an effort to enhance his newly founded music publishing company.[175] Both her parents were children of immigrants and had left school at 14. Bron was evacuated with her mother and two older brothers during the Second World War to her father's cousins in California. She has fond memories of family life. 'My parents were wonderful. We would all sit round and listen to the BBC's *Saturday Night Theatre.* We did things as a family, and it all seemed to centre around the radio'. She considers this is why she has always been passionate about radio work. She recalls that although they were not a very Orthodox Jewish family, Friday nights were special. Home life was a mixture of conflicts and treats and lovely birthdays and that her mother and aunts enjoyed what they called 'a good laugh'.[176]

Bron's family never expected her to have a theatrical career. 'I am a suburban girl. I come from Edgware'. No one in the family had a theatre background.[177] She did comment that her mother was a vivacious outgoing person who would have loved to have been an actress.[178] She attended North London Collegiate School alongside television presenter Esther Rantzen.[179] Another alumni was Fenella Fielding. Bron took the lead part in school plays. At school she announced her intention to apply to drama school and her headmistress told her that all little girls wanted to go to drama school and Bron decided that she did not want to be like all other little girls. Her headmistress urged her to apply to Oxford or Cambridge. 'That generation of women teachers had all been deprived of their dues academically – the possibility of a really good university education – so they wanted it for other people'.[180] She characterised her time at Cambridge as 'three years of unparalleled pampering and privilege'.[181] Cambridge broadened her mind so much that she felt 'like Alice' from Alice in Wonderland in her suburban home in Edgware. 'She could hardly squeeze through the door-jambs'.[182] For her the real education at Cambridge was the people she met. Her outlook on life changed completely and she enjoyed mixing with people from many walks of life and encountering those she never would have met otherwise. Cambridge showed her what she could do with her life and freed her from the feeling that she must marry and have children.[183]

At Cambridge, where she studied French and German, she fell in with a brilliant young group of iconoclasts. She began her career in comedy in a Cambridge Footlights revue *The Last Laugh* in 1959 together with Peter Cook. Footlights, founded in 1883, has been Britain's most illustrious and elite comedy society and where writers, performers and producers meet as students and move into establishment jobs in radio, television and film. Its alumni have set the tone of cultural eras from the 1960s with shows such as *Monty Python* and *Not the Nine O'Clock News* and has been accused over the years of having a lack of cultural diversity.[184]

It is a reflection of Bron's talent that despite her background, she was the first female student to perform in a Footlights Smoker (an informal mixture of sketches and stand up). The addition of a female performer to the Footlights was a departure; until that time it had been all male, with female characters portrayed in drag. It was a triumph in the history of the Footlights. *The Last Laugh* was set in an underground nuclear bunker, where scientists awaited the destruction of the world and included DIY instructions on how to make your own coffin. Each sketch ended with a stated or implied death. The musical accompaniment was provided by a ten-piece modern jazz group. The show was technically complicated, including taped inserts and back projections. After a long campaign by Peter Cook and John Bird, the Footlights' traditional male only rule had been scrapped to make room for Bron. Adopting a political stance far to the left of the Labour Party, the show sought to capture and define the mood that had led 50,000 people to gather for a CND rally in Trafalgar Square at Easter earlier that year.[185] A revue that included Alan Bennett, Jonathan Miller, Dudley Moore and Peter Cook was performed at the Edinburgh Festival and, as a result of its success, the 'satire boom' began. From Prime Minister Harold Macmillan and his Conservative party to the sexual politics of the times, everyone and everything received a quick-witted jab. The arrival of the revue on the West End London theatre scene signalled the official opening of the satirical Sixties. Satire was in and it could not have happened at a more appropriate time when post-war London was revamping itself into the Swinging Sixties.[186]

Cook and his colleagues went on to establish a comedy club, The Establishment, on Greek Street in Soho, London in October 1961, inviting performers such as America's Lenny Bruce to perform and shock the audience. The venue allowed for budding comedians and satirists to perform new material in a nightclub setting outside the jurisdiction of the Lord Chamberlain, whose censorship of language and content was a problem for many performers. *The Establishment*, a tie-in album of comedy routines and sketches featuring John Bird, John Fortune and Eleanor Bron was released on the Parlophone label in 1963. A second club was established in New York that year. The BBC jumped on the satire bandwagon by airing the show *That Was The Week That Was (TW3)*. The irony was that that, as with the Establishment, the objects of mockery (the well-to-do fashionable set) were also the audience. Satire's audiences have always tended to come from the very section of society that is being satirised.

TW3 (1962-1963), produced by Ned Sherrin, took the country by storm and brought in an average of three million viewers. The show covered previously taboo comic subjects such as racism, royalty and religion. Politicians of the day were also fiercely lampooned.[187] By the early Sixties, Britain had had 13 years of Tory government and was ready for a bit of irreverence. Although it aimed to remain apolitical, there was no doubt that members of the satire club were mainly to the left of centre and therefore relished the idea of attacking the Conservatives that were in power. Even Prime Minister Macmillan, a constant source of attack, once wrote to the Postmaster General requesting that no action should be taken against the programme as it was a good thing to be laughed over and better than being ignored. Although satire may not have crumbled the foundations of the nation's elite, it certainly shook it, as satirical publications such as *Private Eye* appeared on the scene that exposed people and resulted in various libel suits. The irony was that the movement was originally established by the Oxbridge set who were in effect members of 'the establishment', the societal elite.[188]

Bron is convinced that she would never have become an actor if she had gone to drama school 'I think I would have found it terribly oppressive and frightening'.[189] She had hoped to be offered a wonderful job after university but discovered that having a university degree was not useful for finding a job.[190] After graduation she took a job in the personnel department of De La Rue, the company that printed banknotes but she found it unbearably boring.

Her career as an actress did not commence in a conventional way. Without a drama school training and only a short spell with a repertory theatre at Bristol, she was fortunate that she was given the opportunity to become well known overnight due to the satire boom. 'I was flung into household-namedom by appearing three times a week live'.[191] Her first professional job was with The Establishment when they did a pilot for BBC's *That Was The Week That Was*. After the pilot she went with The Establishment for a year to the States and upon her return became part of another Ned Sherrin produced show, *Not So Much A Programme, More A Way Of Life*, that featured her as a daft debutante called Lady Pamela Sitty.

In 1965 she came to the attention of a much wider audience, as opposed to the minority that had always appreciated her wit, sharp intelligence and strong-featured beauty. It was at the very height of Beatlemania, when she was chosen to star in the Beatles' film *Help!* (1965). It was an unlikely piece of casting. In the era of the wide-eyed swinging blonde she was a tall handsome woman with black hair and eyes. A television intellectual thrust upon four mop headed millionaires.[192] It was her first film debut and she played the part of the bewitching high priestess Ahme. 'It was a tremendous way to start'.[193] It is said that her name inspired Paul McCartney when he wrote Eleanor Rigby and there were rumours that she had a relationship with John Lennon.

Other films include a doctor in *Alfie* (1966), part of a vacationing foursome alongside Albert Finney, Audrey Hepburn and William Daniels in *Two for the Road* (1967), *Bedazzled* (1967) and *A Touch of Love* (1969). Following her appearance as Alan Bates's wife in *Women in Love* (1969) and a co-starring role in the farce *The National Health* (1973), a satirical comment on England's national health system, Bron was not seen much in film for the next decade and television took up much of her time. In later films she appeared as rather repelling characters (her facial features had become more severe as she became older), such as the arrogant Lady

Wexmire in *Black Beauty* (1994), the harsh Miss Minchin in *A Little Princess* (1995). Other films included *The House of Mirth* (2000), *The Heart of Me* (2002), *Love's Brother* (2004) and the tennis comedy drama *Wimbledon* (2004). Television roles have included appearances in the *Dr Who* series *City of Death* (1979) and *Revelation of the Daleks* (1985). She was Joanna Lumley's horror of a mother in *Absolutely Fabulous* (1992).

Throughout her career she maintained close ties with the classical and contemporary stage and appearances have included *Doctor's Dilemma* (1966), *The Prime of Miss Jean Brodie* (1967), *Major Barbara* (1969), *A Day in the Life of Joe Egg* (1970), *Hedda Gabler* (1970), *The Merchant of Venice* (1975) *Private Lives* (1976), *Uncle Vanya* (1977), *The Cherry Orchard* (1978), *The Real Inspector Hound* (1985) , *Duchess of Malfi* (1985), *The Miser* (1991) and *A Delicate Balance* (1997). More recently she appeared in the musical *'Twopence to cross the Mersey* (2005), *The Clean House* (2006) and *All About My Mother* (2007). She has also performed a one-woman show entitled *Desdemona: If You Had Only Spoken*, a collection of monologues of censored women that could have changed the world.[194] In the 1980s she appeared frequently in Secret Policeman Balls live benefit shows for Amnesty International. She is the author of several books, including *Life and Other Punctures* (1978), an account of bicycling in France and Holland on a Moulton bicycle, *The Pillow Book of Eleanor Bron* (1985) which includes her anecdotes and thoughts and a novel *Double Take* (1996) where the heroine Bella, a Bron figure heavily disguised as a blonde, is one of the acting world's high fliers who embarks on a love affair that is suggested is based on the actor Robert Stephens.

With such a varied career the question remains as to why Bron never quite made it into the topmost rank. She has the view that featuring in satire programmes was not the ideal springboard for a career as a serious actress. 'If you start out associated with comedy and also the handicap of satirical comedy, it's not a line that's easy to cross. If serious actresses like Glenda Jackson and Judi Dench do comedy, it's a delight but it's far harder to cross the other way into serious acting'. She comments that 'I don't think I had in myself the freedom to be able to act and be unconstrained. Also there's a level where, with a certain amount of talent and an enormous amount of determination and a thick skin, you can get somewhere: by being very focused and single minded.' This was not in Bron's character. She always chose things that would interest her rather than those that would advance her career.[195]

She admits that she has probably not pushed herself hard enough to obtain parts. She wonders if her early success as a revue actress may have made it difficult to play straight parts and may also have made directors reluctant to cast her in straight parts. She acknowledges that a number of the big television roles she has had have resulted from other actresses dropping out. 'There was always a point at which I could have done things but didn't', she recalled. I was offered West End plays and *The Avengers*. But I went to Bristol Old Vic and Worthing instead. I felt very much that I ought to have gone to drama school and had sneaked into the theatre by the back door although I was probably wrong to think that'.[196]

Bron did not follow the conventional Jewish path despite the traditional Jewish background of her childhood and attending Hendon Jewish Youth Club.[197] The life she chose for herself, she explained, was unusual for that time. 'My parents were very happily married and they encouraged me to marry. As I never had children nor wanted to have children, I couldn't see the point of it actually. It's the sort of thing, when I was growing up, that people expected of you. But it didn't seem inevitable to me. It didn't seem very desirable, either. It's better to be lonely on your own than lonely when you're married. I think that must be one of the worst things of all. My mother was always worried about me. She wanted me to be secure. I'm sure my parents wanted me to be married and happy, but it didn't seem to me that being married and happy were necessarily two things that went together or that it was necessarily secure'.[198] She was the partner of architect Cedric Price until his death in 2003.

Nevertheless, she explains that in some sense she is a religious person. 'I do think a lot about life and I seem to think there is a higher motive going on in one's life'. Yet when considering the existence of life after death, she cited a Freudian game. 'You go into a wood and you have to describe what sort of trees there are and then there is a house and you have to describe that. One then comes to a wall and you are asked what is on the other side. I then realised that there was nothing on the other side. This is my verdict on life'.[199] Bron herself is full of horror at what religion does to women.[200]

Bron has not been cast in specifically Jewish roles although she was in the ITV sitcom *Fat Friends* (2000) set around a slimming club in Leeds. The characters who attend the club are from various backgrounds and of various weights with each episode focusing on a particular character. Bron played the stereotypically neurotic mother of the Jewish character Lauren Hill. She did not take part in Jewish communal events. When she spoke about her career to Maidenhead Synagogue as part of their jubilee celebrations in 2016, it was only her second appearance before a Jewish audience.[201]

If she had somewhat negative feelings towards organised religion, this did not apply to politics. She was, like Miriam Karlin, active in left-wing politics and voted for Jeremy Corbyn in the 2015 elections. 'I care very much about politics. I am totally bewildered by the fact that I was brought up in a society that seemed to be getting better all the time. I benefitted from the NHS when I had a major operation on my spine soon after leaving university and all the things I acquired – the standards, achievements, how to think — the things which henceforth were going to be for everyone are being diluted. Soon they will only be there for a small minority of people'. She came to realise that she could not take things for granted and how wonderful it was when everyone was striving for a better life for all. 'Now only money buys privacy, clean air, education, health and justice. You have to go on fighting'.[202]

Bron joined Jewish celebrities and representatives from five Jewish gay groups in the 1988 march against Clause 28 of the Local Government Act that stated that a local authority may not 'intentionally promote homosexuality' or 'promote the teaching in any maintained school of the acceptability of homosexuality as a pretended family relationship'. More than 30,000 people took part in the march and it was the biggest demonstration for gay rights to date in Britain.[203] She took part in the 25th anniversary performance for the Jewish Council for Racial Equality that was held at the Tricycle Theatre in 2001. Her views in respect of Israel were left-wing and she attended a fundraising dinner for the magazine *New Outlook*, where Jews and Palestinians joined forces. The magazine was founded by philosopher Martin Buber and it spread the message of peace and reconciliation between Israel and the Arab world. Bron, together with playwright Harold Pinter, read Palestinian and Israeli poetry as part of the programme.[204]

Bron sometimes chose to appear in fringe theatre productions if the cause was close to her heart, such as *Be My Baby* at the Pleasance Theatre, London. She starred as the matron of a home for single mothers in the mid-1960s, the type of establishment where young women had to hand over their babies for adoption after giving birth. The drama referred to 'up the junction side of that decade which co-existed with the Swinging London, Carnaby Street, the Beatles and the group of brilliant satirists which included Bron'.[205]

Bron faced a similar problem to Miriam Karlin and Fenella Fielding in respect of not achieving theatrical fame. She admits that 'I found it difficult to break into serious theatre and I worked hard to move away from comedy to be taken seriously as an actress'. She found that after the age of 50 it was difficult to get roles of any substance that were attractive.[206] In her mature years she has appeared in the BBC Radio 4 soap opera *The Archers*. She played Jill Archer's old friend Carol Tregorran, one of the most iconic characters. Carol Tregorran, who was dining at Grey Gables the night Grace Archer was famously killed in a fire returns to Ambridge to attend the funeral of on-air husband John Tregorran. She was thrilled when she was offered the part. '*The Archers* was part of my history. It is such a valuable part of the narrative of British life'. The character of Carol Treggoran first appeared in 1954 and was a favourite with listeners. Against the social grain of the mid-1950s Carol was a forthright and successful businesswoman. She was thought to be a role model for women at the time and remained in the core cast until 1980. *The Archers* editor Sean O'Conner hoped she would continue to be an independent spirited woman who embraces her later years on her own terms and without compromise. This appears to be very much the character of Bron in real life.[207] She appeared in Age UK's national TV advertising campaign in 2010. The advert highlighted the common problematic areas affecting those in later life and offered solutions through the products and services offered.

Bron's long career stretches back to the 1960s where she found herself in the cradle of the satire boom. She was described as the female Peter Sellers and that her work of characterisation had the validity of social comment that he was famous for.[208] However, subsequent decades saw this quirky yet stylish performer and writer gradually relegated to guest star status.[209] Referring to the start of her career and the 1960s she comments that it was only looking back that she now sees what an extraordinary period it was. She was very much part of the zeitgeist of the decade.[210]

Attending Cambridge University and participating in Floodlights also gave Eleanor Bron's close contemporary, Miriam Margolyes, her start in acting. Like both Bron and Claire Bloom, physical appearance was a determining factor in the course of Margolyes's career. All three women avoided being typecast in Jewish roles, but like many Jewish actresses of her generation, Margolyes felt her appearance limited the range of roles she was offered. Despite an active and wide-ranging career, Margolyes has been defined as a character actress, frustrated in her ambitions to achieve greatness.

Miriam Margolyes (1941 –)

Miriam Margolyes is famously vulgar and outspoken and considers herself one of Britain's best character actresses, describing herself as 'short, fat and curly'. She has enjoyed many years of success as a comedy actress and voice artist, with her work ranging from children's shows to melodrama. She has won numerous awards, including an Oscar nomination and BAFTA award for her Mrs Mingott in the *Age of Innocence* (1993), a Los Angeles Critics Circle award for her Flora Finching in *Little Dorrit* (1987), memorably falling completely head over heels backwards from a sofa, and an Olivier award for her acclaimed solo theatre show *Dickens' Women*. She has had notable roles in *Blackadder* and the *Harry Potter* franchise. She was awarded an OBE for services to drama in 2002.[211]

She was brought up in Oxford, the adored only child of second-generation immigrants Ruth Walters and Joseph Margolyes. The Walters' family originated from western Poland and Ruth's father, who had a furniture shop, was born in Middlesborough in 1867. Ruth grew up in south-east London where her father was one of the founders and first president of the synagogue in New Cross. Joseph Margolyes was born in the Gorbals slum, Glasgow. His father came from Belarus in 1887, working first as a pedlar before opening a jewellery shop. Joseph won a scholarship to study medicine and became a doctor instead of joining the successful family business. He initially worked in East Ham, London and met Ruth at a Jewish tennis club in south London.[212] The family moved to Oxford to escape the bombing. They were members of the Oxford synagogue and Joseph was president of Oxford Bnei Brith.[213] Margolyes recalls that 'in some ways it was not a very friendly community. I don't think they really liked my parents. I don't know why. Some of the community were sort of wide-boys, selling on the black market and rather disreputable and others, the university party, were very charming and interesting'. Miriam went to her local Oxford grammar school and despite later becoming a socialist and a member of the Labour Party, felt hugely indebted to it.[214]

Her mother would have been an actress if it had been acceptable for a nice Jewish girl from her background to do so and was thrilled when her daughter showed dramatic ability. 'I was a show off. I think I came dancing out of the womb. I had big dark eyes and a wonderful smile and people just loved me when they saw me'. As a young child she played Bottom in readings of a *Midsummer Night's Dream* and everyone said she was going to be an actress.[215] She was very happy at school and was the form wag. 'Laughter is like love and I can't get enough of it'. For Margolyes, who needs desperately to be liked, acting is paid 'show off'.

Miriam's Yiddish-speaking father was doctor to philosopher Sir Isaiah Berlin's parents who lived in Oxford and only spoke Yiddish. Margolyes's mother asked Berlin to sponsor her daughter in her university application and she went to Newnham College, Cambridge University. 'It was at Cambridge that my life began'.[216] She focused on performing there rather than her studies in literature. She was the only woman in the 1962 *Footlights* revue, acting alongside John Cleese, Graham Chapman and Bill Oddie and says she was the leading actress of her day there.[217] She admired the comedy *Monty Python* creators and thought they were men of genius but considered them to be horrible. 'In those days women were not meant to be funny. They were meant to be decorative and I was never decorative nor bedworthy and they found me unbearable'.[218] Margolyes found them to be cruel, antisemitic and very cliquey .[219] 'They thought I was a jumped up, pushy, overconfident fat little Jew'.[220] This negative experience differed from that of Eleanor Bron and this might have been due to Bron's more attractive appearance and less confrontational personality. However, it was a useful experience as appearing in *Footlights* enabled her to get an audition at the BBC'. She famously appeared on University Challenge in 1963 when she was the first person to use an expletive on British television.[221]

After Cambridge, Margolyes sold encyclopaedias door to door and did market research. Her confidence at the time stems from her parents. 'I think they believed in me, probably spoilt me and gave me unconditional love and I believe in myself. So much so that when I did an audition at Leeds and the directors asked her whether she was absolutely set on a stage career because they thought she should look elsewhere, she thought 'oh poor fool, you can't see the talent'. Margoyles describes herself as 'untutored'. But there is a freshness and an originality about her which she thinks may be due to not having been schooled in the same way as other actors. Elocution lessons from a good teacher whilst she was still at school taught her what vowels and consonants can do and how they matter when you are acting. 'And it is because of her I have a voice and the voice is what has made me the most money probably and is the reason that people remember me'. Eventually she was hired by the BBC Drama Repertory company and started to appear on radio. From the beginning, it was her voice that made her.[222]

Since that time Margolyes has enjoyed over 30 years as a comedy actress and voice artist and with her distinctive voice has performed countless voiceovers for commercials, including the Cadbury's caramel bunny. A great deal of her work has been on screen, beginning with *Enter Solly Gold,* (1965) and she achieved success in *The Girls of Slender Means* (1975), the BBC adaption of Muriel Spark's novel. Her first major role in film was in *Stand Up Virgin Soldiers* (1977). She is most famous for comedy, appearing in several series of *Blackadder* (1983-89). She came to the notice of a younger audience when she starred in *James and the Giant Peach* (1996).

She was the voice of Fly the Dog in *Babe* (1995) and played Professor Sprout in the Harry Potter films (2002 and 2011). Theatre credits include the musical *Wicked* (2006) and Beckett's *Endgame* (Duchess Theatre, 2009). In 2016 she appeared in the BBC's series *The Real Marigold Hotel*, about retirees moving to India to see if they could have a better retirement there and hosted the BBC series *Miriam's Big American Adventure* (2018) highlighting issues facing the American nation. A recent role was as Sister Mildred in *Call the Midwife* (2018-19), a BBC drama about midwifery and family in 1950s East End of London. She divides her time between England and Australia. She became an Australian citizen in 2013, thereby holding dual British and Australian citizenship.

Margolyes has achieved a great deal and attributes this to her Jewish background where success was important. Her parents wanted her to go to university so that she could meet the right people and 'be able to talk about everything'; to be in some sort of social elite, a feeling that came from being outsiders. Margolyes felt very much at home at university. 'I felt Cambridge belonged to me personally'. Her parents came up to visit so often that people thought they were part of the student body.[223] Her mother was a social climber, shrewd and clever. Her father was a mixture of Scottish and Jewish. Sombre, quiet and full of integrity.[224]

Being Jewish is part of Margolyes' identity and very important to her. As a child she was steeped in Judaism as her parents were observant and so powerful are the traditions that she still fasts on the Day of Atonement, observes the rules of Passover, keeps the dietary laws and has never eaten bacon. 'I feel intensely Jewish'.[225] She chose the Kol Nidre prayer,[226] sung by American operatic tenor Richard Tucker, as one of her choices on *Desert Island Discs*.[227] Nevertheless she considers herself militantly secular. 'Religion has caused so much horror in the world but I believe in tradition. I want to honour the past, honour my parents, my ancestors and all those who died. She is a member of two synagogues, an Orthodox synagogue in Sreatham, south London and the Chabad synagogue in Battersea. 'I may not believe in God but I'm very proud of my roots: they nourish me. I'm fascinated by the pull of Judaism and its culture – the food, the jokes, the vitality, the suffering, the guilt and the history – it's all part of who I am and what I've inherited'.[228]

Her father was the only Yiddish speaking doctor in Oxford so she was used to meeting his refugee patients and learnt about the Holocaust. 'It's no exaggeration to say that every day of my adult life I've thought about the Holocaust. It has coloured my feelings about the world that let it happen and makes me sharp about spotting antisemitism'.[229] For as long as she can remember she wanted to know about the Holocaust and growing up in Oxford, with many refugees in the city, she became used to seeing the numbers on the side of people's arms. A cousin gave her a letter which was a cry for help, written in 1939, and she does not believe that anyone answered it. She went back to where the family lived in Grodno, Belarus and found the home was now a modern block of flats and every trace of them had been obliterated. She says that the Holocaust is the reason why she is an aggressive Jew, forcing her Jewishness on people to show them we are still here.'[230]

Yet Margolyes says but she refuses 'to be trammelled, button-holed, labelled or trapped in a box'. She is not religious. 'I don't like religion' and describes herself as 'a very determined, elderly actress, competitive, kind, Jewish, often melancholic. A performer'.[231] She has great nostalgia for Jewish theatre and likes the mind of the Jew. 'What I can't bear are the North London smarty poos. I don't fit in with them at all'. She avoids going to the Jewish areas of north London and friends bring the chopped liver that she loves to her. Her longing is that Jews do not disappear as a people although she realises that it is the Orthodox Jews who will guarantee their survival. Although she finds their excesses antipathetic, she knows in her heart they are doing more for the survival of Jews than she is. 'It is a paradox and we have to live with paradoxes. It is also a paradox that Jews whose intellectual tradition is one of dialogue are so clamped down on the issue of Israel'.[232]

In July 2006 she was a signatory to the Jews for Justice for Palestinians letter published in the *Times*. She explains that she had visited Israel four or five times before her visit in 1994 when she performed at the Jerusalem Festival. During that period she visited the Gaza Strip and then everything changed. She no longer wants to return for she saw the utter degradation and poverty of the Palestinian Arabs and could not believe that Jews who have suffered as a people could do this to other people. Although she finds it painful to be critical of Israel she believes Israelis are behaving wrongly. 'If I don't speak out then I am condoning it', adding that 'In no way do I condone suicide bombers or that kind of mindless violence. I just want people to sit down and talk and see the humanity in each other'.[233] She wants fellow Jews when visiting Israel to go and see how things are for the Palestinians on the West Bank and in East Jerusalem.[234]

Some people were shocked by her Palestinian support and her friends were divided: Miriam Karlin, who shared her political sentiments, applauded her; actress Maureen Lipman felt differently.[235] 'She is disgusted with me and speaks clearly about that publicly too. The same for the author Howard Jacobson who pillories me, lampoons me in a very public way. I totally accept his right to do so but it doesn't make me happy. It doesn't please me that people see me as an enemy of the Jewish people'. Jacobson has attacked her for her claim that Israel's conduct is behind the rise in antisemitism. Margolyes explains that 'I don't like having to be critical but I am because you have to be very clear about what is right and wrong generally in the world and it is very clear that Israel is behaving wrongly. I don't think they mean to kill innocent people but I don't think they actually care how many Palestinians they kill because they are all enemies according to Israel. It's being done in my name, so to speak, and I simply can't accept it. It's damaging for Israel, damaging for Jews everywhere, fostering antisemitism'.[236]

Margolyes has supported left-wing politics from an early age. 'I came from a very middle-class Jewish background, always voting Tory. And then at University I was changed into somebody with a heart. I've never looked back'.[237] She showed great support for Jeremy Corbyn and the Labour Party. She considers that Corbyn is a man of principle. 'I think antisemitism is throughout the English political system. I don't think Labour have a monopoly on antisemitism'. 'I know Jeremy Corbyn personally and I know he's not an antisemite'.[238] She comments that in the current situation 'governed by a crowd of incompetents', she is going further and further to the left.[239]

Margolyes has never fitted the profile of a conventional Jewish woman and in some ways the intense love she received as a child gave her the confidence to speak out with little heed to what others would think. Being an only child was a mixed blessing. There was always going to be a price to pay for being so cocooned in love by her parents and during her childhood in Oxford they formed what she calls a 'fortress family'. She admits that the umbilical cord was never completely cut and that self-centredness can be a hazard for an adored 'only'. She describes herself as 'appallingly selfish throughout my life'. Her selfish tendency, she believes, led her to cause misery to her parents by coming out as gay when she was in her 20s. The hothouse intensity of her relationship with her mother, in particular, whose wholeheartedness she has inherited, meant that Margolyes told her everything, including details of her sexuality, which she now regrets. Her parents longed for their only child to have a conventional Jewish marriage with children.[240] She is still with the same partner Heather Sutherland, a retired professor of Indonesian history who lives in Amsterdam although they have never lived together. There is some guilt that revealing the relationship led to her mother's debilitating stroke at the age of 63 as the situation was shameful for her, which was then followed by a long period of illness. However, her mother's stroke may have released her to live a fuller life. 'I really believe that if my mother had not had a stroke it would have been hard for me to have a relationship, certainly with a woman'.[241] Margolyes says she was never maternal and did not want children. Although she realises the situation was sad for her parents, one can only live life for oneself. 'So I just did what I wanted'.[242]

Her rich career has seen her work with directors such as Martin Scorsese (*Age of Innocence*, 1993) and Baz Luhrmann (*Romeo and Juliet*, 1996) and she has won awards and acclaim for her film work, her theatre performances and her book readings. Although openly Jewish, she does not portray Jewish characters and instead has become famed for her characterisations of those that are quintessentially English, as shown in her love of Charles Dickens and her portrayal of his female characters. Her one woman show *Dickens' Women* brings to life 23 characters, based on real women in Dickens's life and where they parallel with his fictional characters. The show premiered at the Edinburgh Festival in 1989 and has toured extensively, including a world tour in 2012 as part of the 200th celebrations of Dickens' birth. Margolyes is passionately proud and committed to the show.[243]

In recent years Margolyes has rejuvenated her career with a series of documentaries for the BBC. She was in the first series of the popular *The Real Marigold Hotel* and has presented travelogues on the USA and Australia. She appeared in *Miriam Margolyes: Almost Australian* (BBC, 2020) which sees her travelling 10,000 kilometres through Australia in a camper van and meeting transvestites, farmers and Bondi Beach swimmers along the way. She is outspoken about the plight of the country's Aborigine people. She also makes many talk show appearances. Hayley Freeman has mixed feelings about Margolyes taking part as she considers that they have a tendency to overshadow her work which has been magnificent and that she sometimes she is reducing herself to parody, playing the overweight older lesbian who talks about sex. Margoyles is not concerned about this. 'Not a lot of gay women front up on television so I have to give courage to young dykes to be proud and confident'.[244]

Despite having one of the most sought after voices in the business she says she has not had the career that she aspired to, sentiments that were voiced by Miriam Karlin and Fenella Fielding. She yearned to be taken more seriously and given meatier roles, but she jokes that Joan Plowright[245] always stood in her way. On stage she has the confidence and chutzpah of someone who is beyond embarrassment but she says that in reality, for most of her life, she has simply been a 'frightened little muffin'. The term character actress could have been coined just for her. She has spent her career bringing fruity rich bodied individuals to the screen and yet she has spent her life dealing with the disappointment that she is not the most important person on earth. She blames her parents for that particular delusion. They were a family so wrapped up in themselves that the outside world had no emotional significance for her. She thinks that she should have been treated better and points out that it took until 2008 for her to be included on *Desert Island Discs*. 'I am not happy with what I have given to the world. I think I am underused and undervalued. I have a good voice and my whole life is based on my voice and searching for people's backgrounds using voice as my starting off point. I wanted more out of my skills. I wanted to do Shakespeare, I wanted to be at the National. I wanted to be admired as an actress. I think that at the moment I am just smiled at as an actress. I want to touch people, I want to hurt and astonish.'[246]

She considers being overweight has held her back professionally[247] and comments that until she is invited to work with one of the major companies or directors, she does not consider that she has 'made it'.[248] This in her opinion is not due to lack of talent. 'I think I'm hugely talented and I think I have the potential to be great'. Her great asset is her voice. 'I have one of the best in the world, I think, on stage. I have excellent diction. When I speak I give full value to vowels and consonants. Words are my friend and I know how to colour them, how to use them and I really feel in control when I'm speaking'.[249] Margolyes relishes her outrageousness. She likes to shock and to confront matters that other people are not prepared to do. 'It is a compulsion. A verbal Tourette.[250]I think knickers, lavatories and breasts are very funny. I love the whole physical part of life. I find it hysterically funny'. It is also a way to reassure herself. By saying something shocking gives her power.[251] This compulsion has and continues to entertain audiences worldwide.

Though Miriam Margolyes feels that her appearance has impeded her aspirations, it has not limited her to a narrow range of Jewish roles despite her never having hidden her Jewish identity. In contrast, her contemporary, Maureen Lipman, found national fame in the role of a Jewish mother in a British Telecom advertising campaign and embraced her Jewishness as a positive attribute in a career that has included extensive work in the West End, as well as in television and film.

Maureen Lipman (1946 –)

Described as a female Woody Allen and Lucille Ball[252], Maureen Lipman is one of Britain's best loved stars with more than 90 film and TV credits to her name including the Oscar winning film *The Pianist*. She has appeared in more than 30 West End shows including *Oklahoma* at the Royal National Theatre in 1999. She was awarded a CBE in 1999 and a DBE for services to charity, entertainment and the arts in 2020.

Born in Hull in 1946, Lipman was the daughter of tailor Maurice Lipman and Zelma Perlman. There were three synagogues in the city, the rich one, the average one and the one that the family went to which was just two Victorian houses knocked into one. Her father was the president as he liked to be a big fish in a small pond.[253] She received a very Jewish upbringing but without discussion or questioning of religious practice.[254] Active in the Bnei Brith youth movement, she found post-war Hull a welcoming place for the Jewish community and was proud to be different at school. 'I was born in 1946. We were the good guys, there was no antisemitism. I was glad I didn't have to go to morning assembly and it was like dishes – a set of friends for the weekend and a set of friends for the other days. I didn't feel superior but I didn't feel in any way prejudiced against'.[255]

Lipman never wanted to do anything else but act.

'I was one of those nasty precocious children who used to stand on the sideboard and do impersonations of Johnny Ray and was later on in all the school plays'.[256] It was not a musical family. The first music that affected her was Alma Cogan singing 'Dream Boat'. 'She was big in our house as she was a nice Jewish girl'. She started to impersonate her. Later she played the lead, Doctor Faustus in the school play of the same name and she was sure from that moment that there was nothing else that she wanted to do. Her parents had no objections. Her mother encouraged her and would take her to the pantomime and push her on the stage. She studied at LAMDA (London Academy of Music and Dramatic Art).[257]

Lipman's Jewish background has been very evident in her career. The first main Jewish part was in her late husband Jack Rosenthal's play *Evacuees* (1975), his first full length television play about two Jewish boys evacuated from Manchester to Blackpool. She then became famous as 'Beattie'. Beattie was the archetypal Jewish mother character who fronted British Telecom's advertising campaign in the late 1980s. Mrs Beattie Bellman was created by J Walter Thompson in 1987 and took the nation by storm. She went on to star in 32 television commercials and contributed the world 'ology' to the English language. Having just been told by her grandson Anthony that he has flunked his exams, passing only pottery and sociology, Beattie says: 'he gets an ology and he says he's failed… you get an ology you're a scientist'. Politicians still refer to it years later. The then UKIP leader Nigel Farage blamed 'Beattie' for too many young people going to university to study poor degrees and that telling her grandson that having an 'ology' made him a scientist meant there were many students getting 'ologies' that would be better off studying to be carpenters or apprenticeships.[258]

Lipman has at various times been identified as a Jewish performer and at other times as a performer. David Aaronovich in an interview for the *Jewish Quarterly*, asked her whether when she was training did she think of herself as a 'Jewish actress'? 'I never thought of myself as a Jewish actor. I thought of myself as a Jewish woman who acted and that was my job. I was very up front about being Jewish. I didn't know any better'. She recalls that as soon as she left drama school an agent took her straight to see a plastic surgeon. She did not make any changes but changed her agent. She considered that nobody saw her as a Jewish actress and she played a variety of roles. Then along came Beattie and she was typecast for the next ten years. Lipman does not complain about this as she considers that it gave her the opportunity to appear in Roman Polanski's film *The Pianist* (2002), based on the extraordinary events of a Jewish musician's life in the Warsaw Ghetto and which won numerous awards. Lipman played the musician's mother. 'The Jewish thing has helped me get parts that other people could not get'.[259] She describes being a Jewish actor as 'on the one hand quintessentially precious and all-encompassing, but on the other hand making you an outsider'. The outsider role, she believes allows a distance that provides new insights and stores proportion. She believes that Jews who are 'really out' as such continue to remain pigeonholed within British theatre – like gays. She thinks Jewish actors find it much harder to get cast in classic roles unless the director is Jewish and notes Antony Sher as the exception but in time became relaxed about being Jewish as he was about being gay.[260]

Judaism became more important for Lipman after she married Jack Rosenthal[261] in 1973 and the subsequent birth of their children Amy and Adam. They went to West London Reform Synagogue and became devoted to Rabbi Hugo Gryn. 'He was a rabbi in the true sense of the word, he was a teacher'. She relishes the 'colourfulness' of being Jewish and the feeling of community with people all over the world, knowing that on the first night of Pesach they are doing and saying exactly the same thing. 'If that's globalisation then I like it' and that she becomes more Jewish and more pro-Israel as she grows older.[262] She has involvement in the community and in 2017 launched a pre-Passover Reform synagogues campaign in support of isolated members of its 42 communities, whereby congregants called other members to wish them the best for the festival and ensure that they were not on their own for the Seder night.[263]

Although nationally known for her Jewish character Beattie, she was able to adapt to playing a character such as Joyce Grenfell, who was someone so quintessentially English, on the stage in her one woman show *Re: Joyce* (1991).[264] Grenfell had commented during the Second World War that 'there's something a bit un-cosy about a non-Aryan refugee in one's kitchen'.[265] In her long career Lipman had never encountered antisemitism until portraying Grenfell. She received many letters along the lines of 'keep your hands off Joyce, she was English'.[266] This negativity appears to be in relation to portraying a member of the upper classes and not in respect of other non-Jewish characters. In 2002 she appeared in the ITV soap *Coronation Street.* She played scheming Lillian Spencer, a manageress who beguiles Rovers landlord Fred Elliot before installing her son and daughter behind the bar at the Rover's Return and who clashes with the pub's staff and regulars.[267] In August 2018 she re-joined the cast playing outspoken battleaxe Evelyn Plummer, the long lost grandmother of Tyrone Dobbs. Her character comes into Tyrone's life when he researches his family history after the death of his mother. She was described as 'a 21st century Ena Sharples with added sex appeal'.[268]

In the early days of her career, Lipman appeared at the Edinburgh Fringe Festival. She returned in 2018, the first time in 50 years, with a one woman show of jokes and storytelling *Up For It.* 'Lipman's stories race at a pace with old fashioned Jewish jokes, name dropping and observations on the subjects of public toilets in department stores with doors that do not lock, age and reality tv. A series of interchanging monologues on a defeated mother in discussion with her ex, an insensitive Australian nurse administering a mammogram and a northern café owner. She has the audience eating out of her hand. Lipman has a winning formula – a talented writer and performer who can draw a crowd'.[269]

Lipman has had an illustrious career. She was a member of Laurence Olivier's National Theatre Company at the Old Vic (1971-73) and a member of the Royal Shakespeare Company Stratford season (1973). After early appearances in the sitcoms *The Lovers* and *Doctor at Large* and a role in *The Evacuees* (1979), Lipman first gained prominence on the 1975 TV sitcom *Agony,* in which she played an agony aunt with a troubled private life. She played the lead role in the television series *All At No 20* (1986-87) and took on a range of diverse characters when starring in the series *About Face* (1989-1991). She has continued to work in the theatre for over 30 years with shows including *A Little Light Music* (Menier Chocolate Factory, 2008), *When We are Married* (Garrick Theatre 2010-11), *Old Money* (Hampstead Theatre, 2012), *Daytona* (Park Theatre, 2013), *Harvey* (Birmingham Rep,

2015), *My Mother Never Said I Should* (St James Theatre (2016), *Lettice and Lovage* (Menier Chocolate Factory, 2017) and *The Best Man* (Playhouse Theatre, 2018). She has also taken part in BBC Radio 4's *Just a Minute, The News Quiz, That Reminds Me, This Week* and *Have I Got News for You*. In 2007 she was a celebrity contestant on *Comic Relief Does the Apprentice* to raise money for Comic Relief. In 2008 she appeared in the BBC documentary series *Comedy Map of Britain* and in 2009 in the third series of teen drama *Skins*. She also wrote a monthly column for *Good Housekeeping* Magazine for over ten years which formed the basis for several autobiographical books including *How Was It For You?*, *Something To Fall Back On, Thank You For Having Me* and *You Can Read Me Like A Book*. Her awards include the Laurence Oliver Award for Best Comedy Performance in *See How They Run* (1985) and an honorary doctorate from the University of Hull (1994).

Such a vast output of work reflects great energy and this is not just restricted to the stage and screen. Lipman has always shown a keen interest in politics, both in the Labour Party and concerning Israel. She supported Israel during the 2006 Israel-Hezbollah conflict. In a debate on BBC's *This Week* she argued that 'human life is not cheap to the Israelis, and human life on the other side is quite cheap actually because they strap bombs to people and send them to blow themselves up'. These comments were condemned by the *Independent* columnist Yasmin Alibhai-Brown who said 'brutally straight, she sees no equivalence between the lives of the two tribes'.[270] Lipman responded to Alibhai-Brown's accusation of racism by arguing that the columnist had deliberately misrepresented her comments as generalisations about Muslims rather than specific comments about terrorists. 'Yesterday Yasmin Alibhai Brown cast me in the role of racist. On the programme *This Week* it was perfectly clear to me, if not to her, that I was referring to those who send out children to blow themselves up as people to whom life is cheap. I was referring to extremists, not Muslims in general. I realise to misinterpret my words fitted in extremely well with her premise of the Jew as racist and I hope your readers do too'. Her support for Israel still continues and she was honorary patron of the International Shalom festival event at the Edinburgh Festival.[271]

As many of her background, Lipman was a supporter of the Labour Party all her life. One of the dedications in her book *Something To Fall Back On*[272] is to the Labour Party. She declared in 2014 that she would no longer be voting Labour, after five decades of support, as she denounced Ed Millband's negative stance on Israel after its incursion into Gaza in 2014 and said that she would vote for 'almost any other party' until Labour is 'once more led by *mensches*'.[273] She commented that his support for the motion 'sucks' at a time of rising antisemitism in Europe.[274] A worrying rise in antisemitism caused Lipman to consider leaving Britain, a fact she found very depressing. 'When the economy dries up, then they turn on the usual scapegoat. The usual suspect. The Jew. There is one school of thought that says it is because of Israeli policies in the West Bank. It isn't. There's been antisemitism for the past 4,000 years. When the going gets tough, the Jews get packing. It's crossed my mind that it's time to have a look around for another place to live'.[275]

In a letter to the *Jewish Chronicle* she states that she fully backs the actions of the Board of Deputies, Jewish Leadership Council and the Campaign Against Antisemitism in highlighting the failure of the Labour Party to effectively deal with antisemitism. She considers that only by eradicating this scourge can Labour again become a party worthy of opposition, let alone government. She joined hundreds in a demonstration organised by the Campaign Against Antisemitism outside Labour Party headquarters. She spoke to the crowd telling them that you can easily be antisemitic and still call yourself anti-racist and that was what Corbyn was doing and that everything pointed to the fact that there was an antisemite at the head of the Labour Party. She described herself as a 'disenfranchised socialist' and claimed that Corbyn had made her a Tory[276] and that it was 'scary' to be protesting in 2018 about antisemitism in the Labour Party.[277] She attacked Corbyn for attending a Passover seder organised by left-wing Jewish group Jewdas saying it was 'the absolute cherry on the top' of Jeremy Corbyn's behaviour. 'He is standing with elements who are against everything that we stand for; hardworking, decent Jewish people of whom I am incredibly proud'.[278]

Lipman launched a scathing attack on Jeremy Corbyn as she recorded a mock version of her iconic British Telecom advertisement in which she claimed the party leader had an 'ology in extremism'. She re-enacted her portrayal of doting grandmother Beattie from the 1980s in an online video produced by anti-extremism campaign Mainstream. A lifelong Labour supporter she spoke of her fears of the modern Labour Party and the reason why she will not be voting for them in a mock phone call to her friend Nora. She condemns Jeremy Corbyn and claims they are not a 'socialist party' but are 'extremists'. In the video Beattie tells her friend 'of course we were all Labour, everybody voted Labour. I voted Labour all my life. You know what my late husband said? If you're Jewish they gave you your Labour Party badge the day after your circumcision. They gave with one hand, they took with the other. But this lot… this lot's not Labour. They're not socialists.

You know what they are Nora? They're extremists, that's what my Melvyn says and he's not often wrong.'[279]

With boundless energy, always humorous and forthright, Lipman continues to entertain and make herself noticed. When interviewed on *Desert Island Discs*, she said that her epitaph would be 'only a tailor's daughter but she had them all in stitches'.[280]

The generation of actresses born between, during and immediately after the Second World War, while taking diverse paths to their acting careers and enjoying varying success based on their appearance and early roles, they nevertheless shared similar backgrounds as children of immigrants who openly embraced and even capitalised on their Jewish heritage. The new generation of Jewish actresses born during the post-war 'baby boom' did not always share this easy relationship with their Jewishness, as the career of Tracy Ann Oberman attests. While being Jewish did not limit the range of roles she was offered, Oberman's frequent encounters with overt antisemitism and prejudice caused her to struggle with her Jewish identity for many years.

Tracy Ann Oberman (1966 –)

Tracy Ann Oberman, who was to become the nation's most popular murderess in the television soap *EastEnders*, grew up Stanmore, north London and studied at the Central School of Speech and Drama. She came from a strong legal background. Her family were not thrilled about her desire to become an actress and were always making her watch the television series *Rumpole of the Old Bailey*, telling her that it was just like acting so why not pursue the law. Yet Oberman had wanted to be an actress after going on a school trip to Stratford where she saw *Troilus and Cressida* and was inspired.[281]

Oberman initially studied Classics at Leeds University but switched to a drama course at Manchester University and then spent four years with the Royal Shakespeare Company before joining the National Theatre's production of *Waiting for Lefty* (1999). She returned to the National in 2003 in *Edmond*, playing opposite Kenneth Branagh, in David Mamet's play about a New York businessman's descent from respectability to murder. Her role as Branagh's wife was well received as were her roles in the West End revival of *Boeing-Boeing* (2007-2008) a French farce in which she plays German air hostess Gretchen, one of three trolley dollies being strung along by architect Bernard and whose character Oberman describes as an 'uber-Teutonic blonde, flaxen haired wench who could crush you in her bare hands'[282] and *Earthquakes in London* (2011).

Her very strong work ethic and her drive for professionalism is in part a result of her parents' initial concern with her career choice.[283] She has acted in radio drama and radio comedy, appearing regularly on BBC Radio 4, including *The Way It Is* (1998-2001), the leading role in *The Attractive Young Rabbi* (1999-2002) and *The Sunday Format* (1999-2004). Her first major role on television was in *Casualty* (1998) as a security officer. Her numerous television appearances include sketch shows, dramas and sitcoms, *The Way It Is* (2000), *Lenny Henry in Pieces* (2000-2003) and episodes of *Doctors, The Last Detective, Where the Heart Is* and *The Bill* (2000). She appeared in *Friday Night Dinner* (2011) a Channel Four television sitcom focused on the regular Friday night dinner experience of the British Jewish Goodman family. Set in suburban north London, the episodes follow the family as the sons, musician Adam and estate agent Johnny, arrive at the family home of Jackie and Martin Goodman and proceed to dinner. The meals are often interrupted by Adam and Johnny pranking each other and Martin's oddities. Jackie's best friend is neurotic Valerie 'Auntie Val' Lewis (Oberman), also a frequent visitor.

Oberman's career changed drastically when she joined the British soap opera *EastEnders*, as Chrissie Watts, the second wife of one of the best loved villains in soap history, 'Dirty' Den Watts. She was the voluptuous landlady turned murderess.[284] It was a role that she played for nearly two years. 'By playing Chrissie she found stratospheric fame.'[285] In 2005, over 14 million people watched her character kill Den in a fit of rage with a dog-shaped doorknob before burying him in the cellars of The Vic. She became the nation's most popular murderess and it was commented that 'the actress easily upstaged the rest of the cast with her three dimensional portrayal of a classic soap bitch with steely eyes and barbed remarks.'[286] Chrissie was created to be more the 'equal' of her notorious and villainous husband than his first wife Angie. She became well known for her deviousness and scheming, echoing the traits of her husband. Before long Oberman became one of the leading stars of the show and at the forefront of several storylines. At the time television critics pointed to Oberman's extensive theatrical background and questioned why an actress with such pedigree would agree to be in *Eastenders*. Oberman placed the move in context of her professional exposure, noting her position as a jobbing actress at the time and her desire to return to drama after her recent comic roles and that the offer came at the right time of her career.[287]

Although starring in a soap can prove a curse for actors who can find themselves unemployed after being on television three or four times a week, this was not the case for Oberman and she was hired to appear on *Doctor Who* (2006) opposite David Tennant as human villain Yvonne Hartman, head of the mysterious Torchwood Institute who collects alien artefacts and sees the Doctor as being a prize alien in her collection.[288] Yvonne Hartman is 'a sophisticated sort of baddie' and Oberman was perfect to play the part 'and brilliant at terrorising the next generation of viewers'.[289] She often plays strong, feisty bitchy characters. She appeared in the BBC daytime medical drama *Doctors* as a widow whose two previous husbands had died in suspicious circumstances. She was the evil villainess the Grand Mistress in CBBC's teen spy drama *M I High* who starts a crime wave in a bid to take over the Grand Master as the head of the Secret Criminal Underground League.[290]

She was 'hard as nails' in *Hello and Goodbye* by Athol Fugard.[291] Set in South Africa during apartheid, a brother is reunited with his estranged sister Hester. Oberman plays Hester, a poor white woman in a run down area of Port Elizabeth. As an impoverished prostitute who is 'propelled by a frenzy of money and lust and shamelessly parades her bruised arms and fading beauty'.[292] She was a tough woman in Mike Bartlett's play *Earthquakes in London*, billed as a mixture of 'modern excess, population explosion, family crisis… and the end of the planet?' Oberman is Sarah, the secretary of state for energy and climate change who is in a coalition government and is trying to force through her green message.[293]

She appeared in *Celebration*, one of the short Harold Pinter plays that were put on to commemorate the tenth anniversary of his death at the theatre that bears his name. It concerns two gangster brothers and their molls having lunch at a posh London restaurant. Oberman plays moll Julie, who 'transmits a sexuality from beneath a breaking wave of blonde hair that is as alluring as it is aggressive'.[294] The fact that she appeared in a Pinter play resonated with Oberman. 'He was a brave political writer who was Jewish and faced antisemitism. He inspires me and I take courage from that and my grandparents who did too'.[295]

Oberman has a strong sense of her Jewish heritage. She visited Yad Vashem, the World Holocaust Remembrance Museum in Jerusalem, when she was just six years old. 'This was probably the defining moment in my life. Too young to understand the context but aware that it had something to do with being Jewish. Is this what it means to be Jewish? It's a question I have been asking myself ever since. My early introduction to the Shoah has certainly left me with a survivor's guilt, an inexplicable shame and huge need to stand up to the bully. But also a pride in every single one of us still here, identifying or not, for we are the product of survival'.[296]

For many years she struggled with her identity and to be open about her Jewish identity. 'There was a real shame about feeling persecuted'. There were a few difficult moments of antisemitism early on in her career. The head of her drama school told her she should change her name from Oberman because it was too Jewish and she didn't 'look enough like Anne Frank' to be cast in Jewish roles. She had a real dilemma about this and queried whether she should be called Tracy Denham or Tracy Holland and then she thought 'I am who I am'. Other negative experiences were when a tutor rubbed his fingers in a 'monied way' when talking about Jews and someone who told her she had to choose between being Jewish and an actor as 'there's room only for one religion in this business, Christianity'. She recalls that when she was younger she auditioned for a part in a Jane Austen drama. 'They looked at me, looked at my name and said we don't think people would have looked like you in Jane Austen's time'.[297] This contributed to her hiding her Jewish identity. The turning point had been the BBC show *Goodness Gracious Me*.[298] Watching her friends Anil Gupta and Sanjeev Bhaskhar embrace their cultural heritage 'made me suddenly feel that it was okay to be Jewish and British but it wasn't my defining characteristic as an actress'.[299]

When she was in her 20s and 30s, she did find herself on a path that took her far from her religion. 'Although I always felt Jewish I wouldn't have said it was my overwhelming point of definition. Woman, actor, English may have come nearer to the top of my internal Google search.' She found that she changed after becoming a wife and mother. 'I find that Jewishness is hardwired within me. It is the centre of the wheel from which all spokes emanate'. She describes herself as an integrated secular actress (but not so integrated that she does not feel at home in a synagogue or round the Chief Rabbi's for dinner). She also quotes other attributes such as I am the Jewish daughter who always brings flowers on Friday night. I am the friend who can't help but offer advice and the wife who tries her best to create a moral and embracing home.[300] Her favourite festival is Passover as it covers all bases – spiritual, physical and intellectual. Spiritually it makes her feel part of something ancient and important: a story that has been told for centuries in the same way and with the same never-ending ritual.[301] She is very open about her views and was a columnist for the *Jewish Chronicle* (2009-2017). She supports Israel and in 2012 called on the public to be more active in campaigning on Twitter – 'X' in respect of the campaign to ban the Habima Theatre from performing at London's Globe Theatre international Shakespeare Festival. 'We can no longer rely on the old standards to try and fight back at distorted ideas and interpretations. We need to harness the power of these sites with our own brilliant strategists. We do need to speak out against this new McCarthyism. Quickly, speedily and in numbers'.[302] In April 2019 she was one of over 100 celebrities who signed a statement against a campaign advocating the boycotting of the Eurovision song contest in Israel.

Oberman's great-grandmother Annie Donnoff grew up in Mogilev in Eastern Belarus. After a spate of violent pogroms where her own father was beaten very badly her parents cobbled the money together to send her to England for a safe life. She settled in the East End of London where she worked and slept in a clothes factory for a penny a week.[303] As a child she would watch the musical *Fiddler on the Roof* with her grandmother and Annie would say to her 'this is like a documentary'. Whenever Russia was mentioned, around the dinner table or in a news bulletin, she would spit on the ground and say 'whatever you do, don't go there, they will behead you'. In 2017 she played the part of wife Golde in *Fiddler on the Roof* at Chichester Theatre. She had never been in a musical before. Director Daniel Evans said he liked the timbre of her voice and he saw that she was connected to the material. 'You totally get Golde'.[304] 'Fiddler was my family story. I had a connection with Golde and her hopes and aspirations for her daughters to get them a better life'. She quietly dedicated every performance to her grandmother.[305] 'Fiddler was a seminal moment in owning my culture and who I was'. She also commented that at a time when the Labour Party was turning its back on its Jews, it was a timely reminder that most British Jews came from these shtetls with huge communist and socialist backgrounds.[306]

Her immigrant background served as a connection when she appeared in the adaptation of Howard Jacobson's Manchester-set novel *The Mighty Walzer* at the city's Royal Exchange Theatre. Set largely in Manchester's Cheetham Hill in the 1950s, Jacobson's book is autobiography in the sense that it rises from the community in which the author grew up. The story centres on Oliver, an introverted youth saved from solitude by a talent for table tennis. His mother Sadie (Oberman) is full of fear and inhibitions. She loved being part of the production. 'Here in a room full of Jewish actors there's a kind of shorthand you can tap into'. Again she recalls great grandmother Annie who came from similar stock as the Walzers and spoke Russian and Yiddish and that the one phrase she knew how to say in English was 'look out for the Cossacks'. It is that state of being on constant alert for catastrophe that informs her role as Sadie.[307]

In *Three Sisters on Hope Street*, written by Oberman and Diane Samuels, their story moves Chekhov's famous tale to a tight knit Jewish community in Liverpool in 1946. Oberman explains that it is a family living through enormous social and political change. They completely avoid all big issues by using humour, wit, arguing, bitching and backstabbing and eat all the time and talk all the time.[308] For Olga, Masha and Irina, read Gertie, May and Rita.[309] 'Chekhov wrote about a world I recognised from my childhood – where intense pain is covered by bravura and humour, and where intense longing is masked by self-deprecation and wit. There was the same obsession with death, the same fierce family loyalty, the same tendency toward melodrama – as well as a great passion for food'.[310]

Another personal dimension for Oberman was starring in *Ridley Road* (BBC One, 2021) which revolved around a young hairdresser who starts working with an anti-fascist collective called the 62 Group in the East End in the 1960s. Oberman plays the wife of the group's leader. Her grandparents took part in the 1936 Cable Street march against Oswald Mosley.

Since 2020 Oberman has played Shylock in a production of *The Merchant of Venice* set in the Fascist 1930s. Its original four week run grew into a year-long tour and culminated in a run at the Criterion Theatre, London in 2024. She reframed the courtroom drama from its original setting in Renaissance Venice to the East End of London in the 1930s when Oswald Mosley's British Union of Fascists were attacking Jews. Her great uncle Al was thrown through a window by a member of Mosley's militia. The 1936 Battle of Cable Street in which the fascists were resisted by an alliance of the Jewish, Irish and English class was woven into family lore and forms to backdrop to Oberman's production.[311] She reinterpreted the play from a feminist perspective. Shakespeare's aristocrats were cast as Fascist supporters and Shylock becomes a working-class matriarch seeking a better life for her daughter Jessica. Inspiration again came from her great grandmother Annie who lived through that turbulent time in the city. Annie lived in the Cable Street area with her husband Isaac, going on to run the family's clothing business with 'an iron fist'. 'Women like her were as tough as nails and so I pictured Shylock as a matriarch like that. The 1930s was a very difficult time to be Jewish, to be working-class and to be a woman'.[312]

The fresh version of the play also paid tribute to other Jewish women such as MPs Luciana Berger, Ruth Smeeth and Margaret Hodge who had each spoken out on the issues bedevilling the Labour Party. Oberman feels they have been incredibly brave. 'And the response has been racism and misogyny that hasn't been seen since the 1930s. I have tried with everything that has happened to put it to positive use. After the October 7 attacks on Israel, the play took on a further level of meaning. In performing Shylock's soliloquy in the weeks of October 7 – 'Hath not a Jew eyes? If you prick us do we not bleed?', Oberman has felt that she is speaking for an entire nation and our allies as more Jews were murdered and brutalised in that one day than any other since the Holocaust. Her friend who works in the Mayor of London's office, whose family were also caught up in the attacks, told her that on the same night, before Israel had set a foot in Gaza, they had applications for pro-Hamas demonstrations the next day.[313]

Away from the stage, Oberman has become an avid spokesperson on social media campaigning against injustice and antisemitism in the Labour Party. Her family were life life-long socialists and Oberman was previously a member of the Labour Party but left in 2017 due to its delay in concluding the disciplinary process of Ken Livingstone after he referred to Hitler having supported, when he came to power, Jewish emigration to Palestine. 'Like so many of us whose East End heritage was steeped in Labour, I'm reeling. Resigning my membership. Feel so let down'. She was a fervent social media critic of the party's leadership under Jeremy Corbyn.[314] Her views were also shared by Maureen Lipman. 'My upset is that this was my party, it was my heritage, It was my family'. She notes that the vitriol was highly misogynistic, mainly targeted at women. Her take on *The Merchant of Venice* was more timely than ever. That play has really resonated with me as an activist over the last few years because I found myself on the front line, particularly on social media, of speaking out against a growing wave of antisemitism and anti-Jewish statements'.[315]

In February 2019 Oberman and British TV game show *Countdown* presenter Rachel Riley instructed a lawyer to take action against 70 individuals for tweets which they perceived to be either libellous or tantamount to harassment. Riley and Oberman have criticised Labour persistently and have in return faced substantial antisemitic online abuse. The pair are 'looking to stop vile lies' after their criticising antisemitism in Labour.[316] She was called a Rothschild prostitute, a tax-evading whore, a Holocaust exaggerator.[317]

Oberman is adamant that she had to stand up to antisemitic abuse wherever she saw it. Taking on the abusers meant that she too became a victim. 'As a Jewish woman I have been attacked on my looks, my body, my age, my lifestyle choice, my job. I put in the words 'dirty Jew' into Twitter – 'X' to find out that I came top of the list'.[318] She launched the podcast *Trolled* that shines a light on what it is like to be trolled and is aimed at anyone who is finding it hard to engage about issues that they feel strongly about and are unable to express their opinion as keyboard warriors bully, threaten and attack, claiming that 'this podcast will be a balm to your soul'.[319]

Oberman is a strong personality, as reflected in the roles that she has played during her career. She is a person that likes to 'stand up and be counted' and this is portrayed professionally, such as her role as Chrissie in *EastEnders* where she played a strong woman who stood up to her abuser[320] and in her personal life in her quest for social justice. She was honoured at a Jewish Care's Women of Distinction lunch for her 'courageous work' in fighting antisemitism. She said that despite receiving death threats, threats towards her daughter and warnings her career would be ruined if she did not back down, the thought of those lost during the Holocaust gave her purpose. 'Throughout everything I do, my Jewishness is weaved through it like a golden thread'.[321]

Though Tracy Ann Oberman struggled with her Jewish identity early in her career, as she matured, she has been able to embrace and proclaim her Jewishness proudly and defiantly. Like actresses from an earlier generation she came from an immigrant background and has been profoundly affected by the Holocaust, motivating her engagement in political and anti-racist activism. Her contemporary, Sophie Okonedo, has also confronted her Jewish identity and has had to combat prejudice and racism throughout her career, not only as the descendant of Eastern European immigrants, but as the multi-ethnic daughter of Nigerian and Jewish heritage.

Sophie Okonedo (1968 –)

Sophie Okonedo CBE is an actress who describes herself as a 'north London working-class, black Jewish girl'.[322] She straddles the worlds of kneidlach and fried chicken, klezmer and hip hop.[323] As a child of mixed heritage she overcame prejudice and poverty by developing a sense of pride in her own identity.

Okonedo was born in London on 11 August 1968 to Henry Okonedo, a Nigerian civil servant and Joan Allman. Her maternal grandparents came from Poland and Russia and had settled in the East End. Sophie was just five when her parents separated. Following the breakup her father returned to Nigeria and Okonedo only reconnected with him in later years.

She was raised by her mother and her Yiddish speaking grandparents Max and Jean and spent her formative years living with her mother in the since demolished Chalkhill Estate in Wembley, London, notorious for drugs and criminal violence. Okenedo admits that it was 'very rough'. Former local MP and London Mayor Ken Livingstone said of the Estate 'nobody in their right minds wants to live there. It's a riot waiting to explode'. Even in those uncompromising circumstances her family encouraged her to be artistic. Joan infused Sophie with a sense that she could accomplish anything. Okonedo was an avid reader and her mother would comb second hand bookshops to fill their shelves with books. She remembers how a housing inspector was flummoxed by the family's large collection of books and asked her mother what she did with all those books. She said the remark was made because he considered that poor people did not read. 'My mother never forgot that'.[324]

Her maternal grandmother took her every Saturday to the Wembley Liberal Synagogue, which was local to where she lived. Her grandparents kept a fairly Jewish household. They celebrated all the holidays and spoke Yiddish when they did not want her to understand. They were central figures in her life, regaling her with stories of her ancestors depicted in old photographs.[325] She was the only black congregant at the synagogue. She said she was the only black Jew to grace the steps of the Brady Maccabi youth group. 'I came across as much racism in the Jewish community as I did outside the Jewish community. No more, no less'. She went on to say that 'although sometimes you sort of assume that if a section of society has been through such a hard time themselves, then the way they'd treat you… but that's not the case'.[326]

Eventually her mother, a hairdresser and Pilates instructor, was able to afford a flat above a fish and chip shop in Preston Road, Kenton. Yet in some ways matters became more difficult. The Chalkhill Estate was rougher but there at least she felt that she fitted in as there were many mixed race children. As a teenager she used to be ashamed about where she lived as most of her Jewish friends lived in the more affluent neighbourhoods and if they gave her a lift she would ask them to drop her a distance away from her home. It was some of the parents of her middle-class Jewish peers who were often the cause of her discomfort. 'I certainly felt as a teenager a lot of the parents of the children would have been unhappy if they came home with me. I certainly felt stared at when I went to synagogue'. She remembers on one occasion being picked up from a party by the parents of one of her friends. Before they left she overheard the adults talk about how they were moving out of the area because of the 'wogs' moving in. They then looked down at Sophie, who was about 12 at the time and said 'We don't mean you Sophie'.[327]

It was not easy being black and Jewish as a child in the 1970s but thanks to her mother she did not feel there was anything in her way or any boundaries. This feeling was enhanced when she saw a young black girl perform a routine in the ensemble of the musical Annie during a Royal Variety Show performance. 'It was unusual then', she recalls.[328]

Although a good student and a voracious reader, Okonedo left school at 16 to work on a clothing stall on Portobello Market. Two years later she found her way into acting in a roundabout way after joining a writers' group headed by Oscar nominated Hanif Kureishi[329]. Her work in class led to unexpected results. She did not believe that she was especially talented as a writer but she did have a gift for reading other students' work out loud. Her classmates admired her ability so much that they suggested she try acting. After taking classes at the Weekend Performing Arts and Media College and appearing in performances with the Royal Court Theatre, Okonedo auditioned for and received a scholarship to the Royal Academy of Dramatic Arts (RADA).[330]

As a young actress fresh out of drama school, Okonedo portrayed her raw talent and confidence into stage roles with the Royal Shakespeare Company, the Young Vic and the National Theatre. She also appeared in UK television dramas such as *Sweet Revenge, Clocking Off* and *White Teeth*. However, it was for her edgy and provocative interpretation of Cressida in Trevor Nunn's 1999 London production of Shakespeare's *Troilus and Cressida* which brought critical acclaim.

While concentrating her efforts on stage acting she also scored cameos in a number of Hollywood productions, including *Ave Ventura: When Nature Calls* and *The Jackal*. It was Stephen Frears' 2002 dark thriller *Dirty Pretty Things*, where she played a compassionate prostitute, that was the point that she proved to be a talented lead. In 2005 she burst into the international spotlight when she was nominated for an Oscar for Best Supporting Actress for *Hotel Rwanda*. The film tells the story of Paul Rusesabagina, a hotel manager who saved over 1,200 Tutsis from ethnic cleansing and Okonedo was cast in the role of Tatiana, Paul's wife. She went on to play an emotionally disturbed young woman in civil rights era South Carolina in *The Secret Life of Bees* (2008).

She then tackled her first leading role in *Skin* (2008), based on the true story of Sandra Laing, a bi-racial girl born to white parents, unaware of a black ancestor in their family tree, in 1950s South Africa. The film chronicles the parents' battle for Sandra to be classified as 'white', her rebellion and marriage to a black man and subsequent struggle to be reclassified as 'coloured' to keep her children. At one point in the film Laing's parents learn that their child could not continue to live in their home unless she was documented as a household servant. Okonedo felt a personal connection to the script. 'I could relate to being black and brought up in a white family. She admits that being raised in north London in the 1970s was much kinder than South Africa in the 1950s but it was helpful to understand what it was like to have a family that is a different colour to you – and to question your heritage when people said that 'that can't be your mum'.[331] She would ask her mother if she was adopted. It was hard for people to believe that this young girl with a huge Afro had a Jewish mother.[332]

In 2014 she won a Tony award for the Broadway revival of *Raisin in the Sun* about an African-American clan crowded into a cramped apartment on Chicago's South Side. It starred Denzel Washington and Okonedo is Ruth, his harried wife, a woman drained by the pressures of working as a cleaner while caring for her unhappy husband and son. To find her way into Ruth she worked with a dialect coach for weeks so that she had a faultless Chicago accent and in order to understand Ruth's reality researched the legacy of slavery in America.[333]

The performance earned her a Tony award and in 2016 she appeared in a revival of Arthur Miller's *The Crucible* where she received a second Tony nomination for her portrayal of the betrayed character Elizabeth Proctor. She played the titular role in *Antony and Cleopatra* alongside Ralph Fiennes at the National Theatre which earnt her the prize for best actress in the 2018 Evening Standard Theatre awards. Other recognitions include a Golden Globe nomination for the mini-series *Tsunami: The Aftermath* (2016) and BAFTA TV nominations for the drama series *Criminal Justice* (2009), for a role as Winnie Mandela in the BBC drama *Mrs Mandela* (2010) and Supporting actress in *Criminal : UK* (2021) where she portrays Julia, a woman who is being interviewed as a special witness in multiple murders her husband is suspected of committing.

Many of her roles are challenging. *Ratched* (2020), based on Nurse Ratched in Ken Kesey's novel *One Flew Over the Cuckoo's Nest,* chronicles sadistic villain Nurse Ratched who terrorises a California psychiatric hospital in hopes to set her killer brother free. Okonedo plays Charlotte Wells, an inmate in the hospital who struggles with multiple personality disorders. Okonedo channels several different personas, including a boxer, a baby and the doctor who is treating her. 'She impressively aces a remarkable feat by taking on five characters which she plays in rapid succession without letting one influence the other in the slightest. It takes a seasoned, dedicated actor to masterfully present even one character on screen but she breathes life into five distinct personalities'.[334]

Sophie Okonedo explains her ability to play such a variety of parts throughout her career. 'I'm a north London, working-class, black Jewish girl. I love my upbringing because it had so many different colours: it's given me the equipment to play lots of diverse roles'.[335] She considers the fact that she has a Jewish mother and Nigerian father helped her in her acting. 'I am not a practising Jew and I am not embedded in Nigerian culture but I have a sense of those things inside me which is very handy for acting. There are a lot of things I can draw on.'[336] She is proud to be Jewish and black. 'I find the mixture extraordinary and happy to be both.'[337] She feels very Jewish culturally. 'It's all in my blood.'[338] She has always been out and proud about her Jewish roots and is acknowledged as such in the *Jewish Chronicle*. In her Tony award acceptance speech for *Raisin in the Sun* she thanked the play's producer Scott Rudin 'who brought me over here and had a vision that a Jewish, Nigerian Brit could come over the pond and play one of America's most iconic parts.'[339]

Throughout her career she has played roles where her ethnicity was relevant, such as *Hotel Rwanda, Mrs Mandela* and *Skin* but there were many more where it was immaterial such as Nancy in *Oliver Twist* (BBC 2007) when she was the first black Nancy and Queen Margaret in the Shakespeare cycle *The Hollow Crown: The Wars of the Roses* (BBC, 2016).[340] The feisty monarch, who was married to Henry VI in the fifteenth century, had previously been portrayed by white actresses. Director Dominic Cooke considered Okonedo was the best person to play the part. 'Her visceral power and range is so extraordinary – that's what I was really looking for.'[341] Nonetheless she still has to be cast in a black Jewish role which might suggest a limited vision all round and failure to confront multiple identities.

Okonedo built her career on 'difficult roles'.[342] 'Her success is driven not so much by ambition as by commitment to her art and to portraying the extraordinary potential of people grounded in an unglamorous reality. In that sense the little Jewish girl from Wembley who lights up stages and screens from London to Hollywood never turned her back on the housing estate and the chip shop'.[343]

Conclusion

The lives of the eight actresses profiled in this chapter span nearly a century, and their careers encompass an enormous variety of roles in theatre, film, television and radio. Their paths into acting were diverse and they achieved varying levels of success throughout their long careers. Several were primarily known for their comedic talents, others specialised in serious dramas or as character actors, and generational differences influenced the course of their acting careers. But for all the factors that distinguish these women from one another, they share a common heritage and across the generations they experienced many of the same challenges – and rewards – as Jewish actresses in British theatre.

Each one of these actresses can trace at least part of her heritage to Eastern European Jewish immigrants, and this common background ties them together in significant ways. Though none participated in the Yiddish Theatre of late nineteenth and early twentieth century London, they were all inheritors of that Yiddishkeit cultural tradition and owe a debt to those early East End Jewish actresses for advancing acting as a respectable career choice for young Jewish girls of the interwar period and beyond. As Miriam Margolyes commented: 'My family story illustrates the archetypal trajectory of a working-class Jewish immigrant family: first, a peddler, then in trade, then in professions and then, with me – the third generation immigrant – in the Arts.'[344]

The women in this chapter were all raised in affirmatively Jewish environments – most in the north London suburbs – and acknowledged and even embraced their Jewishness throughout their careers, even when experiencing antisemitism and the perceived disadvantages of being unambiguously Jewish actresses. These disadvantages are richly illustrated by an anecdote concerning a young Jew in an East Surrey regiment who asked the advice of theatre critic James Agate as he was 'wanting to learn the Art of Acting before appearing in the Operatic Stage in opposition to his parents, who desire that he should manufacture brassieres'. Agate asked him: 'What do you look like? Jewish? All right. Too Jewish. Not so good.'[345]

Tracy Oberman was told to change her surname because she didn't 'look enough like Anne Frank' to play Jewish roles and was turned down for a role in a Jane Austen drama because no one looked like her in Jane Austen times. Oberman noted that 'contemporaries of mine like Samantha Spiro[346] were all pretty much told to try and keep your Jewish heritage out of the way because casting directors will see you differently'.[347]

The issues of Jewishness and appearance intersect continuously throughout these women's stories, with distinct impacts on the roles they landed and even the course of their entire careers. For Claire Bloom, who was considered to have classic 'English rose' looks, it meant resounding success in the theatre world and never being cast in a Jewish role, while the striking multi-ethnic appearance of Sophie Okenedo, who has also achieved theatrical acclaim, has similarly been precluded from playing Jewish characters. In contrast, Maureen Lipman, who has consistently been cast in Jewish roles, feels her appearance has on balance been an advantage to her career, while acknowledging her difficulty in landing 'classic' roles on stage. For Miriam Margolyes, it is not so much her Jewishness but being overweight that she feels has held her career back, and Eleanor Bron transcended her distinctly Eastern European appearance to land a variety of roles, but no Jewish parts.

A few of the actresses whose lives have been examined in this chapter managed to scale the heights of acting acclaim, but a number have been markedly disappointed in the outcome of their careers. Certainly appearance has played a part in limiting the scope and range of roles these women were offered, but some were simply unable to transcend being typecast based on their early roles and career choices. Miriam Karlin, Fenella Fielding and Eleanor Bron all believed that their early work in comedy sketches and revues hindered their ability to land serious roles or star in major West End productions. Still an active actress, Tracy Oberman did not express dissatisfaction with the body of her work, but after breaking through as a villainous character in *EastEnders*, she has been cast in a succession of similar roles. Even Claire Bloom expresses some regret at never playing in a romantic comedy, having played serious, complicated dramatic characters throughout her career.

Nearly all of the women profiled in this chapter aspired to an acting career from a young age, and many had understanding parents, especially mothers, who encouraged this goal. Maureen Lipman's and Claire Bloom's mothers actively promoted their early acting ambitions and remained supportive throughout their careers. Both Eleanor Bron and Miriam Margolyes believed that their mothers' encouragement derived from their own repressed desires to take up acting themselves. Family support usually led to the women's enrolment in drama school as a path towards a career in theatre, though Bron, Margolyes and Tracy Oberman all attended university instead. Fenella Fielding and Oberman did not enjoy such family support and forged their own routes to the acting careers that their parents eventually endorsed once they achieved some success.

Several other links, closely related to their common heritage as the descendants of Eastern European Jewish immigrants, unite these renowned actresses. Though all affirmatively embrace their Jewish identity, few consider themselves religious and Eleanor Bron, Miriam Margolyes, and Tracy Oberman consider themselves secular or culturally Jewish. Additionally, for Margolyes and Oberman, the Holocaust has been a formative event in their lives and careers. Most of these women have been the targets of overt antisemitism at some point in their careers, and these experiences, in combination with their upbringing and proud Jewish identity, has led most of these actresses to engage actively in left-wing political causes, campaigning against antisemitism and racism, and taking strong, though divergent stances on Israel and questions of Palestinian autonomy. Her intense reaction to these questions even led Miriam Karlin to renounce her Judaism. Active engagement with politics and social issues connects these actresses as closely as their common experiences as Jewish actresses in the British theatre.

This political activism has intersected with many themes of these actresses' careers in the recent 'Jewface' row over the casting of non-Jews in Jewish roles, such as Helen Mirren as Golda Meir in *Golda* (2023). The issue of casting non-Jews in Jewish roles was brought to the fore in an open letter in 2019 signed by more than 20 Jewish actors and playwrights, including Lipman and Margolyes, criticising the West End Jewish musical *Falsettos*, which had no Jews in its cast or creative team. The letter called it an example of 'overt appropriation' and called for 'livid experience' to be a cornerstone of productions about Jews and highlighted the practice of 'Jewface' as something to avoid.[348] This controversy demonstrates how much has changed for Jewish actresses in the past century. While for Miriam Karlin and her generation of actors, Jewishness was often considered a liability for an aspiring actor, in the twenty first century, Jewish actresses proclaim their prerogative to represent themselves in dramatic roles that highlight Jewish life and experience.

2

Writers

During the Victorian period British Jewish women began to enter the field of writing. They became the first Jewish women anywhere to publish novels, histories, periodicals, theological tracts and conduct manuals. Their romances, some of them which sold as well as novels by Dickens, argued for the emancipation of Jews in Britain and women's emancipation in the Jewish world. 'These texts served as emblems of Jews' desire to become acculturated to modern English life while simultaneously maintaining a distinct collective identity'.[1]

The women lived and worked in accordance with particular pressures. They had to respond to conversionists depicting them as malleable and vulnerable, as too spiritual for the heartless rituals of their dead letter religion. They had to respond to Jewish men who accused them of being undereducated (while refusing to educate them). They tried to define Jewish women's privileges, duties and needs. Their definitions differed depending on a number of factors that included how long their family had been in England, whether they were Ashkenazi or Sephardi, upper or middle-class, traditionalist or reformist. Although they were divided along some lines, they formed a loose community of writers in dialogue about the necessity of women's education. Whilst arguing for women's intellectual emancipation in the Jewish world, many of them were also arguing for Jewish political emancipation in the Victorian world. They worked within the constraints of the time that restricted women's activity to the sphere of the home and to charitable work among the poor but discovered a way to speak in a public voice as if they were merely dispensing maternal wisdom within the confines of the home. They also discovered the romance genre in which they could imagine a release for their heroines from the constraints they experienced.[2]

Their contributions to Jews', women's and Victorian literary history are many. Although not very well known today, early Anglo-Jewish women writers produced the English Jews' most significant attempts at self-definition during the period of emancipation and religious reform (1830–1880). Moreover, they were the pre-eminent Jewish women writers in the world during the first two-thirds of the nineteenth century and among their achievements they wrote the first Jewish novel, the first Jewish women's periodical in modern history and a cookbook in English.[3] The writers included Celia and Marion Moss,[4] Grace Aguilar and Amy Levy.

Grace Aguilar (1816-1847) and Amy Levy (1861-1889) produced important work that is still read today. Both were unmarried and had short lives and were clearly different in their outlook on life. Aguilar's pride in her heritage came out consistently in her writings, whereas Amy Levy was a rebel who examined Jewish life from the outside.

Grace Aguilar's persistence in struggling to launch herself on a literary career despite the ill-health that plagued her throughout her life was similar to that of the Bronte sisters. Most of her output, non-fiction as well as fiction, dealt with Jewish subjects and she won much sympathy from a non-Jewish readership for her writing about Jewish suffering. Aguilar was born in Hackney, London to a Sephardi family that originally came from near Cordoba, Spain. The family moved to the west of England when she was 12, where she spent her formative years amongst Christians. They returned to London and she was forced to earn a living when her father died, which she did partly by writing and partly by helping her mother in a preparatory school for young Jewish boys in Hackney. Her book *The Spirit of Judaism* (1842), a discussion of Jewish practice, argued that the ethics of the Hebrew Bible were more important than the rituals that dominated Jewish life and that a moral life was therefore more important than one that concentrated on the ritual. She explained the differences between Judaism and Christianity, and while favouring a dialogue between both faiths, Aguilar was emphatic that Jews must not be ashamed of what they stood for.[5] She was a forerunner of modern Zionism, even to her insistence that Hebrew should be taught as a modern language and made familiar to every child.

When she died in 1847 at the age of 31 she was remembered as a poet, historical romance writer, domestic novelist, Jewish emancipator, social historian, theologian and liturgist. Her body of work which was translated into French, German and Hebrew, appealed to both Jews and Christians, women and men, religious traditionalists and reformers. 'She developed new and hybrid literary genres, helped to build the Anglo-Jewish sub-culture, advocated Jews' emancipation in the Victorian world, and insisted on women's emancipation in the Jewish world'.[6]

Amy Levy (1861-1889) was born in London to Isabel (Levin) and Lewis Levy, a stockbroker. The family, who were prosperous and middle-class, had roots in England that went back to the eighteenth century and had strong ties to the Anglo-Jewish community. Levy was fortunate to be the child of enlightened parents and they sent her to be educated at Brighton High School for Girls, a school founded by women's rights activists. She went to Cambridge University, where she was the first Jewish student to be admitted to Newnham College. She left Newnham without taking her exams when her first volume of poetry was published. After Cambridge her circle of friends included Eleanor, the daughter of Karl Marx, Beatrice Webb and George Bernard Shaw. Oscar Wilde described her as 'a girl of genius'. She was a New Woman, a rare creature among the largely conformist Jewish community of her time. She pursued an increasingly successful career as a journalist and a poet as well as a novelist, and her poetry is now as much appreciated as her fiction.[7]

Levy wrote essays about secular Jewish identity and challenged the traditional Jewish community's treatment of women. She wrote 'the assertion even of comparative freedom on the part of a Jewess often means the severance of the closest ties, both of family and race'. Her first novel, *Romance of a Shop* (1888), told of four sisters who defy convention to open a photographer's shop but it was her novel *Reuben Sachs*, published later that year, about life in an affluent Anglo-Jewish community that made her name.[8]

It was Levy who first depicted a community caught between religious tradition and secular opportunities. *Reuben Sachs* was the first book by a Jew to open up British middle-class Jewish life to a wider public and is a bitter commentary of Jewish society as Levy then saw it. It tells the story of Judith Quixano, a poor girl who goes to live with wealthy relatives on the opposite side of town. She falls in love with Reuben Sachs, a relative from the other side of this family, and while he returns her affection, Sachs has ambition and knows he must marry into wealth.[9]

It can be seen as the earliest attempt to explore the situation of women in the Anglo-Jewish community. Levy follows in the footsteps of Victorian novelists such as Charlotte Bronte and George Eliot in their portrayal of women's predicament in the wider community. She too explores the women of each generation in her novel, including the unmarried plain (and plain speaking) Esther and the older women compensating for their unfulfilled lives with jewels and pride in their sons, full of unused vitality. But it is in depicting the younger women with the 'narrowest of outlooks' who wait for their only destiny, the marriage proposal, that Levy makes her strongest impact. Even the wealthiest of them says 'no girls like her intended, at first….' Judith is at first fortunate to have her horizons broadened by Reuben Sachs who lends her books. Yet after Reuben has awakened both himself and Judith to his true feelings, he yields to the political ambitions that will rule Judith out as a possible wife. The materialist values in which Reuben and Judith have been raised are called to account for their respective destinies. As a man Reuben has an alternative but for Judith the realisation just brings a lifetime of frustrated desire and a loveless marriage.[10]

Reuben Sachs is one of the earliest examples of the move away from the heavy Victorian multi-plotted novel pointing towards the slim volumes of modernist writers like Virginia Woolf and Oscar Wilde hailed it as a 'classic'. Now regarded as a pioneer of a genre of self-critical Jewish novels, Levy poked fun at the materialistic, somewhat overbearing upper middle-class Jews of Bayswater and Kensington. Much of her writing was coloured by her experiences at Cambridge. She was an early feminist and she was active in literary and politically activist circles in London during the 1880s. Her experience at Cambridge did not turn out as well as expected. It seems to have shown her that she did not fit into either the English or the Jewish world.[11]

There has been greater interest about Levy in recent years and she features regularly in dissertations and courses on Jewish and lesbian literature, nineteenth century feminism, women's poetry and the New Woman. She was a rare creature among the largely conformist Jewish community of her time. Unfortunately, despite her achievements, hers was a troubled life and she committed suicide in 1889 at the age of 27 by inhaling charcoal gas.

Though varied in their background and writing style, these Victorian Jewish female writers provide a rich foundation from which those in the twentieth century and beyond could build. The following authors have been chosen to represent the cosmopolitan nature of British Jewish writing and cover the whole of the twentieth century from Naomi Jacob born during Queen Victoria's reign to those currently writing.

Naomi Jacob (1884-1964)

One of the most popular writers of her day, Naomi Eleanor Clare Jacob was born in Ripon, Yorkshire. Her German-Jewish father Samuel Jacob was a schoolmaster and her mother Selina Collinson, who was not Jewish, was a writer. At the age of 15 Jacob became a teacher in Middlesbrough to augment the family's income. After leaving teaching she became personal secretary to Marguerite Broadfoote, a variety performer, who introduced Jacob to appearing in Vaudeville during the First World War. Jacob's first novel, *Jacob Ussher*, was published in 1926 and became a bestseller. Her

Jewish family Gollantz series of novels extended her popularity, in particular *Four Generations,* published in 1934. Harking back to her upbringing she would write stories set in Yorkshire, such as *Late Lark Singing* (1957). Jacob wrote two books a year, including her *Me* memories, culminating with *Me and the Stage* (1964) written in the year she died from a heart attack. Jacob was famed for her bold appearance, complete with crew-cut and monocle. There was talk of her various lesbian romances, including the variety actress Marguerite Broadfoote, but she never wrote about them.[12]

Jacob had a somewhat unusual background. Her mother 'Nana' Selina Sara Collinson was the daughter of Robert Ellington Collinson, a considerable figure in Ripon society who ran a well-known hotel The Unicorn. He was an alderman and justice of the peace but also a gambler and heavy drinker. Although Nana had numerous suitors she surprisingly chose the physically unprepossessing Samuel Jacob, despite her reservations about his older age and appearance, for a variety of confused reasons. She was desperate to escape from the Unicorn and her stepmother and she was jealous of her sister who had just got married and was living in a fine house.[13]

Although Samuel's first language was German he spoke English fluently, if over correctly. He was cultivated, had renounced his Jewish faith and belonged to the evangelical section of the Church of England. He had come from Manchester to Ripon to take charge of a private school for boys and was subsequently appointed headmaster of the choir school at the Minster. Jacob's parents married in Ripon Minster with most of the city dignitaries present. Only two members of the Jacob family were there, Samuel's sister and brother. His father Samson Jacob did not attend for although not strictly Orthodox he still felt uncomfortable at the thought of being associated with a Christian marriage but sent the couple his blessings. Samson had escaped from Poland as a child during a pogrom in which his parents were killed. His mother died of a brutal flogging and his father, a cantor in the synagogue, had his tongue cut out and bled to death. Samuel was brought up in Germany by relatives who had left Poland earlier. He came to England in his twenties with his wife and young family and set up a tailoring business in Manchester. He became a naturalised Englishman and although he spoke German to his family, his principal language was Yiddish and if he ever reverted to it Samuel would explode at him to stop.[14] He was a great linguist, a prominent Leeds social worker and presented to one of the Leeds synagogues a *Sefer Torah*[15] which had been in the possession of his family for many years.[16]

Jacob's parents' marriage was an unhappy one. Samuel Jacob was unfaithful and became known as the 'gay Lothario of Ripon society' that would result in his losing his headmastership of the choir school. 'Did I ever imagine a daughter of mine marrying a dirty undersized foreign piece of scum?' said his father-in law. There was no great love between Jacob and her father. When she was born he was disappointed that she was not a boy and when he first saw her said she looked like a boiled monkey. She despised him growing up and he is an anonymous shadow in her earlier autobiographies, a 'he' or 'him'. After he died she wrote about him in *Robert, Nana and – Me*, and spoke about his unstoppable sexual appetite, his drunkenness and his inability to show affection. His most grievous fault, however, is one she dwells on in other books, especially the novels concerned with the fortunes of the Gollantz family. She could not forgive him for wanting to be accepted as an upper middle-class Englishman, the equal of her maternal grandfather and his friends. She presents him always as the upstart Jew, an embarrassing misfit in the drawing rooms of Ripon, lacking the proper social graces. In her fiction he is transmogrified into a variety of 'bad Jews' – men or women who think they are clever, renounce their faith who pretend to be more English than the English, who bring shame on their race. Her 'good Jews' by comparison remain Jewish, make their money through hard work, manage to be at once proud and modest.

Jacob always proclaimed her Jewish ancestry. Her mother reverted to her original name Nina Collinson after divorcing her bankrupt husband and she urged her daughter to follow her example. She suggested this in 1899 just before her departure with her other daughter Muriel to America. She left 15-year-old Jacob, who was estranged from her father, to fend for herself. She never understood why her daughter retained a surname that was synonymous with so much unhappiness.[17]

Erratically educated but widely read, Jacob left school at 15 to train as an elementary school teacher in a church school in a Middlesborough slum. She was in constant conflict with the narrow-minded disciplinarian regime at the school as her own teaching was imaginative and inspiring. At 18 she began to visit music halls in Leeds. By going to the stage door she met the actress and singer Marguerite Broadfoote. She left the teaching profession and became her secretary and lover. Jacob loved the theatre world and mixed with the big names of the day, including the Du Mauriers, Henry Irving, Sarah Bernhardt and Marie Lloyd (after Lloyd's death she wrote her biography). In time Jacob became a character actress and had a successful career in the West End and in touring productions. Most notably she appeared opposite John Gielgud in the Edgar Wallace play *The Ringer*.[18]

Jacob liked to astonish new acquaintances by telling them the story of how she smuggled herself aboard a destroyer during the First World War. She masqueraded as a 'matelot' with absolute confidence, speaking in the light baritone voice that would deepen over the years. She boasted that she took part in two naval battles before leaving the ship and returning to her life as an independent woman. These exploits are not mentioned in her autobiographies as if revealed would have caused havoc at the Admiralty as such unnatural behaviour constituted a threat to national security and might have ended in a trial or imprisonment. It might not have happened. Perhaps it was invented by Jacob to impress the girls she met in the 1920s and 1930s when she was already becoming established as a popular novelist.[19]

Jacob did not take up writing until she was in her forties and her first novel, *Jacob Ussher* was published in 1926. She was at that time working on the stage as a comic actress in light drama. Resurgence of tuberculosis a few years later meant that she needed to find other means of support in order to live in a dry climate. From 1929 she lived in Italy and during the next 30 year period she published over 80 books. These were mainly light fiction but she became a celebrity through her stream of nonfictional works about her own life and opinions, commencing with *Me: A Chronicle About Other People* (1933). After the war she developed her celebrity status with talks on the BBC radio programme *Women's Hour*.[20]

At the peak of her activity in the 1930s she was churning out at least six novels a year. Apart from the sequence concerned with the fortunes of the Gollantz family she was also writing sagas of Yorkshire life in the nineteenth century, often featuring the token wicked squire, virginal heroine and hard-hearted mill or mine owner; love stories set in London, Paris, Venice and Milan. The diverse subjects included *The Irish Boy* a romantic biography of Michael Kelly, the Dublin born tenor whose singing enchanted both Haydn and Mozart and the two great composers appear in the novel.[21]

Although she was christened and received into the Roman Catholic church, many of her novels had Jewish themes. She remained proud of her Jewish heritage and this is evident in the Gollantz saga which she began writing just before the Nazis swept to power in Germany and the series made her name. 'Full of charmed and fascinating characters, Jacobs was a consummate storyteller, and the family come to life on the page imbued with warmth and humour as well as psychological and emotional truth'.[22] The seven novel series traces the lives and loves of several generations of Jewish antique dealers in Europe and explores how one family's destiny is shaped by the politics and attitudes of the time as well as by the choices and actions of its own members. The saga opens with Emmanuel Gollantz moving from Vienna to London at the end of the nineteenth century and remaking himself as a rich Englishman art dealer.

Claire Tylee comments that readers probably enjoyed the vast pace of the narrative, the exoticism of a family of continental Jewish antique dealers. A family saga, these books enabled their female readers to identify vicariously with the activities of the male protagonists whilst secure in the cocoon that protected the female members of the family. Like other popular fiction it diverts readers from the stress of their own lives. The books included the reinforcement of moral certainties by the containment of evil and the reward of happiness to the good. Jacob's saga reassures its readers that although there are Jewish bounders, the majority of Jews are respectable, decent, honest people with firm family values and strong community connections that do not exclude gentiles. Britain is shown as right to provide a haven to such immigrants who will certainly contribute to the economy, encouraging a sound business ethic whilst not disturbing the moral fabric of society. Jacob normalises Jewish people and their customs, integrating them into British society. In the 1930s when Britain was recovering from the Depression and the 1929 crash and suffering from the loss of Imperial confidence of late Victorianism, Jacob's series of novels about family continuity and social integration, with the luxury and prosperity of an antiques business, provided just the hope and reassurance people needed from the drug of light fiction.[23] Bryan Cheyette considers that a great deal of Anglo-Jewish writing can be divided into those novelists who feel the need apologetically to 'explain' Jews to others and those who satirically poke fun at Anglo-Jewry's complacently respectable self-image. The apologetic tradition can be seen in the Jewish family sagas of Naomi Jacob in the 1920s.[24]

Jacob's novel *Barren Metal* was also a study of the Jewish environment and was written in 1936 at the height of her writing career. Claire Tylee considers it is a novel she obviously planned with great care in order to engage directly with antisemitism in Britain and apathy towards the political situation in Germany. The novel was not a political tract. It is genre fiction designed for ideological purposes and aimed at a particular readership. Jacob drew on the entertainment skills she had learnt from music hall culture using pathos, melodrama, romance and comic dialogue to amuse her readers. It was Jacob's effort to adapt popular culture conventions in the direction of social realism. Instead of showing women as baggage to be comfortably carried by their male relatives, this novel focused on the ability of a working-class Jewish woman to break tradition, to escape domesticity and to take responsibility for her own life. In this novel Jacob expresses the socialist feminism of the Women's Social and Political Union campaign for women suffrage and enables her heroine to play her own small part in opposing Nazism. She finds a way to convert popular fiction into an unthreatening vehicle for her radical politics of class, gender and race.[25]

Barren Metal begins in 1880 with the arrival in the East End of London of a poor immigrant family from Hamburg, Leah and Israel Pardo with their small son Meyer, who come to live with Leah's brother Benjamin. The Pardos are less religious than Benjamin but the family's week is structured around the joys of the Friday night meal. Living all together in two rooms they survive as tailors. Meyer is encouraged to be ambitious and by borrowing and inheriting some money when Benjamin dies he sets up a workshop and employs young Jewish seamstresses. He eventually makes a fortune by providing uniforms during the First World War. At the age of 28 he marries Rachel Jacob, a beautiful orphaned Jewish waitress he meets in a kosher restaurant. Although they are not Orthodox they have Jewish friends and keep a kosher diet. Their twin sons are sent away to boarding school and the family move to a large house in Maida Vale. The boys are forbidden to use Yiddish expressions. We read about Meyer's determination to move on in the world and Rachel's efforts to retrieve him from the money machine and his Jewish and non-Jewish associates who have dubious values in order to save her marriage. Meyer abuses her, claiming 'You were born in the ghetto and you don't take no trouble to climb out of it. You want to bring Whitechapel and everything about it up to the West End. You let everyone know you're a Jewess, you can't forget it, you won't let other people forget it. All right! Cut off your hair, wear a *sheitel* (wig) and go to *shool* (synagogue) live kosher – I don't care. Only you damn well do it without me!'[26]

One son David plans to train as a film director in Germany; the other, Ike, aims to become a gentleman's tailor in Savile Row. He marries wealthy Helen Neubauer and they change their names to George and Henrietta Samson. Ike asks his mother not to call him by his birth name or to use Yiddish words. Helen mentions the German movement against the Jews 'is dreadful but you must remember that many of the Eastern Jews have brought it on themselves' and that her family have almost forgotten that they have Jewish blood. Rachel does not understand the reference to Nazism as she is practically illiterate and does not read the newspapers. She later learns about the situation from David when he returns from Germany. David hates Ike's hypocrisy and snobbery. 'I'm David Pardo, I'm a Jew, and I'm not going to pretend to be anything else'. This ethic, repeated in the

Gollantz saga, is not to deny one's ethnicity. When Meyer is imprisoned for embezzlement, Ike disowns him. Rachel stands by Meyer and while he is in prison sets up a small workshop in order to pay off his debts.

The other original aspect from a feminist perspective is that the novel argues for the right of a woman over 40 to have a sex life, even an adulterous one. While Meyer is in prison Rachel has a relationship with a non-Jew Sholto Falk whom she marries after Meyer dies. Jacob is quietly opposing the Nazi law that forbids such a relationship. 'The novel subverts dominant cultural ideologies of race, class and sexuality' and draws the reader to empathise with a working-class Jewish woman who demands a life of her own. The novel is innovative in telling the story to the background of Jewish immigration and to the contemporary situation of Jewish refugees from Nazi Germany. They learn about how David is unable to get his articles published and about the situation for Jews in Germany when he returns to Britain in 1934. 'They won't look at it or listen to me. One man told me that Jews had ceased to be an item of news'. Rachel's advice to David is not to be bitter over his sense of powerlessness and to recognise the limitations to reorganise a whole state and to help in whatever way one can. In Rachel's case she was employing a woman refugee from Germany. Tylee considers that *Barren Metal* made a significant contribution to the pressures working against the racial hegemony of British culture during the interwar years.[27]

Barren Metal is a good example of Jacob's ability to identify with a despised people and their temptations to hopelessness. It concerns a working-class Jewish woman Rachel who marries a successful businessman but becomes disoriented by his rejection of their Jewish identity. As Rachel grows in confidence she finds a way to take her own independent political stand against Nazism. She understood despair and found ways of suggesting positive activity without being patronising. This particular novel was designed to confront the persecution of Jews in Nazi Germany and to oppose the weaker antisemitism of British society. Written in 1935-1936 in Merano, north Italy, where Jacob was living, the book was presumably prompted by the antisemitism and violence against Jews that erupted in Nazi Germany in the summer of 1935 and made news in the British newspapers and which were followed by the institution of the Nuremberg Laws in November 1935.[28]

Jewish themes were also introduced into the novel *Seen Unknown* with the publisher's statement that it is a portraiture of Jewish life and characters and *Time Piece* where she returns to a pastoral setting 'through one delicate daughter of the English soil marries the wastrel son of not unsympathetic Jewish parents and thus introduces a Semitic strain into this country stock'.[29]

In *The Morning Will Come,* Isaac Noelle, a Polish Jew born in 1867 is brought up in Berlin. He loves and marries an English Christian and they have four sons and one daughter raised in the Jewish faith. As a family they are not deeply concerned with observing Judaism but they are concerned with living an upright life. Jews, says Isaac's second son who has become an American citizen 'have got to learn a heck of a lot. They've got to learn not to make difficulties, imagining that the length of this border or the way something's killed or things that have got to be done when folks die make all the difference to life. It's essentials that matter – those things aren't essentials'. This son fights in the American army in the 1914 war. The eldest son has become a British citizen, while the third son, the only son to fight for Germany later, becomes a high-ranking Nazi official. The family reunite after the war and Isaac makes a toast to 'what is essentially good all over the world'. *The Daily Telegraph* commented that the elderly Jew was 'drawn with great understanding'. Jacob has conviction that good will triumph in the end.[30]

Jacob made no secret of her Jewish origins and her prolific output touched on Jewish issues, pogroms and prejudice. She refused the Eichelberger award, a coveted literary honour when she discovered that the joint recipient of the award was none other than Hitler. She wrote about her reasons for refusing the award. 'I am fifty per cent Jew and have identified myself with that splendid race through my novels. Though not a Jew by faith I have a burning admiration for this noble and dignified race. To have accepted it would have been to – almost – betray those people to whose race I partly belong and who have been my good and loyal friends all my life'.[31] She had broad views on religious matters. Although partially Jewish and a Catholic, she states in her book *More About Me,* 'I know Jews who are among the grandest Christians I know or shall ever know. They are men and women whose whole lives – consciously or unconsciously – are lived according to the Sermon on the Mount, the Lord's Prayer and the belief that the greatest of these is charity – which is love. That is what I mean by being a Christian'.[32]

She supported Jewish causes and spoke at the Anglo-Jewish Association (May 1954), the women's appeal luncheon at the Midland Hotel, Manchester in aid of Jewish child victims of persecution who were now living in Palestine (1938), the Bnai Brith lodge in Edinburgh (1937) and the women's lodge of Bnai Brith London (1936).

Her own life was at least as colourful as that of her characters. She was politically active, campaigning for women's suffrage. She was boldly transgressive in gender, class and race. She lived a lesbian life, sharing her house with two other women. Although she was discreet about sexuality in her books, there was nothing ladylike about her behaviour which could be described as hearty. As her maternal grandfather was a north country publican, she was at home in the public house culture of drinking, jokes and loud talk.[33] Her sole concession to femininity was to put on a skirt when she attended Mass. She kept her hair cropped short and wore men's tailored suits. She was seldom without a collar or tie. She wore brogues, boots and lace-up two-toned shoes.[34] Jacob, known not as Naomi but Micky, looked like a man and a very masculine one at that. As she was also part Jewish, she had two battles to fight. She could not fight the very obvious fact that she was a lesbian and the name Jacob (which her mother wanted her to change) was clearly not Anglo-Saxon. She turned herself into a 'character' to keep a certain protective distance from the ordinary world.[35]

Her personal courage is most evident in regard to racism. Her mother's family had roots in Yorkshire going back centuries; her father was a Jewish immigrant. He converted to Christianity and worked in an Anglican school. He despised Jewish culture but she was much attached to her Yiddish speaking paternal grandfather, a tailor, who although not Orthodox still maintained Judaic traditions. After her parents' divorce Jacob never changed her name, adopting neither a stage name nor a pen name. In a period of antisemitic prejudice she drew attention to her Jewishness. Her alertness to racism, well before the era of political correctness, is one of the most significant features of her writing.[36]

Claire Tylee points out that as a writer in the early part of the twentieth century, Jacob's Jewishness may have been more outspoken than other Jewish female writers, such as Anita Brookner and Ruth Prawer Jhabvala, that followed her. She contributed coherently to the consistent picture of prejudice, persecution, diaspora and exile and to the central themes of identify, alienation and assimilation that are typical of Jewish writers. Jacob wrote best sellers, particularly family sagas, for a working-class readership, combating the antisemitism of the 1930s. Although forgotten now, she was a celebrity in her own time, transgressing codes of femininity, class respectability with great good humour. Behind her generous laughter was a serious purpose.[37]

It was not until the late 1950s and 1960s that a new wave of Jewish playwrights and novelists made an impact.[38] In the late 1950s the Holocaust cast long, mostly silent shadows over the British Jews. Many had settled in the suburbs and were struggling to be Jewish at home and British in the streets. External evidence of Jewish life was found only in the Grodzinski signs above the bakers. Jewish babies were named Susan and Stephen while their Hebrew names memorialised dead relatives from Poland. As the world edged towards 1960 the transition to the next generation of traditional Judaism, whether that meant Orthodoxy, socialism or a cohesive family life, was a precarious one. The challenges to the Jewish community now were to integrate their traumatic previous decade with the turbulence of the coming one. Their place in this country felt relatively secure, hence their literary self-expression was more public, even experimental, gradually gaining in stature. Jewish writings in the late 1950s showed a tense, uneasy community, raising its head above the parapet with confused diffidence as well as emerging confidence.[39]

Gerda Charles (1914-1996)

Gerda Charles was the pseudonym of Edna Lipson, an award-winning Anglo-Jewish novelist and author who belonged to the 'new wave' of Anglo-Jewish writers who emerged in the 1960s. She started writing in the late 1950s and while her fiction began by describing the Orthodox background of her youth in Liverpool and the 'insensitivities' of provincial life, she went on to use the more general theme of marginality in order to avoid the problems of limited readership. Her works include *The True Voice* (1959), *The Crossing Point* (1960), *The Slanting Light* (1963), which won the James Tait Memorial Prize and *The Destiny Waltz* (1971), her last novel, which won the inaugural Whitbread Novel of the Year award. Charles worked as a journalist and reviewer for various newspapers including *The New Statesman, Daily Telegraph, New York Times* and *Jewish Chronicle*. She described her writing as being about 'the job of maintaining sanity, dignity and order' in a world in which she seemed to be increasingly marginalized and alone. Her introspective and inward-looking battle with the world prevented her from producing more novels in the last 20 years of her life.[40] Charles is an unusual British-Jewish novelist as throughout her life she remained an Orthodox Jew, at the centre of Jewish communal life in England. Her novels, which tend to have moralistic themes and content, reflect her religious commitments.[41]

Charles was born in Liverpool into an Orthodox Jewish family. Her father, who came from Lithuania, was a draper who abandoned the family when she was a year old. Although she was too young to remember him, the event dominated her life, shaped her attitudes and coloured her work. Her early years were bleak. Her mother had been left almost destitute, ran a succession of small boarding houses in and around Liverpool and the little education Charles had was sporadic as they were continually moving. She left her ninth and last school at 15 to help her mother as chambermaid, cleaner and cook.[42]

She deeply regretted that she had no formal education. She believed that a university education formed a logical and articulate mind. She remembered too vividly the narrowness of her own youth where she was derided if she used a word of more than two syllables and will never forget the provincial narrowness of Liverpool. She attended evening classes at the City and Guild Institute and wrote an article on the forgotten books of her childhood. This was printed first in the college magazine and then by the National Book League and she began to write short stories. A perceptive tutor encouraged her to write a full-length novel which resulted in *The True Voice* (1959).[43] 'Lily Frome, the subject of *The True Voice*, is an angry young woman. The story of struggle to find a niche in the world of art and intellect, told with insight and understanding, makes fascinating reading'.[44] It was commented that she was an extremely perceptive writer. 'Everything she saw was carefully noted and registered. Her characters were usually drawn from people she knew and the events from incidents – mostly unhappy ones – she had experienced'.[45] The novel was published under the pseudonym Gerda Charles as her relatives 'treated writing as something to be ashamed of'.[46] The forename was an adaptation of Gertude (her mother's name) and Charles, derived from the name of her great grandfather Rabbi Charles Cohen of Sunderland, known as Reb Chatze who had published a book of essays in Hebrew.[47]

Jews and Jewish life were at the centre of most of her books and her second novel was *The Crossing Point* (1960), an informed and somewhat critical novel about Anglo-Jewry at that time. It was considered an able and ambitious piece of work that set out to describe Jewish life in England with particular reference to lower middle-class suburban society. 'Her observations are a north west London area which she calls Manor Green and this she divides into various income strata. She is a courageous chronicler, rigidly honest in her examination of Jewish character and paradox and she does not allow prejudice or sentiment to introduce on her hard hitting yet commentary. She relates her drama through the examination of an unmarried middle aged rabbi whose personal problem balances between his sensuality, materialism and spiritual morality. Sara, the woman who Rabbi Leo Norbert almost selects as his bride, reveals the sensitive poetic intellectualism of her race and her battle to control the fanaticism of her hysterically Orthodox father serves to focus all the characters involved'.[48]

Writer Alexander Baron considers that it is the first novel about Anglo-Jewry that can stand as a work of art. The hero is not a rebellious young man or woman but a Jewish minister, a sensitive and intelligent man, whose community is a prosperous north west London suburb. He is middle aged, personable and unmarried. And this, as much as his spiritual duties, brings him into a particularly intimate contrast with his congregation. He is the target of a hundred ambitious mothers. All their homes are open to him, their daughters on display. And because of his own loneliness he is able to perceive not only the social and cultural shortcomings of these typical Jewish households but to sense the other loneliness, the other lonely hearts that exist within a way of life that is crammed with every material comfort. The other main character, a person of integrity equal to his own, is the unmarried girl Sara Gabriel, who is stifling in the home of her bigoted Orthodox old father but whose distress and rebellion are the more moving because in all questions of religious and social duty she accepts her father's values. Around these two are gathered a whole pageant of Jewish characters, beautifully drawn and a picture of Jewish social life that is almost panoramic in its scope.[49]

Baron discusses the relationship of the Jewish writer to the community and that the point people miss when they rail against the writers as being antisemitic, or showing the bad side of the community, is that these writers launch their attacks not out of hatred but out of love. However, there is indeed a certain excess of heat, an anger. A long section of *The Crossing Point* is a series of satirical pictures of the smart Jewish seaside hotel and the drawing rooms of wealthy and charitable ladies. For Baron this anger, frantic quality arises from the writer's concern for the people he is attacking, whom he regards as his own kinsfolk. The writer is deeply concerned with his Jewish heritage. But his slogan is 'gefilte fish is not enough', Jewishness is more than cosy habits. Baron believes Charles felt deeply drawn to the spiritual essence of Judaism 'the perfect compound, the perfect fusion, the one perfect medium between man and God. In Judaism we have the exact and central heart. It may be that he feels that this is the heritage of which most Jews, practising their observances complacently are unaware'. He considers that this is a work of art because it is different from its predecessors due to the fact that unlike them it is more than a social document. 'It is primarily concerned with throwing light on the nature and motives of human behaviour and in this sense its interest is universal'.[50]

Charles writes disdainfully of money worship and spiritual confusion in the middle-class community surrounding Rabbi Norberg. This was one of the novels written by Anglo Jewish authors at the time that signalled the birth of the so-called 'Golders Green novel'. The wealthier members of the Anglo-Jewish community were made aware that there were intellectual critics in their midst with a penetrating eye for their faults.[51] These writers were rebels kicking against the now secure middle-class Jews and who mocked and criticised the Jews of Golders Green, Stamford Hill and Ilford.[52]

The novel was considered to be of great interest to those outside the Jewish community. The *Birmingham Daily Post* commented that 'the stringent arresting analysis of the characters, problems and way of life which is the material of *The Crossing Point* will be a revelation to most people, like the exploration of an exotic new country. Charles as a guide has a gift for presenting her community of suburban London Jews in a striking way, unemotionally and with keen intelligence. Loneliness nags at Leo, a worldly but thoughtful middle aged rabbi always on the look-out for a wife but unable to find one who will both suit him and accept him. Few will read this absorbing novel without feeling enriched'.[53] Writer Kingsley Amis commented that the novel was 'brilliantly talented… with an energy and curiosity that makes the average novel look tired and bored'.[54]

A Slanting Light, her third novel which won the James Tait Prize,[55] effectively announced that Charles had arrived.[56] The novel concerns Bernard Zold, an American Jewish dramatist who comes to London to help in the production of his latest play and the English woman whom he engages as a housekeeper in his home in St John's Wood. Zold is a gentle, helpless man who lives with his wife, mother and daughter in utter loneliness. They are unaware of his needs. They trample his life into misery, acting sometimes from selfishness, sometimes from possessive affection. He is unable to communicate with them. He struggles to make them understand him but they will never know him, his work or his true purpose. His family life drags on in messy failure and he fares no better with other people. His work is applauded but he is neglected. He meets literary people who are eaten up with malice and egotism. He is too kindly, too bewildered to defend himself by striking back.[57]

The novel received positive reviews 'Charles is an impressive novelist because of her ability to explore one aspect of human personality at great length and with great vehemence but never tediously. She reiterates her point but develops it with each restatement'. We learn at the start of *A Slanting Light* that in spite of his literary reputation Zold makes a poor show personally. We hear the story through his housekeeper Ruth Holland 'a lower middle-class provincial Englishwoman with immoral longings'. The *Times Literary Supplement* commented that 'even though Zold is explicitly said to personify the role of the Jew – and Miss Charles is exceptionally acute about Jewishness - it is as a man that he interests the reader as a creative writer bogged down in real life by an inadequate wife, a lumpish child, a twisted mother and a brutish brother. The point about Zold is that he will not cast off the responsibilities of the family, he knows it is the morality of the character that counts and not his external features'.[58]

After receiving an award for *A Slanting Light*, Charles entered into the brief golden phase of her life. She was on radio and television and in wide demand as a book reviewer. Her fourth novel, *A Logical Girl* (1967), set during the Second World War, dealt with the arrival of American soldiers in an English seaside town. *A Logical Girl* is full of woes on the meanness, shoddiness and moral vulgarity of provincial life as seen through the eyes of Rose Morgan. She records the appalling humiliations, the snubs, duplicities and insults inflicted chiefly by her sister-in-law. Rose, so conscious of her own superiority, so keenly aware of the shortcomings of other people, is powerless to intervene. She is a bungler by nature. 'My ideas coming out in raw, pure chips like coarsely grated carrot, unpeeled and with bits of earth still in them, quite unlike the cooked potato of other people'.[59]

Her fifth novel *Destiny Waltz* (1971), which won the Whitbread award, was Charles's crowning achievement. One of the judges, J B Priestley said 'of the mass of 100 odd novels submitted for the prize, many of high literary quality, Charles's book stood out easily and clearly as the best'.[60] *Destiny Waltz* tells how a TV documentary is produced on the early background of a famous Jewish poet from the East End of London who died young. An elderly bandleader, who knew him as a child, is brought in to help. The team visit an East End grocery shop, a school and the lavish home of a Jewish couple who patronised him. The drama is all interior, as the bandleader ruminates on the ups and downs of life, feeling his way through memory and the banalities of daily existence. Tender and trenchant in describing a Jewish background, it is a portrayal of the life and fate of a Jewish poet and of Jewish social life in London before the Second World War.[61]

T R Fyvel comments in the *Jewish Chronicle* that Charles has deserved praise in the highest reviewers' circles, especially in respect of the satirical passages about Anglo-Jewish life. He points out that the Jewish community formed only one percent of the population and what is striking is that the general British reading public have developed a new curiosity about Jewish life. Jewish writers were now writing in an atmosphere of cultural philosemitism where the Jewish background in their work is an asset rather than drawback. They were writing mainly and naturally about the world of their own Jewish life and imagination and this was now readily acceptable by a non-Jewish public. He considers that after the Holocaust there appears to be something like a new attitude towards Jewish matters by non-Jews which seems touched confusedly by a sense of guilt, a sense of duty and puzzlement, all adding up to a certain cultural philosemitism.[62]

Charles felt that non-Jewish demand was basically responsible for the contemporary upsurge of Anglo-Jewish writing. Whereas Jewish creative writing in the English speaking world was virtually non-existent until the twentieth century, recent years had seen the gap filled by new talent. It was the non-Jewish reader who called the Jewish writer into existence because of the desperate need and desire to learn from him. The Jewish writer's chief concern was with the place of man in society. Whereas Catholic writers such as Graham Greene and Muriel Spark concentrated on problems of faith, the Jewish writer was preoccupied with problems of behaviour.[63] She also pointed out that Anglo-Jewish writers were now for the first time writing with authority as they were the third generation in their land of domicile and therefore deeply rooted enough to be creative.[64] She placed herself differently from other Anglo-Jewish writers that she divided into two main groups – East End writers from working-class backgrounds such as Arnold Wesker and West End writers from wealthier and better educated backgrounds such as Peter Schaffer and Frederick Raphael. She differed because she was not from London but from the provinces – lower middle-class Lancashire – and she believed she was the only Anglo-Jewish creative writer to lead an Orthodox life.[65]

Charles maintained a strictly Jewish Orthodox way of life. 'We live by the thousand small decisions of every day. These decisions make our morality. The intended function of small, daily religious observances is to keep our self-discipline and our sense of marvel constantly exercised and supple and responsive'.[66] She cited the importance of Yom Kippur (Day of Atonement). 'The most important thing about Yom Kippur is the self-discipline, a discipline that comes from within. I find it an enormously optimistic day. The idea that all vows and promises and commitments should be allowed to be rescinded and remade is a marvellously helpful thing. It means that one is never wholly condemned and that one is given an opportunity to undo whatever one has done wrong. 'Prayer, repentance and charity avert the evil decree'. This is one of the most hopeful things in the Jewish religion'.[67] She was a believer in a Jewish destiny whereby Jews have a moral obligation to behave well and that if they do not they will be punished and that to behave generously and well is their job in life. 'The Jews are destined to be moral champions. They are the chosen people in the sense that they are chosen for responsibility'. She was of the belief that if people suffered, one could not question why and one could not judge the Almighty.[68]

Such beliefs hopefully helped her to deal with her disappointments with life. She regretted she had never married and she reflected that she would rather have had a happy life than her books. She only wrote books because she had no one to talk to.[69] At the height of her powers she was destined to spend many years caring for her ill mother as she had no siblings or children and it became impossible for her to write. After her mother died in 1981 it was too late. Her old publisher had been taken over and the new publisher was no longer interested in her. She talked about a novel in progress, a second or third draft but nothing materialised. She was somewhat resentful of her lot, often antagonising people in the process. This was reflected in her writings as she had her own real problem of creating close relationships.[70]

Between 1959 and 1971 Charles wrote a succession of five novels which established her, for a time, as one of the foremost women writers in Britain. Chaim Bermant considered her perhaps the most gifted of a whole spate of Anglo-Jewish writers that included Wolf Mankowitz, Frederic Raphael, Bernice Rubens and Bernard Kops. They were all more or less on the fringes of Jewish life. Charles was at the heart of it. *The Crossing Point*, built round the efforts of a middle aged rabbi to find a suitable wife, gave a panoramic view of Anglo-Jewry at a crucial point in its fortunes. It was not a pretty picture for it suggested shallowness, hypocrisy and philistinism. However, it was a richly informed one and a sociologist attempting to write a study of the community in the early post war years would find it a most authoritative text. She gained respect in the non-Jewish world and even Kingsley Amis, who was often accused of being antisemitic, considered her to be brilliantly talented and that although her subject was Jewry she raised all sorts of wider questions about group feelings in general, about morality.[71] Lauded for her intelligence and the perception of her writing, it is hoped that such critical acclaim served as some compensation for the disappointments of her personal life.

A British Jewish voice to impact seriously on the literary scene in this period was Bernice Rubens with *The Elected Member*. She was the first woman to win the 1970 Booker Prize with this, her fourth novel, a surprise winner against strong competition which included well known literary figures such as Irish Murdoch, William Trevor and Elizabeth Bowen. Its 'outsider' status fitted well both Rubens' writing style and her analysis of her life and work.[72] She published 26 novels which won critical acclaim, popularity and prestigious prizes.

Bernice Rubens (1923-2004)

Bernice Rubens, one of four children, grew up in poor circumstances at 9 Glossop Terrace in the Splott district of Cardiff, Wales. She considered Splott, which was not a Jewish area, to be 'the unmentionable and indisputable armpit of Cardiff'.[73] Her father Eli Rubens was a Lithuanian Jew who left his home in 1900 at the age of 16 and went to Hamburg. From there he hoped to join his brother in New York. Due to being swindled by a ticket tout Rubens never reached America, his passage taking him no further than Cardiff. He was in Cardiff for three weeks before he realised that he was not in New York. This was the only story that he told about his youth.[74] This account is rather mythological as this would not have been the route from Hamburg but whatever the reality, he decided to stay in Wales and there he met and married Dorothy Cohen, whose family had emigrated from Poland and whose father Wolf was a tailor. Dorothy had trained as a primary school teacher and volunteered for local Jewish charities for the elderly and infirm. Eli Reuben was a travelling tallyman/credit draper, buying suits and shoes and selling them to miners for a shilling a week.[75] The family took in lodgers to supplement their meagre income. Rubens attended Cardiff High School together with her sister Beryl and the sisters shared the Panama hat that was obligatory wear in the summer term. After the Second World War the family became more prosperous. There was a car, a fridge and a new home in the middle-class suburb of Penylan.[76]

Rubens grew up in tight knit Jewish community of 600 families. She recalls going to synagogue on a Friday night. There were only two synagogues, both Orthodox, and no Reform. 'It was the kind of community where everyone knew what everyone else was doing'. It was a disgrace to marry anyone non-Jewish. 'It was a case of don't do that, what will Mrs so-and-so say'. Rubens' parents were staunch Zionists and she joined the Habonim Zionist Youth Movement. 'I had the sort of parents who thought everyone should go to Israel but not their own children'.[77]

The family were musical. Her mother played and taught the piano and her father was originally a violinist. When he came to England he arrived with a full-size fiddle and a half size fiddle. 'In our family we handed down instruments like you handed down clothes and when the half fiddle was handed to me, when my sister became too big for it, I passed on that one as the noise of a young musician practising was horrendous'. Rubens was desperate to play the cello, but poverty precluded such a purchase and it was only later in her life that she learnt to play the instrument. At the time she became 'the listener' in the family, a role that stood her in good stead when as a young mother she sat down to write her first novel. Her brothers Harold and Cyril became classical musicians. Harold was forced to quit playing through illness, but Cyril was a violinist in the London Symphony Orchestra.

Rubens did feel resentful as she felt that she was an outsider in the family not being a musician, especially when the extended family used to visit on Sundays and marvel at her siblings' playing. Her mother used to comfort her by saying that there had to be a listener in the family. 'Looking back it was the greatest gift she gave me because the ear has to be practised as carefully as any fiddle and in those growing up years I listened and I think that is a wonderful gift for a writer who has to listen with skill and to enjoy listening'.[78] Rubens considers that she has always had an outsider complex but realised that it was a benefit as a writer to be both an observer and to be part of life. 'Most of my novels are about survival and that is a Jewish area'.[79]

Rubens read English at the University of Wales, Cardiff where she was awarded a BA in 1947. She married Rudi Nussbauer, a wine merchant who also wrote poetry and fiction and who came from a family of rich assimilated German Jews. He came from a totally different background and Rubens said that she fell in love with him because 'he knew about Camembert and I did not'.[80] They had two daughters Rebecca and Sharon. She taught at a grammar school in Birmingham (1950-1955) and then worked in the film industry where she made documentaries. Rudi left her in the late 1960s and she was devastated. At the time she refused to take money from him because she did not want to ease his guilt.[81]

Rubens became a writer by chance. 'I thought I would have a go. I was lucky to be published'.[82] Winner of the Booker Prize (*The Elected Member*, 1970), shortlisted for the Booker Prize (*Five Year Sentence*, 1978), she was described by an *Evening Standard* reviewer as, 'exotically swarthy, gypsily beringed, small, plump… at one remove from the seemly, London Library circuit of modern letters'.[83]

Her first novel *Set on Edge* (1960) is based on the life of her maternal grandmother and describes the mixed blessings of parental expectation and shows how destructive possessive relationships within the family can be.[84] She took the title from Ezekiel: 'The fathers have eaten sour grapes and the children's teeth are set on edge'. She dedicated it to the memory of her father who had died in 1968. Her family provided her with material throughout her writing life.[85] Although she went on to write about everything from the trials and tribulations of a male gentile transvestite (in the first person) in

Sunday Best (1971) to sinister goings on aboard a cruise ship full of genteel widows (*Birds of Passage*, 1981), she frequently returned to Jewish themes and characters. As she explained: 'Everything that happens in family is more so in a Jewish family. In a Gentile family someone may have a cold. In a Jewish family it has to be consumption'.[86]

Nowhere is this more poignantly demonstrated than in *The Elected Member*. Norman Zweck is the clever one of a close-knit Jewish family who are still living in the East End of London and have not yet moved out to the suburbs. A rabbi's son, infant prodigy and brilliant barrister, he is the apple of his parents' eyes until he becomes a drug addict aged 41, confined to his bedroom, at the mercy of his hallucinations and paranoia. As a child Norman had shown an extraordinary ability to pick up languages, but to highlight his genius his mother lied about his age and even delayed his barmitzvah by three years. Saddened and shamed by what he sees as his son's failure, Rabbi Zweck muses that to be driven mad by one's own genius would not be so bad 'an inverted *nachus*[87] almost but drugs?'[88] For Norman, his committal to a mental hospital represents the ultimate act of betrayal. For Rabbi Zweck, his son's deterioration is a bitter reminder of his own guilt and failure. Treated as a scapegoat for the failures of the rest of the family, including Rabbi Zweck himself and his two daughters, driven by the pressures of parental expectations into drug addiction and incarcerated in a mental hospital, replayed a desperate period when Rubens's older gifted brother Harold suffered a similar confinement.[89]

The portrayal is nothing short of terrifying. The Zweck family inevitably loses the all-important struggle to maintain an image of normality in the outside world. Rubens fearlessly explored their loneliness, craziness and painful destructiveness. At the close of the novel, Norman, cries out in a frenzy of pain and loss: 'You', he screamed to the ceiling 'and you bloody well know who I mean'. He sank weeping onto his bed. 'Dear God', he said. It was a word after all, that covered everybody. 'Look after us cold and chosen ones'. *The Elected Member* kick started a bold new era for British Jewish literature. It was not for the faint hearted.[90]

Still drawing on personal experiences, her second novel *Madame Sousatska* (1962) was the story of a child prodigy. It deals with the relationship between a devoted piano teacher, the Madame Sousatska of the title, who specialises in child prodigies, and an aspiring young Jewish pianist, and is based on the experiences of her brother Harold and his teacher Madame Maria Levinskaya. The story was made into a film in 1988 starring Shirley MacLaine. Her third novel *Mate in Three* (1963) concerned her collapsing marriage (her husband had fathered a son by another woman) and her sixth novel *Go Tell the Lemming* (1973) covered their divorce.

As first generation British, it soon became obvious to the family how lucky they had been to have escaped from Europe. During Rubens's childhood the family home was a refuge for some of the last Jews to flee the Continent. One boy from Austria stayed for five years. All this had its impact, as did her father's awareness of his 'guest' status in Britain, and many of her female characters are stunted by irrepressible feelings of gratefulness. In *Birds of Passage* (1981) Alice on a well-earned cruise with her neighbour, was constantly grateful to the dapper Mr Bowers 'for each bowing and scraping of Mr Bowers' feet, she felt the need to offer him at least her body if not her spirit'.[91]

Sue Lawley, in an interview on *Desert Island Discs*, asked Rubens how important her Jewishness was to her. 'It is me. It's not a question of importance. It's like saying "how important are your brown eyes", they are there and they have great deal to do with my vision. My writing vision is a Jewish vision'. She also queried whether Rubens felt a sense of Welshness. 'My father used to say, remember you are a guest in this country and he would say it all the time. Although he was naturalised he felt an immigrant. I used to feel a guest until he died and was buried in Cardiff along with my mother and that six foot of earth gave me a territorial right to the land and so I didn't feel a guest any more but it took my father's death to make me feel Wales was my home'. Now she had a sense of belonging.[92]

A number of her novels focus on Jewish issues. *I Dreyfuss* (1999), an updated spoof of the Dreyfuss affair, is a clever reprise of the French legal scandal at the turn of the twentieth century turned into a drama of contemporary Britain. The book's hero is a 'closet Jew', a type of concealment that stirred Rubens's anger and scorn. The novel tells of his journey through the trauma of his conviction and incarceration for child murder into a transformed relationship with his Jewishness and the suffering of his Jewish ancestors.[93]

The novel deals with antisemitism. Rubens notes 'the English are known to be of a polite persuasion and their antisemitism is of the most courteous kind'. Alfred Dreyfus, a worthy schoolmaster, is unjustly convicted of a murder and the literary agent who persuades him to write an account of his unfortunate story is not much liked because 'he too was one of "those".[94] *I Dreyfus* is her most polemical novel. Its protagonist Sir Alfred has lived life as a 'count me in Jew', belting out hymns louder than anyone else in church and gleefully exposing his uncircumcised member at the urinals. Ultimately this offers no protection and his Jewishness screams out to all but himself. Gradually he realises that by denying his Jewish identity he has been living in a wilderness and it is only when he can accept himself for who he is that he is truly released from his cell. The novel offers a bleak prognosis of antisemitism, as Rubens explains in the author's note: 'This novel makes no attempt to update the Dreyfus story. Rather it is concerned with the Dreyfus syndrome which alas needs no updating.'[95]

Rubens admitted that she had not personally suffered from antisemitism as being a writer she was not mixing with people all the time. 'But there's no question that it exists in England. It is in the upper classes and is very polite. Because it's so polite it's difficult to fight'. Although not all her books deal with Jewish subjects, Rubens accepts that she is still known as a Jewish writer. 'I think that's because my vision is Jewish if you can call it a vision. It's a vision of survival – that's a kind of Jewish syndrome isn't it? I feel Jewish. I was brought up in a reasonably Orthodox home and the ritual of it became part of me'.[96] Rubens said she felt more and more Jewish as her life went on.[97] There was something of the Jewish mother lurking behind her small frame.[98]

In her later books Rubens moved from family life to broader historical subjects. The theme of Jewish identity surfaced repeatedly in her fiction. It found its fullest expression in *Brothers* (1983) a novel that follows several generations of the Jewish Bindel family through a fight for survival that takes them from nineteenth century Tsarist Russia to western Europe and Nazism, then back to modern Russia and its continued persecution of the Jews.[99] In *Mother Russia* (1992) a tumultuous tale of that country's passage through the twentieth century, Sonya's husband divorces her because her Jewishness will hinder his party career. 'Soon will come a time when such things will not matter', he opines, to which she replies 'there has never been such a time, nowhere in the world'. Elsewhere Mrs Feinberg, the 'token Jew' at the exclusive Hollyhocks nursing home of *The Waiting Game* (1997) is welcomed by matron with an over-understanding that 'bordered on racism'. Rubens's finely tuned ear for the unspoken truths that hide behind even the most inane social banter is crucial in pinpointing that particularly British brand of antisemitism.[100]

She talked and worried about antisemitism and Israel and her growing concern came out in books such as *I Dreyfuss* and *The Sergeant's Tale* (2003). 'Since the 1970s Rubens has delved into chapters of Jewish history, creatively embellishing events and individuals from the shtetl to Salonica with wit and wisdom'.[101] *The Sergeant's Tale*, loosely based on a true story, is set in 1947, one year before the Israeli War of Independence when Palestine was still under the British mandate. Young Israelis are flocking to the leadership of Menachem Begin and his Irgun terrorist movement in an attempt to overthrow the British. Two British sergeants are kidnapped by the Irgun. They will be executed unless there is a widespread amnesty for the Irgun freedom fighters. A hunt takes place throughout Palestine to find and liberate the two men. 'There are two distinct sides to Bernice Rubens. One is the gently humorous chronicler of strange suburban foibles. The other is a deeply committed historical writer dedicated to the exploration of her Jewish heritage. It was her most astringent and militant work to date'.[102] The novel went some way to explain the continuing complexities that existed both in the retelling of the early history of the State of Israel and in the largely unrequited love affair between the Israelis and the British.[103]

Rubens enjoyed the respected place she had achieved in the literary world. She was an honorary vice-president of Pen International (global association of writers that advocate for freedom of expression and literature) and served as a Booker Prize judge in 1986. She was a compelling storyteller, weaving her novels from many strands: her own vivid experiences, her friends' and family's lives, centuries of Jewish tradition and history; above all her remarkable and disturbing imagination in everyday places – a suburban villa, an English public school, a home for the elderly. She showed the horrors that can lie behind net curtains and, polite conversation or an unexplained wink.Though her novels had many themes she admitted that she really only wrote about human relationships and these were the core material of her books. To this subject she brought her unsparing scrutiny, ruthless candour and a dark, unquenchable humour. Yet success did not cure the insecurity she felt. 'Better than most, not as good as some'.[104]

Her insecurity probably stems from her position as a child of Jewish immigrants. As David Herman explains in the *Jewish Chronicle*, she was part of an explosion of Jewish literary talent from the mid-1950s onwards that included an exciting new generation of Jewish playwrights such as Harold Pinter, Arnold Wesker and Bernard Kops and new Jewish novelists such as Rubens and Gerda Charles. Several things were striking about this generation. Many chronicled the move from slums to suburbia and were the first in their families to find their voices in a new country. They grew up in an increasingly prosperous and liberal post-war Britain and had one foot in the old immigrant communities and another in the new world of the late 1950s and 1960s. This gave the writing of their generation its tension and energy. They came from working-class homes and built middle-class lives. They grew up listening to Yiddish but wrote in English and were secular not religious. They felt cut off from Anglo-Jewry but didn't fully belong to gentile Britain either, with its literary traditions and landscapes.[105]

Anita Brookner mirrors British Jewry's preference for keeping a low profile in relation to her background. Her writing reflects the way in which it has been easier for some Jews in Britain to assimilate within society.

Anita Brookner (1928-2016)

Anita Brookner was born in Herne Hill, a suburb of London, the only child of Polish-Jewish parents, Maude and Newson Bruckner. She was educated at James Allen's School in Dulwich before going on to King's College, London where she graduated with a First in art history in 1949. After completing her doctorate at the Courtauld Institute of Art in 1953, she became a visiting lecturer at Reading University in 1959, where she remained until gaining a lectureship at the Courtauld in 1964. She was the first woman to hold the Slade Chair of Fine Art at Cambridge University (1967-68) and was promoted to Reader in Art History at the Courtauld in 1977, where she worked until she retired in 1988. She was eminent in the field of art history with a passion for French eighteenth century painters such as Watteau, Greuze and David. She wrote many art history books and turned to writing novels in her 50s, publishing roughly one novel a year. Her fourth novel *Hotel du Lac* (1984) won the prestigious Booker Prize. She was made a CBE in 1990. Many of her characters are children of European immigrants to Britain and despite her illustrious career she often spoke of how her family's roots made her feel like an outsider in the UK.[106]

Her father, Newson Bruckner, was a Jewish immigrant from Poland who came to Britain at the age of 16, served in the British Army during World War One and then went to work in the Schiska's tobacco factory where he met and married the owner's daughter Maude. The family changed their surname to Brookner because of anti-German sentiment in Britain at that time. Newson was a gently failing businessman who at one point owned a lending library. Marriage and motherhood spelled the end of Maude's professional singing career, an experience that left her 'inclined to melancholy' and was a major source of conflict between her and her husband. The disappointment that Maude felt clearly made an impact on her daughter and can be viewed as a template for many of the characters, especially female, whose lives fail to live up to expectations.[107]

Brookner had a lonely childhood although her grandmother and uncle lived with the family and her parents opened their home to Jewish refugees escaping Nazi persecution. Living in such an environment led to a feeling of displacement. 'They were transplanted and fragile people, an unhappy brood, and I felt that I had to protect them. Indeed that is what they expected'.[108] In regard to her parents she explained that 'I loved them painfully but they were fairly irascible and unreliable people. They should never have had children; they didn't understand children and couldn't be bothered'. Her parents were 'mismatched, strong willed, hot tempered with a great residual sadness which I've certainly inherited. We never had much fun'.[109] The melancholy that permeated the household in which she grew up had possibly as much to do with the temperaments and trials, particularly of illness, of its members as with their reception in Britain.[110] 'I think my parents lives were blighted — and in some sense mine too – largely by the fact of being strangers in England, not quite understanding what was happening and being done to them.'[111]

She grew up in a secular Jewish household and never learnt Hebrew, which meant that she could never 'join in fully'. With feelings of being displaced in some measure from her Jewishness, she confessed to having no religious faith but wishing she had. A sense of being part of two cultures – but also *apart* – was clearly the legacy of the Brookner family. She describes her maternal grandfather, who had come to England at the end of the nineteenth century, as having 'adopted every English mode that he could find' but for whom 'European habits of thought – melancholy, introspection – persisted'. The combination, according to Brookner, was anything but a positive one.[112] 'My Polish father, who remained very Polish, thought that the best thing he could do for me was to unveil the mysteries of English life which could be found in the novels of Charles Dickens'. She was set to read his novels from the age of seven. Despite her father's endeavours, she commented 'I've never been at home here. I took on protective colouring at an early age but it didn't stick'. She describes her academic and working life and nursing her parents until they died as 'a dreary Victorian story with this added complication of not being English'.[113]

Already a published author of non-fiction, as well as a critic, contributing to the *Art Review* in the late 1950s and early 1960s, Brookner published *A Start in Life* (1981), the first of 24 novels, at the age of 53. Many of Brookner's characters are children of European immigrants to Britain; a number appear to be of Jewish descent. Their quiet service flats off London's Edgware Road render a slight foreignness to works that are essentially about reticence. Brookner's Jews are émigrés rather than immigrants.[114] Writer and broadcaster Maureen Kendler points out that her voice, faint and ashamed, seems a throwback to a previous timid generation. The overwhelming theme of Brookner's novels is loneliness, a sense of being unfulfilled and of being the ultimate outsider. Her protagonists, usually but not exclusively, unmarried and female, are unable to join in the sweep of life. Somehow the mechanism for doing this, the necessary joie de vivre, energy, good looks and self-esteem, have eluded her narrators. Those who do possess these qualities are often vain and shallow in their successes but they are also life's winners.[115] Brookner's protagonists are typically academic women with attachments both to the intellectual life and to an old fashioned model of femininity in which a woman waits to be discovered, looking her best.[116] Brookner represents the old dichotomy between male and female, with men getting the best out of life. Her heroines, however intelligent, are restricted by their sentiment, their gentleness, their sense of duty, whereas her male characters are freer emotionally and can live by their own logic.[117]

In considering whether Brookner's Jewish background had any influence on her work, it is interesting to note that Brookner, although she described herself as a 'lapsed Jew', did refer to herself as 'inescapably Jewish', and commented 'you're never really free of your own history'[118] and that 'I have never learned the custom of the country because we were Jews, tribal and alien'.[119] In terms of Judaism 'one can only opt out of it, never be free'. She felt herself to be an external outsider, born to immigrant Jewish parents whose failure to acclimatise seems to have scarred their only daughter, leaving her trying to understand life here through the rules of a game that was ever mystifying and elusive.[120]

Cheryl Alexander Malcolm considers that although Brookner's writing exhibits few of the features commonly associated with Jewish writing she may be writing in a more varied, subtle and less obvious way. A straightforward dramatization and discussion of Jewishness in her novels is relatively scarce but what is constant in her writing is the complex dialogue she establishes with the elements of her inherited Jewishness that concern her most. The most intense connection with Jewish culture that her heroines and heroes are endowed with is twofold: First, most of her characters undergo a lifelong determining experience in the complex and ambivalent relationship they have with their mothers. This is a particularly strong feature in Jewish culture, especially in exile. Secondly, most of her characters share a constant state of displacement and a strong desire for another place. The responsibilities to aging mothers for extremely dutiful daughters and the complex and ambivalent relations that derive from such commitments, as well as their nostalgic desire for other places become the most idiosyncratic and permanent features in all her novels and both attitudes are centrally related to Jewish culture.[121]

Adrienne Baker comments that the family is central to Judaism simply because dispersion strengthened the need for family stability and it became a 'domestic religion' to resist public antisemitism. The Jewish family plays a central role in the transmission of Jewish identity especially through the cultural and religious ritual that women preserve in the home. It is therefore unsurprisingly that the family figures prominently in Jewish women's writing. Brookner, like Bernice Rubens, is concerned with domestic life. Brookner has been recognised as central to the genre of 'the women's novel' fiction concerned with domestic life, written by well-educated women for a well-educated bourgeois readership. Rubens and Brookner take the family as their major subject, particularly the expectations forced on children by their parents and the destructive love-hate relationships that result. Themselves the daughters of European Jewish immigrants they assimilated into British culture. Their ambivalence about this gives depth to their writing. Yet a sense of insecurity lies behind the pressure to conform and achieve.[122]

Brookner emphasises the isolation and lack of roles for single women. Though a successful career may occupy her working hours, her leisure time seems to drag endlessly. *Providence* (1982), *Look at Me* (1983) and *Hotel du Lac* (1984) all focus on this situation. Brookner shows that there is little to be gained from the company of gloomy women who share a similar plight. Her heroines reflect the traditional Jewish desire for marriage and a family. Like Gerda Charles, she condemns those men who use vulnerable, not especially attractive, women for brief pleasure then pass on, oblivious to the expectations they have aroused. She condemns too that aspect of human nature which makes us prefer the carefree and careless, in spite of their shallowness and immorality, to the good and deep thinking, simply because they are more attractive.[123]

In the 1980s Brookner openly confessed the close connections between her own experience and those of her heroines and heroes. Yet Jewishness is very rarely referred to directly in her novels. It is mostly introduced in disguised and oblique ways. Like Brookner herself, most of her heroines and heroes are the children or grandchildren of Central European Jewish exiles and this played a central role both in her characters' destinies and in Brookner's artistic purposes.[124]

In *A Start In Life* (1981), Ruth Weiss's grandmother has a 'sad European past' and is surrounded by the dark heavy pieces of furniture brought from Berlin and enjoys as a source of warmth and security the food she knew back home — the buttermilk, rye bread, caraway seeds. The alienated and introspective narrator is 40-year-old Dr Ruth Weiss, her carefully chosen name suggesting the biblical Ruth 'amid the alien corn' and the purity of

Snow White (Weiss). Ruth's initiation in this coming-of-age novel is a meal in a Paris restaurant where 'for the very first time she ate lobster, forbidden on her father's side', a reference to Jewish dietary laws which prohibit shellfish. The qualifiers possessed by the heroine Ruth Weiss – brains, a capacity to take pains, patience and naivety – render her invisible and useless for anything other than acute observation of others' knack of enjoying life.[125]

Family and Friends (1985) focuses on the children in the Dorn family under matriarchal Sofia, who is ill-equipped to control her beloved children as they grow up. The two good looking ones escape to become raffish bohemians. The plain stolid siblings stultify in frustration at being unable to take such bold steps. When Sofka dies, her son Alfred stands at the foot of her bed, has his jacket cut and drapes the mirror with a shawl[126] – announcing what the astute reader knew all along – this was a Jewish family.[127] The Dorns are one of those rich Mittel European families who settled in England with their fine linen, silver and furniture decades before Hitler. The words Jew or Jewish are not mentioned once in *Family and Friends*, their origins only indicated in slipped in details, like after death, the ritual cut.[128]

Although the Holocaust provides the backdrop to *Family and Friends* (1985) in *Latecomers* (1988) it is centre stage. The novel is a moving depiction of two aging Englishmen Thomas Hartman and Thomas Fibich who are sent to London as refugees just before the Second World War and who become lifelong friends and whose beginnings as child refugees from Germany colour the remainder of their lives.[129] There is not a mention that the protagonists are two Jewish Kindertransport[130] survivors who suffer survivor guilt. We are aware of the Holocaust only in its absence. Hartmann has come to terms with survival by 'consigning certain memories to the dust' and sedating himself at night to ensure untroubled sleep. Fibich is troubled by haunting memories, of separation from his parents at the train station and returns to Berlin in a journey to redeem the past.

In *The Next Big Thing* (2002), the protagonist Julius Hertz is clearly a Jew although this detail tends to be expressed in Brookner codes which refer to the 'ancestral religion'. He and his family are refugees from Germany and Brookner is at her most explicit about the effects of this start in life: these include the mental illness suffered by Hertz's brother, the intense loneliness of the whole family and an ongoing sense of exile and rupture from the life that should have been theirs.[131]

Brookner's preference is discretion to disclosure. She says of Jane Austen what could well be applied to her own writing. 'I think she made a tremendous far-reaching decision to leave certain things out'. The words 'Jew' or 'Jewish' rarely occur in Brookner's writing. It may have proved easier for her to reach an English audience by drawing a discreet veil over her many Jewish characters. Her people are subject to doubt and dislocation, despondency and alienation; they are aware, like her 'of what it is like to be lonely, perceptive, an observer'. At the same time Brookner mirrors the way in which British Jewry has preferred to keep a low profile. Her writing epitomises the way in which it has been for some Jews in Britain to assimilate within society. Yet they may find themselves with a poignant sense of loss, the loss of Jewish warmth and community while enduring the contradictions of diaspora life.[132]

Although Brookner does not speak of antisemitism as such, in interviews she does refer to 'the English' as separate and different from herself. The 'us and them' polarity she uses on these occasions is in itself very revealing, suggesting confrontation and opposition or at the least the divide separating outsiders from insiders. She is noncommittal about exactly where her Polish roots lie. What she does say is supported by her more autobiographical novels. Relatives on her mother's side had been well-off entrepreneurs. In their case England did not offer them the opportunity to find work so much as to continue business. In the family chronicle *Family and Friends* which was inspired by an actual photograph, this is what happens. Here, as in *Latecomers*, the protagonist's background is German. In *Hotel Du Lac* (1984) and *Dolly* (1993), family roots go back to Vienna at the beginning of the century. Although these settings might seem at variance with anything autobiographical given Brookner's professed Polish origins, they are considerably more than mere backdrops picked randomly off a map of continental Europe. In fact, the Jewishness of these characters serves to link these origins to Brookner's own.[133]

Brookner's father had changed his name from Bruckner. As in real life, name changes in Brookner's novels generally do not succeed in transforming characters any more than they do succeed in turning them from outsiders into insiders. Closest to her father's experience of anglicising a name too difficult for the English to pronounce is that of Mrs Miller in *Altered States* (1996). She changes her Polish name of Jadwiga to Jenny but still lingers on the margins of a family and culture not her own. Another example is the father in *The Debut* (1981). He is German born and with his mother he is 'Georg' and with his English wife the more easily pronounceable 'George'. The implication is that he moves between two worlds. Brookner parallels name changes with the desire for leaving and entering other worlds in *Providence* (1982). Here the protagonist goes by the name Kitty Maule with her English university colleagues and by that of Therese with her foreign born grandparents. The result however is that she feels fully at home with neither.[134]

A similar situation is in *Hotel du Lac* (1984) that tells the story of romantic novelist Edith Hope, who is banished by her friends after breaking off an engagement, and goes to stay in a hotel on the shores of Lake Geneva. There she meets an assortment of people and observing them helps her to understand what course she should take in her life. It became one of the top ten bestselling books of the 1980s and was adapted for a BBC television drama in 1986. The protagonist has two names, a given name and an adopted pseudonym representing the actual and fictional worlds between which she moves. When her real life German middle name of Johanna draws the attention of a Swiss hotel clerk, the suggestion is that she does not fit precisely in either. 'An unusual name for an English lady. Perhaps not entirely English'. As a symbol of belonging, names and name changing feature repeatedly in Brookner's writing.[135]

Despite the fact that Brookner makes no secret of her Jewish upbringing and regrets that she missed out on Hebrew lessons because her parents thought her health too delicate for her to withstand such demands, her writing exhibits few of the features commonly associated with Jewish writing. The absence of characters clearly designated as Jewish and the omission of the word Jew entirely from novels in which they do feature have led some critics to accuse her of a 'self-conscious refusal to engage with this Jewish culture'. Others strictly regard Brookner's writing as English and find it difficult to group her with other Jewish writers. But like the intelligentsia Jew who tells the former *shtetl* dweller 'your Warsaw is not my Warsaw', Brookner's London is not an East Ender's London. Brookner was born into a well-off family of continental European entrepreneurs that went on to have its own factory in Britain. As a child she had a nanny and there were servants in the house. Where memoirists such as Emanuel Litvinoff[136] recall the material poverty of a Jewish immigrant community, Brookner writes about emotional need among well-off second and third generation non-English and English alike.[137]

Brookner said she does not want to be 'ghettoized' and deplored any 'Jewish eagerness to claim lost souls'. Instead she preferred to be known as an 'English' writer and has achieved fame and recognition as one of the most accomplished writers of British fiction. She is known for her elegant turn of phrase and elegiac description of mood, often a deep well of inner loneliness.[138] Bryan Cheyette comments that Brookner, like Pinter, are uncomfortable about their Jewishness being thought of as a central aspect of their work.[139] She rarely gave interviews or attended Jewish communal events although she did take part in 1986 in a book fair organised by Ben Gurion University to raise money for projects and a fundraiser for the Jerusalem University library, and signed a petition in 1988 with other writers for Jews for a Just Israel protesting against the situation in Gaza and the West Bank.

Brookner died on 10 March 2016. She had requested not to have a funeral which was inkeeping with her very private persona and showed she had no interest in conforming to Jewish custom. Her publisher Judith Annan remarked 'I think what people miss is that her novels are some of the most shocking of the twentieth century, for underneath the veneer of novel plots about women failing to marry, failing to see the venal in those around them, failing to make successful lives. She wrote about the biggest fears we have: loneliness and death'. In later years Brookner spoke frankly about her regrets at not marrying and having children while conceding that motherhood might have impeded her writing. 'That's why I write because I have no children'.[140]

Brookner's accessible prose style confirmed her as a writer of great depth and integrity, offering insight into the searing isolation suffered by outsiders. Her vivid analysis of humanity came from her constant observation of people, her acerbic humour and her intellectual rigour. She was celebrated for both her incisive style and her empathy with the lonely and loveless. She was also a keen exponent of the Jewish angst that often typified her era, but she preferred to be taken seriously as an English writer. Ron Charles, book editor at the *Washington Post* considered that no one captured the rhythms of loneliness as brilliantly as she did.[141] As Brookner commented, 'I feel like I am walking with the mark of Cain on my forehead. I feel I could get into the Guinness book of records as the world's loneliest most miserable woman'.[142]

The 1960s was a time of waiting for British Jewish writing. By the 1970s Jews were in a far more settled, successful and secure position in Britain. East End life was a distant memory; a new generation was going on to further education and entering the world of the professions. Jewish literary voices were more confident. In the 1970s and 1980s respected acclaimed authors were putting Jewish lives, rituals and families centre stage. Upwardly mobile Jews were trying to penetrate the middle-classes and Hampstead intellectuals craved acceptance into fashionable media circles. 'With their noses pressed against the window of Britain they could see their dream of belonging and being truly established and accepted as part of society grew even nearer, yet they still stayed frustratingly just out of reach'.[143]

Linda Grant (1951 –)

Linda Grant was born in Liverpool and read English at the University of York (1972-1975), before moving to Canada for her MA and postgraduate studies at McMaster University and Simon Fraser University. In 1985 she returned to England and became a journalist, working for the *Guardian* and eventually writing her own column for 18 months. She published her first book in 1993, a non-fiction work, *Sexing the Millenium: A Political History of the Sexual Revolution.*

Her debut novel *The Cast Iron Shore* (1996) won the David Higham Prize for Fiction and her second novel *When I Lived in Modern Times* , about a young Jewish East End hairdresser who sets out for Palestine in the aftermath of the Second World War and becomes enmeshed in Zionist politics, won the 2000 Orange Prize for Fiction. In 2002 her third novel *Still Here*, set in Liverpool and about a middle-aged romance, was long listed for the Man Booker Prize. *The Clothes On Their Backs*, a story of survival, was shortlisted for the Man Booker prize and longlisted for the Orange Prize in 2008. Set in a small flat in central London where Vivien grows up the only daughter of ultra-cautious Jewish parents, she finds new, thrilling and tragic possibilities through her slum landlord. It won the South Bank Show award in the literature category.

Other works include *The Thoughtful Dresser* (2009), *We Had It So Good* (2011), *Upstairs at the Party* (2014) and *The Dark Circle* (2016). Her second, non-fiction work, *Remind Me Who I Am Again* (1998), a personal memoir of her mother's fight with vascular dementia, won both the Mind and Age Concern Book of the Year awards and was cited in a discussion about ageing in BBC Radio 4's *Thinking Allowed* in December 2003. Known for her journalism, particularly her features and blogs on fashion, Grant was appointed a Fellow of the Royal Society of Literature in 2014.

Grant, whose grandparents were Russian and Polish immigrants, was the oldest child of Benny Ginsburg and Rose Haft. The family adopted the surname Grant in the 1950s. Her father left school at ten and went on to make and sell hairdressing products. Her mother's siblings went barefoot to school; the only reason her mother wore shoes was because she was the youngest. There was a sense of 'We came here with nothing and you can achieve anything through brains and hard work'.[144]

Grant grew up in Liverpool, in what she refers to as a small first generation ghetto. 'When you are growing up the world you live in seems rich solid, unquestionable. The Jewish community of Liverpool seemed more authentic than that of London. It was more innately Jewish. Not because of its diversity but because of the very lack of it'. Grant explains that although there were a few versions of the Hampstead Jewish intellectual, some refugees and émigrés, they held themselves slightly aloof from the great mass of immigrant life that had arrived in the city at the turn of the century. To be a Reform Jew was radical, to be Liberal was so exotic as to be unimaginable. 'As for the Chasidim, I had never heard of them. To be Jewish was to watch clean-shaven Jewish men walk along the street to their synagogue holding velvet embroidered Tallis bags (that contained their prayer shawl) or drive there, parking the car round the corner out of respect for the feelings of the rabbi'. She describes how the wives would arrive later in their suits from Jaeger and hats from Cresta, and left earlier. The Kiddush (prayer and blessing over wine) was full of men with gefilte fish breath, sweet red wine staining the tablecloth. It was more authentically Jewish because it was, due to its conformity, still really a shtetl'.[145]

Grant did not know anyone who was not a member of the United Synagogue. Most people were in business and had little connection with anyone non-Jewish. 'Sometimes I feel like I come from nowhere, it's like me and six people'. She went to York University at a time and in a place where girls like her were expected to marry young, live round the corner from their parents and provide grandchildren. She was 'at war' with her mother's expectations. Being a nice Jewish girl would have been 'like being walled up'. Her mother's bitterness at not having a typical Jewish daughter came out in explosions to total strangers in front of her daughter, when her mother was suffering from dementia, described in Grant's book *Remind Me Who I Am, Again*.[146]

For Grant, the child of Jewish immigrants who grew up in post-war Britain, a sense of internal contradiction was formative 'while slavishly trying to imitate *them*, the English, I also became self-divided'. Reflecting on memories of her loud, generous and to her teenage eyes, embarrassing father, she observes that she took for granted the 'vulgar luxuries' that he could provide yet she also longed for 'a dry, mild laconic father with a name like James or Charles or Timothy and a distinguished war record'.[147] This suggests a particularly complex aspect of identification that British Jews of this generation had to negotiate.[148]

Despite numerous uncles and aunts nearby the family tree grew in unstable ground. Antisemitism loomed large in their stories about the past and neither of her parents ever shook off what Grant describes as a paranoid, insular mind set. Grant's aspirational snobbish mother tended to airbrush out of the picture her own impoverished start; her father was a cobbler who repaired and sold shoes of the nearly dead. Grant was sent aged seven to a girls' private school in order to equip herself for marriage to a Jewish solicitor but ended up becoming something else. 'I was embarrassed by my parents and thought they had nothing of interest to say or contribute to anything'. She rebelled against her parents, rejected religion and the 'densely Jewish' atmosphere and 'very Jewish food regime' of her parents' household in which Marmite, honey and marmalade were treated as alien substances. After completing her A-levels Grant spent a year working for Oxfam and then went on to study in England and overseas and for a long time hardly looked back at the environment in which she had grown up. Grant sees herself as having been tracked down by her past. Her father died when she was 32 and around the same time she began thinking differently about the attitudes that shaped her.[149]

Her fiction draws heavily on her Jewish background, family history and the history of Liverpool. In an interview with Emily Parker for the University of Leicester's July 2008 'Unsettling Women: Contemporary Women's Writing and Diaspora' conference, Grant explained that she had always wanted to be a writer but as she was unable to get a job as a writer she concentrated on reporting and did not write her first novel until after the age of 40. It took her a long time to find her fictional voice which was to do with being Jewish. She had tried different voices but found none adequate. There were two modes open to her. One was to have a voice like the Jewish author Howard Jacobson which was absolutely embedded with a recognisable Jewish community (Manchester) but she was from a community that was not recognised as Jewish. People would often say to her that they never knew there were any Jews in Liverpool. Also, growing up in a middle-class family made her marginal to the Liverpool voice which had always been working-class or Irish. There was also the generalised middle-class English voice that always felt to her like ventriloquism.

Her first novel *The Cast Iron Shore* was about someone who feels marginal. 'It was only when I started writing about people who are marginal, who have problematic identities and problems with belonging that I found my voice'.[150] Jo Roselman comments 'that there are many chains that anchor us to our social moorings: family, culture, religion, gender, politics, sense of place. But sometimes history's bludgeon severs the chains and sets us adrift'. This novel charts the life of Sybil through the second half of the twentieth century whose chains were always fragile. She was born into a family free of close ties. Sybil's father is a Jewish furrier and she goes with him to the synagogue where she feels alienated, sitting in the ladies' gallery, not understanding Hebrew and listening to the other women gossip about her parents' marriage. Her mother is also an immigrant, a non-Jewish

German; style and fashion are her religion. Between the wars they live a life of material comfort, cultural numbness and social isolation. When she is 14 she meets a Stan, a sailor, who although from a different world is also rootless. Together they witness the horrors of the Liverpool Blitz and after the war, Sybil who is now in her early 20s, follows Stan and emigrates to the United States. Here begins a life torn between the desire to belong and an independence and attraction to the outsider.[151]

The protagonists in Grant's novels tended to be, like Grant herself, second generation immigrants who feel like outsiders. Grant sees the outsider as paradigmatic of the position of Jews in Britain. The sense of marginality was exacerbated by the strange dissonance between the stereotypical English character, which is defined by tact, reserve, good manners and Jewish identity which is all about screaming rages. Her own sense of being an outsider was complicated because she grew up in a house where Yiddish was spoken, her parent's first language, and there was a different religion to the mainstream. Once she left the house she was not treated as a member of an ethnic minority because she was white. 'So I was in the strange position of always 'passing' and that is why there is a great deal about women in disguise in my first two novels. That's the way I felt when I was growing up, like someone who was to some extent in disguise outside the home. But I also felt alienated from the world inside the home because I wanted to be part of the outside world. So I always had two compartments inside my head. The fractures and tensions were great and these permeate everything I have written.'[152]

The migrant's search for self in the face of homelessness is reflected in Grant's characters who are chameleons who adopt various disguises and constantly reinvent themselves. Grant explains that when her grandparents arrived in Britain in 1900 from Eastern Europe they discovered a very rigid class system and this rigidity was reinforced by the clothes people wore. They realised they could use clothing as costume in order to reinvent themselves; they could wear whatever they liked and they would be taken at face value. Therefore appearances had enormous significance as one could always pretend to be somebody else, identity was mutable.[153] (Clothes feature a great deal in Grant's work, including *The Clothes On Their Back* and *The Thoughtful Dresser*).

Grant considers that despite the problems engendered by a sense of homelessness, diaspora had some positive effects. 'If you are a writer because you are by definition an outsider you observe society all the better. The condition of being part of a diaspora is that of being transitional and cosmopolitan, usually urban, not particularly attached to landscape, constantly in flux'.[154] She points out that Jews have the habit of thinking and perceiving from the outside, the capacity to be an observer, poised between the two worlds which is a special gift that all Jews bring to the diaspora they inhabit.[155]

Grant does not have any religious affiliation to Judaism but grew up with an acute awareness of her ethnicity and of the particular difficulties it posed in assimilating into English society. Grant observes that it was 'hard to tell' what class her parents belonged to since they were 'neither part of the great proletariat nor of a peasantry'. What their class really was, she concludes, was immigrant.[156] She emphasises her family's sense of its Jewish heritage. 'In her kitchen my mother cooked recipes that her own mother had brought from Kiev, and the dishes that came to the table were our link to the vanished communities of earlier times; they traced the wandering of the Jewish people across the earth'.[157]

By the time Grant was in her late 30s she reflects that she had explored various avenues and that 'she had done hippy, done communist'. It was then she realised 'with a sudden grasp of revelation' that she'd been formed by growing up in a Jewish community. It was a shock to her to realise how much this influenced her. 'I had slammed the door on it, thought none of it had any relevance to me. Then I thought about Jews not having a sense of knowing their place and about the sense that you can do whatever you want'. These two themes underpin Grant's writing. She describes her own Jewish identity as completely secular. 'I think a fairy blessed me at birth by making me Jewish, it's a thing of enormous value, such extraordinary diversity, so fascinating. At the same time you can feel quite smothered. I just have to return to my upbringing, there are so many fascinating things to write about and that's just my family. When I venture beyond into contemporary Jewish history it's a treasure trove'.[158]

Her books truly reflect her background. There is a stereotypical perception, perpetuated by many Jewish writers themselves that Jews are temperamentally unsuited to the countryside, the suggestion is that Jews are in essence urbanites who can only belong in the shifting and impermanent environs of the city. The major cities have traditionally accommodated different waves of immigrants whereas the countryside has been regarded as far less progressive and flexible terrain. This perception is central to a number of Grant's journalistic essays and her novels, many of which reflect specifically on Jewishness in relation to politics and place in the late twentieth century. In her first novel *Cast Iron Shore*, Grant narrates the story of Sybil Ross, daughter of a Jewish immigrant furrier, who like Grant was born and brought up in Liverpool. Sybil is preoccupied by transitory, rootless, surface performances of identity. She has been formed by the perpetual passages and rhythms of the port. 'I understand ports. No one who was born in a port knows who they really are.'[159]. When she has to take her Yugoslavian cousin to the countryside she only sees nondescript colours and is unable to name trees or flowers or recognise foxes and minks when they are running around before they are made into fur coats. The implication is that surface appearance and the values of acquisition are more significant than a natural world with which the transitory Jew has no real or deep connection. Such moments of disconnection tend to lead to an awareness that is sharpened rather than muffled by a sense of not belonging.[160] Her parents associated the rural with shtetls 'where villagers were massacred by the Cossacks. Once when they drove through the Lake District, her grandfather who didn't speak a word of English said, 'here they could build houses for the workers'.[161]

Grant keeps revisiting the theme of belonging, not belonging and a sense of place. Her main characters in *The Cast Iron Shore* and *When I Lived In Modern Times* (2000), are both young women who leave home to make a journey and find a new life. Alix in *Still Here* (2002) returns home to Liverpool from France as her mother lies dying. There are repeated themes of being half German, half Jewish, being an outsider, searching one's place. 'You're neither one thing nor the other and that drives people mad', Stan says to Sybil at the end of *The Cast Iron Shore* (1996). But Sybil is looking towards the sea at Liverpool docks and there is a sense that she accepts that she will always be looking elsewhere, at another place, a potential journey.[162]

Interwoven in her search for what it means to be Jewish are her writings about Israel. Israel was a place where her parents could stand proud in the world that took their victimhood and fear away. It turned their eyes away from the past to the future. The understanding of the creation of Israel as representing a move away from a painful and fractured past towards a confident future is a potent theme in British Jewish writing. Grant's parents' joy in relation to Israel's creation was undercut by a sense that the British who had abstained in the UN vote had once again failed to fully endorse support for the Jews. Therefore the moment of Israel's creation, whilst not exactly making them Israeli, also somehow made them even more not British than they were already.[163]

For Grant, part of the post-war generation brought up in Britain, feelings about Israel were complex. For this generation rejecting Zionism was often bound up with familial tension as well as political conviction.[164] Yet for Grant, a left leaning British Jew, Israel invoked in her an uncanny sense of connection. She spent four months living in Israel and she found herself drawn there, not out of Zionism or interest in the Middle East but because the moment she put her foot down everything was half familiar. 'I had half the story already in my head'.[165]

In *The People On The Street, A Writer's View of Israel,* Grant describes her relationship with Israel and Israelis in all its complexity. She went to stay in Tel Aviv with the intention of writing a novel but ended up so intrigued and enchanted by the people she met there that she wrote instead this non-fiction work. She stressed that while she was not a political analyst or expert on the Middle East she brought the distinctive view of the novelist. It was very much the personal stories of the real life characters in the book that enthralled her. Her affinity for the people she meets is a result of their Jewishness and more specifically their Jewish histories. It is clear that Grant's own Jewish identity is founded on the history of her family, refugees from antisemitism in Eastern Europe and pervading the book is her sense of wonder at a whole nation made up of people like her: Jews with complicated family histories; people whose parents or grandparents fled countries all over Europe as well as the Middle East. Grant complains that the varied and fascinating people she meets and talks to in Tel Aviv do not find their way into news reports on Israel and that journalists head straight for Jerusalem (a city for which she has little affection) and meet politically obsessed Jews and Arabs who are not representative of the Israel she loves. Those living in towns and cities on the coast are the real Israelis, living ordinary lives.[166]

Grant has a sense of belonging in Tel Aviv. Although she has lived in London longer than she has lived elsewhere she does not feel like a Londoner. She considers her personality is far more suited to the New York Jewish community than its British counterpart but 'no one accepts me there because I'm English. A New York American Jew said that English Jews are not real Jews, they speak with a la di da accent. I feel completely erased, my Britishness was seen as making me not really Jewish, yet in Britain my Jewishness makes me not really British'. She concludes that in Tel Aviv everyone comes from somewhere else and that she has as much right to be there as anyone else who lives there.[167]

Post-war Jews were stained by the long shadow cast by the Holocaust. Grant recalls that 'history breathed down our necks as we were growing up, a constant reminder that where there were suburbs and houses and trees and allotments and W H Smith and Tesco and Marks and Spencer, a kind of mental chasm yawned beneath our feet into which we were always fearful that we could fall'.[168] This sense of history, 'breathing down our necks' was a key theme in accounts from the immediate post-war generation as they negotiate their British and Jewish identities in a post- Holocaust world. These post-war children lived in an unsettling environment that combined the apparent comforts of Anglo-Jewish life with the dawning realisation of the horrors that had beset European Jewry.[169]

The post-war period in Britain is explored in Grant's work. In *The Clothes On Their Back* (2008) Grant writes about a sensitive girl growing up in 1950s London, sealed off from both past and present by her timid refugee parents. The dramatic arrival of a glamorous uncle, violently unwelcome by her parents, changes everything. A story of concealed pasts, stark choices and how the clothes we wear define us all. Post-war London is the beginning of the novel *The Dark Circle* (2017). It tells the story of Jewish East End twins Lenny and Miriam Lynsey who are diagnosed with tuberculosis and sent off to Gwendo, a Kent sanatorium to recuperate. Antisemitism lurks around many corners. The Gwendo is a social melting pot in which people across the class spectrum are trapped together with no chance of escape, allowing Grant a prism through which to view the social, political and cultural mores of the period. *The Dark Circle* is a fascinating portrayal of the authoritarianism inherent in post-war British healthcare. Some of the treatments are brutal and improved yet there is a dictatorial assumption that doctors' orders should never be questioned. Lenny and Miriam face antisemitism from all quarters: 'who on earth was that hairy Jewish gorilla? Was he bothering you? We can put in a complaint, you know'.[170]

Ruth Gilbert considers that writers such as Grant have contributed significantly to recent developments in British Jewish women's writings. As these women engage with history and reflect what it means to be a British Jew, so British Jewish women's writing is becoming an increasingly notable aspect of the contemporary literary field.[171]

Maureen Kendler is of the opinion that *Remind Me Who I Am Again* occupies a key place in the move towards Jewish writing becoming mainstream. 'Grant writes passionately and with great intelligence about her past and present and is deeply rooted in her Jewishness. But what she has to say moves easily from the particular to the universal, so while her Jewish audience will recognise its authenticity, her non-Jewish readership will appreciate and understand too'. Writers at this time are ever sensitive to the horrors that happened in the distant past but respond thankfully second hand. 'We look over our shoulder with nervousness, always alert for antisemitism but for the moment we are safe and our writing reflects that. We can take our place proudly and confidently on the bookshelves that explore life lived here'.[172]

'British Jewish writers today are shaking off a culture of reticence and self-censorship which inhibited previous generations of Anglo-Jewry. They are raising their Jewish voices unabashedly and in public'.[173] Naomi Alderman is an example.

Naomi Alderman (1974 –)

Naomi Alderman belongs to a generation of British Jews that has been able to declare themselves more loudly and proudly than those that came before them. Whereas their parents had been wary of being too noticeable – unsure even about using the J-word too audibly in mixed company – these younger Jews have been much bolder as shown by Alderman's novel *Disobedience*. There is an ease about 'outing' oneself as a Jew that did not exist in the same way 30 or 40 years before. This was partly due to the confidence that came with feeling settled and accepted that was not always available to previous generations.[174] From the 1970s on monolithic Englishness was crumbling and gradually it became acceptable to be British and something else.[175]

Alderman is the daughter of Marion, a retired art teacher and Geoffrey Alderman, a journalist and British historian specialising in the Jewish communities in England in the nineteenth and twentieth centuries. They were 'unorthodox Orthodox Jews' who brought their daughter up to be intellectually curious but culturally conservative.[176] She went from a state Jewish primary school in Colindale, north London to the highly competitive South Hampstead High School. Her parents were both from solidly working-class backgrounds. 'We weren't particularly wealthy so I was quite out of place. What these schools do if you come from a background like that is essentially a process of deracination. For years I looked down on my mother for shopping at Asda and now I feel very ashamed of it'. Her home life in her teens was overshadowed by the suicide of her uncle when she was 14 which traumatised her parents and 'broke' her grandmother. 'It meant that I didn't have a period of adolescent rebellion. To rebel you need to feel safe that your parents will still love you and that they'll be ok, and after my uncle's death it was clear to me that my family were not ok, so I was a very good girl'.[177]

Literature was an everyday source of personal growth for Alderman when she was growing up. She read the Bible in Hebrew from an early age and her mother would take her to the library every few days.[178] School was a nurturing place where she flourished academically. It was not until she went to read PPE at Lincoln College, Oxford University that she found how hard it could be to live by different rules. On arrival she was excited to find a room full of state-of-the-art computers so that she could play games that she had not played before. She then found it was full of boys swapping pictures of topless women 'and I was this good Orthodox girl'. The college kitchens would not cook kosher food so she ate at the Jewish Society six days a week and once a week had a potato wrapped in double foil so that she could have some vestige of college life. On the eve of each Sabbath she would leave her files in the library and her toothbrush in the bathroom to avoid carrying them.[179] From time to time she would find her toothbrush missing and her papers torn. Years later at a college reunion someone confessed that 'me and my friends used to mess with your stuff on the Sabbath'. Alderman considers this to be a case of antisemitic bullying.

After university she briefly worked as a PA at a children's publisher then edited publications for an international law firm which sent her to its New York office. New York introduced her to the Orthodox gay community 'who had these terrible stories: rabbis who said if you didn't marry and have children you were completing Hitler's work'. She returned for an MA in creative writing at the University of East Anglia with the seeds both of serious religious doubt and her first novel.

Disobedience was published in 2006 when Alderman was in her early 30s. She submitted her manuscript on a Friday and it was snapped up by Penguin Viking on the following Monday. It placed a New York Jewish lesbian at the heart of the novel set in the north London home of an Orthodox rabbi, offering a rare glimpse into a hidden world. The book caused some distress in Orthodox circles. It marked the end of Alderman's life as a practising Jew. 'I went into the novel religious and by the end I wasn't. I wrote myself out of it'.[180]

In what surely is the most transgressive novel by a British Jewish woman writer in recent years, Alderman turned to a subject that has been all but absent since Grace Aguilar and Lily Montagu first wrote about God and gender in the Victorian period. *Disobedience* is set in the insular community of north London ultra-Orthodox Jews, synonymous in the mind of the alienated Ronit, with sexism and social conformity.[181]

The publication of *Disobedience* made Alderman the most exciting young Jewish novelist in the country. It was translated into ten languages, earnt her the 2006 Orange Prize for new writers, the 2007 Sunday Times Young Writer of the Year and a place among Waterstone's 25 Writers for the Future. The novel charts a lesbian love affair within the Hendon Orthodox community and tells the story of two childhood friends, Ronit and Esti, whose friendship had over time blossomed into romance and then faded again when Ronit left England.

When Rav Krushka, hallowed leader of an Orthodox Hendon congregation dies, his daughter Ronit returns to London from a decade self-imposed exile in New York, where she has dropped religion, become a career woman, slept with her boss and undergone extensive therapy. Eagerly awaiting for her return is Esti, the wife of Ronit's cousin Dovie who is the congregation's heir-apparent – and Ronit's former love interest. The reunion forces Ronit to come to terms with her lingering feelings about religion while Esti – who is regarded by the community as frail and strange – must come to terms with her lingering feelings towards Ronit and confront the state of her marriage.[182]

We follow the characters through a number of very closely told experiences, dreams, narrations, conversations and physical experiences. Deborah Smith comments in *Jewish Renaissance* that Alderman links the two narratives beautifully and creatively so that they become almost like a harmonious duet. Throughout the book Alderman shows that she has a vast knowledge of Judaism. Each chapter is opened by a short teaching from Jewish texts that is meaningful beyond the context of the book. *Disobedience* is imbued with Jewish humour, Jewish words and Jewish feeling and could only be written by someone who feels great love for her community whilst at the same time being alive to its failings. There would be people that would not be comfortable and would not want the community discussed or who do not like to see Jewishness so 'out there' and for it to be intertwined so closely with themes and questions about sexuality and what it means to be gay.[183] The book was serialised on BBC Radio 4's *Book At Bedtime* with Sara Kestelman and Tracy-Ann Oberman as narrators. It was made into a film in 2018 that starred Rachel Weisz and Rachel McAdams.

Miriam Shaviv of the *Jewish Chronicle* considers that Alderman deserves praise for discussing openly the issue of sexual orientation in the Orthodox community which although had received more attention in recent years was still largely a taboo. She makes a bold attempt to portray the Orthodox community sympathetically yet critically. Despite all the 'lesbians in Hendon' hype the climax of the entire novel is a brief kiss in a park. Shaviv wonders whether this is an attempt by Alderman to show sensitivity towards the community about which she is writing.[184] 'Alderman's commentary on Orthodox Judaism in the twenty first century is thought provoking and illuminating and she has the comic's gift to assassinate from within with compassion.'[185]

Alderman explains that her interest in writing about homosexuality was due to her Orthodox upbringing as Judaism does not have a lot to say about straight women's sexuality and the basic attitude is that it does not exist. 'So I have empathy with people who are told that their sexuality, their desire, is not something that can be spoken about'.[186]

Disobedience points toward new directions for British Jewish women's writing at the beginning of the twenty first century. While earlier generations were haunted by a traumatic European heritage or wary of a history of British antisemitism, poets and novelists now imagine relationships to Jewishness that are no longer exclusively dominated by the past. The ongoing story of Jewish writers' vigorous engagement with a religious establishment and social conventions that constrain women's public freedoms nonetheless continues. And while the theme of conflicted Jewish identity still forms the core compelling subject of their writing, it no longer leads inevitably to bleak paralysis but opens up instead to a future of new retellings.[187]

Writing *Disobedience* had a profound effect on Alderman's life. 'I kept myself very religious whilst I was writing it because I thought it would be bad faith not to', she explains. 'For a long time I had known morally that I was not in agreement with Orthodoxy but I was still doing all the practices. After the novel was published I came to feel that I couldn't call myself Orthodox anymore. It's so patriarchal, anti-women, anti-gay'. After the book was published Alderman referred to herself as 'used to be Orthodox'. However, she observes practices that still have meaning for her such as Passover.[188]

She acknowledges that Judaism had a profound influence on her approach to books. 'They do say that writers should be outsiders and I am interested in the combination of insider and outsider of being a Jewish person in a Christian country'.[189] For Alderman being Jewish 'is a bit of a blessing, a bit of a burden. For myself I've managed to turn it from a prison cell into a toolkit. Learn what wisdom there is from Judaism. Use what's useful, disregard the rest. And if nothing is useful, throw it all out without fear'.[190] Nevertheless she does acknowledge that for some 'the *frum* (Orthodox) life can be a very good one – purposeful and filled with meaning, warm social bonds and the comforting joyful round of ritual and routine'.[191]

Although no longer a believer Alderman continued to be fascinated by religion. Her third novel *The Liars' Gospel,* (2012), told an alternative life of Christ in which Jesus has become the religious preacher Yehoshuah, son of Miryam, who may or may not be a worker of miracles. It too caused offence in some quarters. 'Before writing it I felt oppressed by Christianity because it's responsible for so much persecution of Jews; since I wrote it I think of Jesus as my friend. I haven't allowed him into my heart, just into my sitting room'.[192]

The Liars' Gospel is an unusual take on the life of Jesus. It sets the story of Jesus in the context of Jewish history, as a chapter in a bigger tale. This version like the original is told in four gospels; the testimonies of four people whose lives were changed by this wandering preacher. One gospel concerns his mother Miryam who is torn with grief over his death a year before and fury at the trouble he is still causing and that she is an attraction for his followers. Another gospel is about Judas who betrayed Jesus and then hung himself. In Alderman's version he becomes a successful after dinner speaker on the Roman party circuit. She writes acutely about his loss of faith in Jesus and he becomes a hero rather than the traditional villain. The other two voices belong to the High Priest Caiaphas whose life is a nightmare of appeasing the Romans and Barabbas the political rebel released by Pontius Pilate because the rabble preferred him to Jesus. By turning this well-known story on its head, Alderman places the beginnings of Christianity against the chaotic background of an occupied country.[193]

Alderman's second novel was *The Lessons* (2012). *Disobedience* was set in the self-contained world of Orthodox Hendon. *The Lessons* is set in Oxford University which is a similarly cloistered environment. The hushed quads and ancient spires are a far cry from Hendon's suburban semis and urban parks yet both worlds have their own calendar, culture and customs and both are shaped by a tradition so intense it can feel stifling.[194]

The Lessons is a louche campus novel about a young man's obsession with a magnetic, obscenely wealthy gay fellow student. It abounds in bright young things making lofty pronouncements over expensive wine and wheels of ripe cheese. It has the glamour, the wealth and the classic fall from grace. The themes of *Disobedience* resurfaced as it explores sexuality, the demands made by family and community, the gay love circle. Oxford, where Alderman studied, was not so far from Hendon as both the ancient university and Orthodox Judaism are hothouse communities where rules and rituals must be observed in order to preserve identity. Both are worlds where the self can be swallowed.[195]

Alderman felt that Oxford was not intended for her although her father had studied at Lincoln College and took her there when she was eight and told her that it was her future place of study. Alderman considers that Oxford was an institution for monks and wealthy Christian men and two hundred years previously she would not have been admitted because she was Jewish. 'Something of that spirit has remained. It seems to me that Oxford would like you to pretend that you're a toff'.[196]

In contrast is *The Power* (2016), a sci-fi/dystopian novel, which tells the story of what happens after a genetic mutation gives young women the power to electrocute people. What starts out as a fantasy of female empowerment deepens and darkens into an interrogation of power itself, its uses and abuses and what it does to people who have it. In *The Power* a convent gives sanctuary to the newly empowered young women when the male establishment is hunting them down and despite the doctrinal problems that they pose goes on to preserve their stories and to sanctify their conclusion that God must be female. It is no coincidence that the novel seems 'Atwoodesque' in its evocation of a closed order of women. It developed after Alderman was 'adopted' by the author Margaret Atwood in a mentoring scheme for young writers and is dedicated to Atwood and her husband 'who have shown me wonders'.[197] The novel won the Baileys Women Prize for Fiction 2017. 'Feminist writing has shown me purpose. My book shows what women can do'.[198] Speaking at the awards ceremony, Alderman said that 'the women's movement is more vital to me than running water'.[199] It was among the New York Times's 100 notable books of the year and former American president Barack Obama chose it as one of his favourite books for 2017. It has now been adapted for Amazon Prime Video.

Alderman has extended her creative writing skills. She is not only an award-winning young novelist but a successful games writer. She has written online games for Penguin and the BBC and was the lead writer (2004-2007) on the alternative reality game Perplex City which was nominated for a BAFTA. In 2012 she co-created and wrote the smartphone audio adventure app *Zombies, Run!* which was shortlisted for Five Develop Awards and has sold more than half a million copies. Each episode sends runners on a 'unique mission in the zombie apocalypse' which is dramatized in audio, with interludes for runners' own music playlists. Besides the games and original fiction Alderman wrote a tie-in novel *Borrowed Time* (2011) for the *Doctor Who* television series. In addition to her literary prizes and professorship of creative writing at Bath University, she was elected Fellow of the Royal Society of Literature in 2018.

Alderman is very much an example of a new generation and a contrast to British Jewish writers of the immediate post-war period. Although Alderman was a further generation away from the war, the Holocaust was still a pervasive presence throughout her childhood. Noting the difficulties of having been educated to 'imagine myself in a camp' she was aware of an ongoing sense of anxiety about the potential re-emergence of antisemitism. Like Linda Grant she grew up with a consciousness of the 'mental chasm' into which post-war Jews were always 'fearful that we could fall'. But Alderman also recognises the paranoia that accompanies such fear. 'Except it's not here. Right now, right here, life is about as good for us as life has ever been for anyone in the history of the world. Probably better'. She acknowledges that 'we have an impossible task: to hold onto something at the same time as letting it go. The fact that it's impossible doesn't mean it's not worth trying. Remembering. And at the same time remember that it's over'.[200] This enabled her to write from a position of safety and she shows great confidence in all that she does.

Popular awareness of British Jewish women writers in recent years has been augmented by the work of Naomi Alderman and Charlotte Mendelson. Alderman's *Disobedience* focuses on Orthodox Jewish life in suburban Hendon, north-west London. Mendelson's *When We Were Bad*, set in the Belsize Park area of north-west London, also depicts British Jewish life but from a less Orthodox perspective. Both novels were highly publicised and both have contributed to a sense of growing visibility in the representation of British Jewish women.[201]

Charlotte Mendelson (1972 –)

Charlotte Mendelson's novels are full of close, competitive families, of fierce love and troubled filial loyalty; of lesbian yearnings both acted upon and ignored; of being Jewish in Britain. She comes from a close, academic Jewish family. Her own background is cockney mixed with Mittel-European Jewry (her grandparents were 'Hungarian-speaking-Czech, Ruthenian for about 10 minutes, Carpathian mountain-y, impossible to describe') who left Prague in 1939. She grew up in Queensway, a cosmopolitan area of west London until she was two years old when the family moved to a house in a cobbled passage next to St. John's College, Oxford, where her father Maurice Harvey Mendelson, a barrister, taught public international law. Oxford gave her the voice. 'I sound like a pre-pubescent Etonian'. She went to Oxford High School and New College, Oxford where she read ancient and modern history. She considers this a terrible mistake as she should have read English. She describes Oxford as 'incredibly retro' and explains how she spent her years growing up in navy corduroy, mixing interesting paints out of broken bits of brick and feeling very fashionable if she listened to the Beatles. She considers it a good place to grow up as it was full of lots of other brainy weirdos – a fact she mocks in her novel *Daughters of Jerusalem*.[202]

Mendelson was an archetypal swot and never more than 'low-key troublesome'. As a teenager she cried if she scored less than 80 per cent, deliberately picked the most self-punishing option every time. She took up the French horn because it had a reputation for being a most difficult instrument to play and chose Greek A-level because it was harder than Latin. She studied Ancient and Modern History at Oxford but later had regrets that what would have suited her best was English literature at somewhere like Leeds. Instead 'I can act out Athenian naval battle manoeuvres. But who needs that?'[203]

She found it hard being a woman at university. 'It felt like either you had to be decorative or you had to be a sort of un-female super brain. I wasn't posh and I wasn't confident. I was really hideous'. It was an unhappy time. She had dreamt of lying under trees reading Keats and instead she was in the library reading book 17 on Merovingian archaeology and thinking it was hell. She wanted to be a writer. She learnt to touch-type first like a 1950s debutante and then worked as an editor at Jonathan Cape (1996-1997). She found herself frustrated and there was a lot of 'going sadly home alone'. She considered an escape to law school, applied, deferred but did not go.[204]

It was the Oxford based poet and critic Craig Raine, the editor of the anthology *New Writing*, who helped set Mendelson on her writing career. He heard her give a very rude account about someone she had just split up with and he encouraged her to write the story which was published.[205] This was followed by *Love in Idleness* (2001) *Daughters of Jerusalem* (2003), *When We Were Bad* (2007), *Almost English* (2013) and *The Exhibitionist* (2022). She was an editor at the *Headline Review* (1998-2014) and is a visiting professor of creative writing at Royal Holloway, University of London and a Fellow of the Royal Society of Literature. She has also published a book on gardening, *Rhapsody in Green* (2016) and is the gardening correspondent at the *New Yorker*. She was longlisted for the Man Booker Prize (2013), the Baileys Women's Prize for Fiction (2014) and the Women's Prize for Fiction (2022).

One way of describing Mendelson's books would be to say that they are about the private lives of children. *Love in Idleness* is about a girl's first months alone in the big city, separating herself from her mother, establishing her individuality. *Daughters of Jerusalem* begins with a child's-eye view and like her other novels explores the clash Mendelson believes exists in families, however outwardly functional: between people's inner lives, and what their family thinks and expects of them; how that clash shapes the adults they become.[206]

Love in Idleness is a classic coming of age: arriving in a big city, not knowing anyone and spending far too much time thinking. The protagonist Anna Raine is desperate to break free from her mother's bonds when she returns home to Bath after university. Provincial middle-class Magda is dismayed when her daughter opts to take up the offer of staying in a flat in London. The flat belongs to Magda's bohemian sister Stella. Thoroughly disapproved of by Magda, Stella is just the sort of woman that Anna longs to become. While Stella is away in Paris, Anna explores her aunt's flat and tries to unravel some mysterious secrets. So begin Anna's adventures in the capital where she strikes up tentative friendships during the day but is left lonely at night. As Anna uncovers more about her aunt, she learns more about her own awakening sexuality.[207] It ends with Anna who had suffered loneliness and inappropriate crushes, beginning to get back on an even keel by exploring the attractions of women. The switch from heterosexual to lesbian mirrors Mendelson life. She had boyfriends until she was 23. 'Not a whiff of lesbianism. Not even a thought. But I am very all or nothing. It was all that and now it is all this. There was about a 10-minute cross over period of uncertainty'. She also adds that she was every mother's nightmare. 'You think you've got a nice heterosexual daughter, and then suddenly, oh my God'.[208] The family did not take it well. 'I told them on Christmas Day which is fantastic for a Jewish atheist'.[209] She met novelist Joanna Briscoe in 1997. They appeared in the IOS's pink list in 2007, the annual celebration of the great and the gay.[210] Mendelson has two children from her former marriage to Briscoe.

Her second novel *Daughters of Jerusalem* won a Somerset Maugham award and the John Llewellyn Rhys Prize for an under 35s author. It is set in Oxford in the mid-1980s and Mendelson employs her insider knowledge of the city. Victor, an ageing Jewish history don, is obsessed with his chances of giving a prestigious lecture at his college; his wife Jean, some 20 years younger, toils away as a librarian while dreaming of escape. Their oldest 16-year-old daughter Eve is brilliant but is vehemently jealous of her younger prettier sister Phoebe and cuts herself regularly in the privacy of her room. Phoebe, 14, is spoilt and does everything for attention: she smokes, drinks and plays truant from school. As Victor and the two girls become more distant, Jean explores her sexuality and embarks on an affair with her best friend Helena. Meanwhile, Victor's arch enemy, the academic Raymond Snow arrives in Oxford and threatens Victor's chances at the lectureship and worms his way into the affection of the two young girls.[211]

Almost English is a tale of adolescent insecurity, secrets and lies and the eccentricities of the émigré. The heroine is Marina, an intelligent but naïve teenager growing up in west London in the 1980s. Her life, and the lives of those she lives with, specifically her mother, grandmother and two great-aunts, is turned upside down when she goes to boarding school. The world that she encounters there is one of teen vindictiveness, sexually entitled teenage boys and Sloane Ranger types. A vague romance offers Marina a ticket to a very different life from her own as she gets to know the upper class Viney family. The novel, set over a term at Combe Abbey School, follows Marina as she attempts to reconcile who she thinks she wants to become with her eccentric Hungarian immigrant family. The reader is introduced to them by large amounts of food and accented English.[212]

Almost English is sparked by memories of her Hungarian grandparents, the family is, as she puts it 'the really embarrassing foreign kind'. Where her characters are Jewish they tend to be gently, subtly so. Gerald Jacobs points out that they are not 'in disguise' as gentiles, which is how Jews intent on reading between the lines view characters unattributed ethnicity created by such Jewish writers as Anita Brookner and Harold Pinter.[213] Mendelson comments that 'they were definitely Jewish but I didn't say that because I wanted to write about the immigrant thing more than the Jewish thing'. She agonised over writing about the Holocaust. The characters are some old ladies and their granddaughter who lives with them. The old ladies went through the Holocaust and she was unsure what to do with that. She spoke to her father who told her it was not her job to write about the Holocaust, not a burden she had to take up. In the end she wrote about not knowing what happened to the grandparents – about the gap itself.[214]

Nowhere in this novel is there overt Jewishness. 'But the origins of Grandma Rozsi and great aunts Zsuzsi and Ildi, so redoubtably corseted, and redolent of *Je Reviens* (with undertones of poppy seed pastry) are unmistakable'. So is the subtle reference to their unease about Marina attending daily chapel at her new boarding school. There is a mystery surrounding the pre-war leaving of Hungary. It is understood that the family once owned a thriving business. The novel is a tribute to her own vanished Hungarian family.[215]

When We Were Bad is Mendelson's first 'Jewish' book. All of its several main characters are Jewish and the text is strewn with Hebrew and Yiddish words and phrases, all untranslated and without a footnote or a glossary. The novel, with the London locations of Belsize Park and Gospel Oak, centres around Claudia Rubin, a charismatic female rabbi – wife, matriarch and communal leader – and the Rubin family that exists within her shadow. The magnetic and media savvy Claudia is the heart and hub of a family full of secrets. She has a 'brain that women envy' and a 'body that make men weak'. She overwhelms all those who come into contact with her. During the novel the tight family circle that she has built around starts to unravel and Rubin family members are forced to question what it means to be a Rubin and what it means to be an individual within the Rubin family. Claudia is the centre of the family with a weak, less successful husband. Her four children have either chosen Jewish partners or are still living at home. Em and Simeon appear unable to leave home and form lasting relationships. Frances has married someone of her mother's choosing and fights feelings of disappointment in marriage and Leo agonises about breaking the family bonds in order to forge new ones.[216]

The lives of the four children of Rabbi Claudia Rubin have been deliberately moulded to fit the image of an ideal family. Now in their 30s, the image, obsessively nurtured by their mother, is about to shatter. Leo, the eldest son, runs away on his wedding day and goes off with the officiating rabbi's wife. This somewhat absurd situation sets off a series of events. The book focuses mainly on Frances, the oldest daughter and major source of disappointment, because of her absence of looks and inability to fit in. Yet she does everything right by the family, marrying a man approved for her, organising the practical details of their daily lives, dropping everything at a moment's notice to give support and not getting thanks in return. By contrast, her over-indulged younger siblings do nothing but exude charm yet are thoroughly approved of by their mother. Claudia is painted as the age-old caricature of the Jewish mother controlling and manipulating all those who purports to love. The fact that she is also a public figure means that what she does is magnified and the damage inflicted is multiplied. We are told she believed that if the family appeared to be perfect, the rest would follow. Having set herself up as the goddess of the family she becomes imprisoned in her own illusion and will do anything to preserve it not only before the public but within the family. Her first reaction to her son's flight is to worry about what the media would say. Then anger that he could betray what she believed in.[217]

For this book Mendelson did have to do her own research. She grew up in a completely Jewish but virtually non-practising family. She thought all rabbis wore beards until she met Rabbi Julia Neuberger who became her friend and mentor in Jewish practice.[218] 'We lit holiday candles in a desultory way, had a seder every year for the grandmothers but never did Friday night'. She says that as she has got older, she wanted more. 'As a Jew living in England, writing a novel about London Jews felt very brave and scary. Partly I wanted to engage with my Jewishness and explore it, but above all, I was preoccupied with the idea that all families give their members roles, which you can only be happy completely accepting or escaping'. She adds that she loves writing about families. 'There are so many things you must not talk about: burning secrecy, dark family history, especially among Jews.[219]

Mendelson had a meteoric rise with these novels that were about close competitive families and about being Jewish in Britain. After a lull for almost a decade came *The Exhibitionist* that is set in the London art world and centres on a dysfunctional family and about the choices they must make in balancing their needs and relationships. The Hanrahans are a family in crisis. Ray, an artist with a huge ego, is about to have an exhibition that will make or break him. It is his first solo exhibition for many years and his wife Lucia, a former student, is now the more acclaimed artist and he is resentful. Their children are also facing personal troubles and are about to make big changes in their lives. Although Mendelson made her name with a series of Jewish family dramas, *The Exhibitionist* does not have any Jews or Jewish issues.[220] Mendelson comments that 'it is specifically not about a Jewish family. They are Anglo-Irish. At first I tried to write just about the 'English' and found I couldn't do that. Some of the family's 'otherness' is a bit like Jewishness'.[221]

When discussing what makes a 'Jewish book', Mendelson considers that it is anxiety, food and jokes and when questioned as to what makes her a Jewish writer, she commented that she talks about despair in a way that she hopes is funny. *When We Were Bad* was her first novel to explicitly concentrate on a Jewish family and she agonised that it was too Jewish for non-Jews and not Jewish enough for Jews. 'I was being out about Jewishness. It felt scary'.

Making the leap into thinking that a Jewish family might be as interesting as a Bangladeshi family was huge. 'I read Monica Ali and Zadie Smith. It was just about being an immigrant – insecurities about immigrant families, grandmothers with embarrassing accents and weird food in the fridge. The same was for families if they were Greek or Irish. The Jewishness is just the texture'.[222]

Mendelson writes about people under pressure and considers that families are the most interesting to write about because that is where everything starts. 'We are the weird, troubled people that we are because of our families'. She wanted to ramp up the pressure in *When We Were Bad* and that is why she made the Rubins the children of a rabbi. 'Who could be more prodded and looked at than children of a rabbi. They are under the spotlight and I wanted them to be in a situation where they had to choose to be happy, which might mean trying to escape their family expectations. That's obviously a classic lesbian dilemma.'[223]

Although the novel features a rabbi as a central character and depicts key moments of Jewish ceremony and celebration, it is a relatively secular work. Jewishness is articulated here through family, ritual and culture rather than religion. Unlike Alderman who drew directly from her own Orthodox background, Mendelson has a less secure relationship to Jewishness and her account of her experience of being Jewish in Britain. In an interview with Laura Phillips for the *Jewish Quarterly*, Mendelson confesses that it is scary coming out as a Jew: 'Because although I'm very proud and very open about being Jewish… I am not all that confident about being Jewish. I am not a member of a shul… It did feel a real head-above-the parapet thing'. She was also worried about what other Jews would think; whether it would be a case of keep your voice down and don't draw attention to them or that she did not know what she was talking about.[224]

Ruth Gilbert considers this to be an interesting and very current dual anxiety about belonging in relation to both Britishness and Jewishness. As a minority within the mainstream of British life, Mendelson perceives the novel to be a 'coming out' in terms of identifying publicly as Jewish. The fear expressed by Mendelson is that the novel might expose her as an ignorant and ultimately unconvincing Jew; not to non-Jews but to a Jewish community in Britain of which she is not really a part.

Although generally well received, some of Mendelson's apprehensions were realised in reviews in the Anglo-Jewish press. Rabbi Sybil Sheridan picks up on some 'inaccuracies' in Mendelson's depiction of Jewish life and finds Claudia unconvincing as there is an absence of Jewish values and no feeling that she cares for people.[225] Deborah Smith reviewing in *Jewish Renaissance* points out that there are some jarring aspects of the religious elements of the book that make it appear as if it was written by an outsider. This is illustrated by a rabbi, whatever denomination, serving chicken and Camembert together at a Friday night dinner.[226]

Nevertheless, Gilbert points out that the question of authenticity is complex. Perhaps what is most authentic to contemporary experience for Jews in Britain is, in fact, a somewhat fractured relationship to Jewishness, characterised by insecurity, displaying pockets of ignorance but demonstrating curiosity and a sense of engagement with what it might mean to be a contemporary Jew. The women in this novel, as contrasted to those in Alderman's work, represent different ways of being Jewish women in Britain today.[227]

Conclusion

From the late Victorian period to the present, Jewish women writers have been interested in exploring themes arising from their own lives as women within a Jewish religious and cultural world and as Jews within a larger, non-Jewish society and culture. Though the seven gifted women writers profiled in this chapter hailed from across the UK, varied in their educational and religious backgrounds, and wrote in a variety of genres, they share much in common. Writing across the twentieth and twenty-first centuries, their novels vary widely in settings and plot and include both explicitly Jewish and entirely non-Jewish characters and themes. Yet a number of common themes predominate in their work, especially those that focus on problematic identities and difficulties with belonging—all tied to their own identities as Jewish women born and growing up in Great Britain.

Nearly all became novelists later in life, after pursuing other careers, and only Bernice Rubens followed the conventional path of marriage and children while both Naomi Jacobs and Charlotte Mendelson lived or came out as lesbians, though the cultural shifts that occurred between their lifetimes meant that issues of religion, gender and sexuality and even one's own sexual preferences could be more explored openly in writing by later generations of writers. Not coincidentally, all of these women were the children or grandchildren of Jewish immigrants or refugees, and this background contributed significantly to their feelings of being outsiders who did not fit into British society. Most of these women's writings drew on autobiographical elements to explore themes of alienation and family conflict. Jewishness and being brought up in a specifically Jewish milieu remained a fundamental identity for all these women, even Naomi Jacobs, whose non-Jewish mother urged her to renounce her Jewish name. The fact that Anita Brookner and Linda Grant's families anglicised their names and Gerda Charles chose a pen name reflects the tensions between Jewishness and belonging. Most tellingly, all of these women turned their conflicted identities and feelings of estrangement and marginality into powerful writing that earned many of their novels critical acclaim and awards.

3

Popular Singers

The story of modern pop music is largely the story of the intertwining popular culture of the United States and the United Kingdom in the post Second World War era. Bombed out Britain, at the turn of the 1950s, looked to America for inspiration and to Hollywood and Broadway for entertainment.[1] Women on both sides of the Atlantic played their part in the construction of modern-day pop, from blues to rock and roll, and were at the forefront of the promotion of new formats.

A new type of female star emerged after the Second World War. During the war many women took over men's jobs which had given them a sense of freedom. Once the men returned many women became housebound again with a sense of reluctance. To make it vaguely palatable, their return to the 'domestic' had to be sugared and heavily sold. One of the most effective ways to market the image of domesticated femininity was through postwar pop – an ideal personified in Doris Day, the wholesome peroxide blonde Hollywood star. Day presented a screen version of ideal womanhood while women working in more popular music also played out a role of glamour and glitz. While most female singers up to the end of the 1940s were usually attached to big bands, by the next decade they were emerging as soloists and stars. As economic restraints on touring big bands signalled the decline of the swing era, popular taste shifted to smaller combos and individual artists and there was greater pressure on women visibly to be stars.[2]

In 1952 Britain had little self-confidence and no reason to believe it could compete with the likes of pert, blonde Doris Day.[3] Alma Cogan was to change the situation. She created a complete 1950s fantasy, a combination of Dior's New Look and Girl Next Door.[4]

Alma Cogan (1932-1966)

When on 26 October 1966 giant headlines across the front of newspapers informed a shocked public that Alma Cogan, Britain's greatest female recording star of the 1950s and early 1960s, had died from cancer at the tragically young age of 34, there was universal grief and incredulity. It just didn't seem possible that the bouncy, bright and bubbly Alma with her sequinned, voluminous dresses and wide dynamic smile was no more. During her life Alma's vivacity and talent had brought her extraordinary fame. In a brief but meteoric career, Alma packed theatres all over the country, dazzled millions of television viewers and clocked up 20 hit records, more than any other British singer, spending an astonishing total of 109 weeks in the charts. As she belted out one novelty hit after another – 'Bell Bottom Blues', 'Dreamboat', 'I Can't Tell a Waltz from a Tango', 'Twenty Tiny Fingers', 'Never Do A Tango With an Eskimo', 'Cowboy Jimmy Joe', and 'Just Couldn't Resistor' – her style was the very quintessence of kitsch and the height of high camp.[5] She specialised in the novelty end of the market and was the brightest star in an otherwise drab postwar Britain.[6] She became the most successful female recording artist of the 1950s and was the first female singer to have her own major television series.

Alma was born in Golders Green, London in 1932. Her sister Sandra Caron describes the family as a typically warm, loving, hugging and kissing, outgoing immigrant family. Their father Mark Kogin came from Vinitza, Russia in the 1890s and then lived in London's East End (Whitechapel) with his parents and five siblings where his father Phillip Kogin worked as a tailor. Their mother Faye came from a similar background. Her maternal grandparents had a shop on the Old Kent Road and in Whitechapel. Alma's parents met during a tea dance at the Café de Paris, London and were married at Heygate Synagogue in Walworth Road, south east London and the reception for 300 people was held at Portman Rooms, Baker Street. Soon after his marriage, their father started to sell ladies' clothing and called his shops Mark Cogan (rather than the family name Kogin). He never became wealthy because he was too impatient. No sooner was a shop set up and running well, he would sell it and buy another.[7]

Alma was brought up in a middle-class home with nannies as both parents were working in the family business. It was at family gatherings and singalongs that it became evident, even from an early age, that Alma was a 'natural' with an unusual quality to her voice. By the age of four she was singing 'Begin the Beguine' and it was against this background of approval that Alma developed her love of performing. During the war the family moved to Slough and then to a large high street shop in Reading where they lived above the shop. They went on annual holidays to Torquay, staying at the Imperial Hotel. The children went to private day schools and Alma and her sister were educated at St Joseph's, a Roman Catholic convent. Sandra explained that their parents wanted to send their children to the most conventional school they could find. The choice of a convent school was due to the fact that their mother was convinced that as the nuns had no social life they would be able to concentrate exclusively on the children. There was only one other Jewish girl in a school of 500. When harassed in the playground for being Jewish, Sandra recalls that her mother told them they were to be proud of their heritage and to learn to stand up for themselves.[8]

Their home was always filled with music as there was a vast collection of records, from the Andrews Sisters to Al Jolson. The records were there to enjoy and also for inspiration. The parents wanted their children to be able to perform and to do all the things that they had been unable to do. 'We were expected to become stars'. Alma had her first singing lessons at St Joseph's and aged ten sang at a Sunday charity concert at the local Palace Theatre. Her parents soon realised that there was something unique in the way that she sang and that she was capable of far more than charity concerts and family singalongs. They decided to investigate the possibilities of performing at tea dances and took Alma round the tea-dance circuit, to cajole the bandleaders into letting her sing. They moved to Worthing and Alma took every chance she could to sing with the local bands and her parents encouraged her. She would enter talent competitions and at the age of 14 won the 'Sussex Queen of Song'. This led to her first engagement at the Grand Theatre, Brighton in June 1947. She started to appear in cabaret in London and as an extra in films. The family moved to Stafford Court, Kensington High Street. Her parents could not see a future in the level of work she was doing and insisted that she went for auditions as they wanted her to be a top star. 'How could anyone fail with parents like that?' said Alma.[9]

Through Wally Ridley, a contact at HMV records, and Alma's persistence, her first record 'To Be Worthy of You' was made and it caught the attention of BBC radio producer Roy Speer who was looking for someone for the series *Gently Bentley*. The show was a vehicle for Australian comedian Dick Bentley who wanted someone to add variety to the show by contributing at least one song. The power of radio then was unique. Alma now had entry into virtually every home in Britain. Alma and Wally started to look for a song that would put her in the charts. Day after day they searched to find something different and happier. Wally recalls 'one day we were going through a couple of songs in the office, there was a soppy line that was all wrong. Alma and I had a fit of giggles and she went on singing, still giggling'. At last they found what they were looking for. It was a giggle in the voice. It was distinctive – no one else sang like that. It also fitted her personality and ebullient stage performances. It would become her hallmark and make her a recording star.

The breakthrough was perfectly timed as this style was suited to the type of song that was to become identified with the 1950s – the novelty song.[10] There was a growing trend for these upbeat numbers that told a story. She then became successful on a radio show *Take It From Here*. Her first appearance on television was on a Garrison Theatre show for the navy in February 1954. Her new song 'Bell Bottom Blues' was a great hit with the boys in blue. She was the first girl singer to become a major star on television. Due to the broadcast of the Queen's Coronation in 1953 millions of people had rented or bought sets. After the Coronation television had to broadcast new types of shows that were different from radio and to find stars to suits the medium. Just after Alma's first television triumph two relatively unknown comedians from the variety theatre, Morecombe and Wise, started their series *Running Wild* and Alma was asked to be their resident singer.[11] She became the first British female singer to have her own television series while her glamorous showbiz parties and luxurious collection of clothes also made her the gossip column favourite.

Her clothes were another hallmark. She designed her own dresses and developed quite a reputation for gorgeous and outrageous gowns. Her dresses were an important part of her act. When presented to the Queen at the Royal Variety Show in 1955 her dress was a vast mauve crinoline with 14,000 beads on it and 200 yards of net in the skirt which was quite a post-austerity statement. Her fans loved her glamour and therefore glamour was what she gave them: hundreds of yards of petticoat, flounces and feathers with diamanté earrings to match. One famous dress for an ATV show had 12,964 diamanté beads and seven skirts and needed two men to carry it.[12] She travelled in Rolls Royce cars that could accommodate her dresses.

Alma had a strong Jewish connection that was evident at all times. 'If you have seen Alma in person or on television you will have probably noticed that she always wears a Magen David (Star of David) and has a collection of about 30 of them. She always takes pride in showing her Jewishness. She is Orthodox, so far as it is possible for anyone in her profession to be so, and wherever she may be touring she attends a Sabbath service if there is a synagogue in the vicinity'. [13] When young she was a leading light in the Maccabi Association drama section and a member of the reception committee of 'young ladies'.[14] She gave dozens of performances for Jewish charities and took part in several communal projects that included Youth Aliyah, Jewish Child's Day and the Maccabi Association.[15] She was deeply religious. She found consolation, as she so often did in times of stress, in religion and prayer. On all her travels she carried her lucky Bible with her. When she was released from hospital after an operation she went to the synagogue to give thanks for her return.[16] Her sister comments 'we were raised in an Orthodox home and were brought up not to drink or smoke'.[17]

Her non-drinking and smoking was surprising considering the extravagant parties she held at the flat where she lived with her widowed mother and sister at Stafford Court, Kensington. It became a meeting place for everyone in the public eye during the late 1950s and early 1960s. An incredible mix of people gathered there that crossed all social barriers and included actors, entertainers, politicians and titled folk.[18] The Cogan flat was probably the most celebrated show business salon in London at that time. Guests included Princess Margaret, Cary Grant, Audrey Hepburn, Tommy Steele, Noel Coward, Elizabeth Taylor, Ethel Merman, Danny Kaye and Sammy Davis Jr. The Beatles were regular visitors. John Lennon's nickname for Alma was 'Sara Sequin' and he called her mother Ma McCogie. It was on Alma's piano that Paul McCartney composed 'Yesterday'. It was 3am and Paul first called it 'Scrambled Eggs' because that was what Alma's mother had just cooked them. Cynthia Lennon, Lennon's first wife, recalls that before they met her they considered her out of date with her old fashioned cinched-in waists and wide skirts of the 1950s. 'But in the flesh she was beautiful, intelligent and funny, oozing with sex appeal and charm'. She recalls walking into Alma's home for the first time and that it was like stepping into another world as it was decorated like a swish nightclub with dark, richly coloured silken fabrics and brocades everywhere. Every surface was covered with ethnic sculptures, ornaments and dozens of photographs in elaborate silver, gold and jewelled frames.

There were rumours of a secret affair with John Lennon who at the time was married to Cynthia. Sandra Caron knew there was a close connection between the two of them, but it was something that no one admitted because John was married. 'We had a very strict Jewish upbringing and my mother would never have approved of a relationship between Alma and a married man'. Alma had an incredibly close relationship with her mother and wherever she was in the world, she would ring her every night.[19] Ironically before the Beatles rose to fame and Lennon was a student at Liverpool Art College he used to make horrible jokes about her, impersonate her singing and adopt crazy facial expressions to try and imitate her. But in 1962 when the Beatles appeared with Alma at the London Palladium, it appeared that Lennon revised his view of her. 'John was potty about her', George Harrison revealed later.[20]

Alma had a clean image. Her sister said she did not take pills or drink. She loved her fans and worked unendingly for charity.[21] The two Jewish men that regularly escorted her, composer Lionel Bart and Beatles manager Brian Epstein, were both gay. Bart referred to Alma as his girlfriend and how he introduced Epstein to her and her parties when Epstein first came to London from Liverpool. 'Brian was very taken with her as we all were'.[22] Sandra Caron recalls how Bart had bought a large flat in Chelsea and was at the height of his success with *Oliver!* and was rich and famous. It was said that he hoped Alma would share her life with him and rumours were rife. Alma had to deny very firmly that they were engaged.[23] Epstein's friendship with Alma was one of the few enduring connections that he made. 'The male-female aspect was irrelevant. She was a forceful, imaginative, naturally enthusiastic woman who loved her show business life. Epstein admired the theatrical flair deep inside her. They socialised and spoke by phone extensively; he took her gifts from foreign trips. Seen together, they seemed perfectly at ease, a couple destined to be together'.[24] She was the perfect 'nice Jewish girl' to accompany both Bart and Epstein who could not at the time reveal their homosexuality. The last man to be officially in her life was Jewish. Brian Morris, who managed the Ad Lib, one of London's trendiest night clubs, was desperate to marry her. It was a serious relationship and they became engaged in 1965 but no wedding date was ever announced.[25]

Her star status lasted until television began to kill off the variety-theatre circuit that sustained her.[26] As the emergence of the Beatles and younger female singers such as Lulu, Sandie Shaw and Dusty Springfield came on to the pop scene, Alma's records ceased to become hits and her star dimmed in Britain although not internationally. In Japan her recording of 'Just Couldn't Resist Her With Her Pocket Transistor' topped the charts for an unprecedented ten months. Yet the 1950s that was truly her decade were over. Her fun hit songs had made her the most highly paid woman in British show business in the 1950s. She was more than a singer; she was a 1950s legend. From the mid-1950s to early 1960s she was one of the most familiar faces on British television and one of the first beneficiaries of the emerging television industry to create a celebrity. Actress Val Williams commented that she was a large presence and represented a kind of escape, Film historian Richard Dyer said she was the kind if daughter that everyone wanted 'She was happy without being threatening. If you were happy everything would be alright'. She provided lightness in post war austerity Britain. Wally Ridley said she did not have a great voice but she delivered a package to an era struggling out of war and rationing with her over the top style and baroque dresses. After the 1953 coronation when many bought television sets for the first time and the television industry took off, she was an idea whose time had come. 'She was ideal for family viewing as she appealed to everyone: catchy tunes for recalcitrant five-year-olds; unthreatening sexiness for dads and cosiness and surreal dress patterns for mums'. Brian Tesler, a BBC producer, commented that she was everybody's favourite. 'She could sing, dance, engage in cross talk and handle a funny line. And she looked good. She was a gift to any television producer'.[27] However, what suited the 1950s was not wanted for the next decade.

Whilst touring Britain and Sweden in 1966 Alma collapsed twice, leading to a cancer diagnosis. Within a few weeks she was dead. Although she was a sensation overtaken by rock and roll, news of her death made front page news as far afield as Australia and Japan.[28] Yet she did become a cult as was shown at the 25th anniversary memorial of her death, held at the Cumberland Hotel, London where she had made her debut at the hotel's regular tea dances in 1948. Tony Mallerman said she became famous again 25 years after her death as the nostalgia industry had reinvented the undemanding 1950s and Alma was its icon, a retrospective role model; the quintessential girl of her time. However mindless her songs, she put them across with such resolute happiness they helped keep fans spinning for a decade. They were uplifted by the laughter in her voice which was expanded into a gimmick. The austere post war gloom met its match with Alma. 'The pop world finally shucked its dun-coloured utility clothing and a bright butterfly of peace emerged'. Alma soared with ease, protected and encouraged by parents, loved, adored and feted. 'There were no sexual scandals. Perhaps her genius was that she presented no challenge to her fans, was neither mistress nor rival, just a bubbly big sister with silly songs, a laugh in her voice and those dresses!'[29]

Alma's style of performance was replaced by rock and roll and teen pop. The period 1958-1963 was the age of the 'teen idol'. A new sound had emerged on the west coast of America embodying the clean, healthy image of the American teenager. The 'surfing scene' was about having fun and groups such as the Beach Boys emerged. Record companies recognised the potential of teenage romance and the teen idol particularly with the large record buying group of girls in their mid-teens. They realised if they could control teenage tastes they could control the market and the profits. The idea was to decide on a look and a sound, choose a safe respectable teenager to fit both and produce records about teenage concerns. The music contained in the lyrics was to be basic to teenage life — falling in love.[30] Again, a Jewish figure was to represent that shift.

Helen Shapiro (1946 –)

The period from 1960 to 1963 was a strange period for British pop — a hiatus, a low before the storm. From the United States there were still singers in the rock and roll tradition, such as Sam Cooke and Chubby Checker, but from Britain there was only one new artist who generated excitement among young people, a 14-year-old school girl Helen Shapiro.[31]

Britain was the world's centre of pop in the 1960s. Although male groups dominated the UK charts, record labels needed a girl singer to satisfy those teenagers in need of a female to emulate. The person that met their requirements was East End Jewish girl, Helen Shapiro. She took the charts by storm in the early 1960s with her songs 'You Don't Know', 'Walking Back to Happiness' and 'Don't Treat Me Like A Child'. Her big deep voice that belied her years catapulted her to the top of the charts. Heading the bill at the London Palladium by night, the youngest girl ever to do so, whilst still at school, she led the kind of life that other teenagers could only dream about. She was supported by the Beatles on a nationwide tour and appeared on the Ed Sullivan Show in 1962, a rarity at the time as The Beatles were yet to explode into the United States and very few British artists toured there. 'It happened like nothing ever happened before. It was success to the tune of about £600 a week and it happened less than 12 months after Helen first opened her month and sang to the tough professionals who risk their reputations and careers by saying whether young pop singers can be successful. The Shapiro success had no matching partner because it was the first time for any girl singer on either side of the Atlantic'. Nothing new happening in the music business and feelings were low.[32]

Such an overnight phenomena was in stark contrast to Helen's humble beginnings. Her maternal grandmother Sarah came to England at turn of twentieth century from the *shtetl* Asia Polya, about 15 miles from Odessa, Ukraine. She was one of seven children and her eldest brother Lewis came first to the East End where he set up a tailoring workshop and then sent for the rest of the family. They were not a particularly religious family but a musical one. Her husband Samuel, also from the Ukraine, was a master tailor with his own workshop in Old Montague Street, just off Brick Lane. They had nine children, including Helen's mother Rachel, and lived above the shop. Unfortunately Samuel was a gambler and at the age of 46 had a stroke and the rest of the family kept the workshop running. There was very little money. A large extended family of aunts, uncles and cousins lived in the neighbourhood. Helen has memories of a happy childhood with typically Eastern European Jewish cuisine and celebrating Chanukah.[33] Her brother Ronnie played the banjo and all her relatives loved to make music. It was a family united by music.

Helen was captain of the school netball team at Clapton Girls School by day and ballad singer at Clapton Jewish youth club by night. She launched her own career by answering an advertisement in the *Jewish Chronicle* for singing lessons. Her teacher, Maurice Burman, who had taught Alma Cogan, became her manager.[34] In six months she rose from unknown East End schoolgirl to pop star of international fame. Her first four hits spent an impressive 77 weeks on the charts, two of them hitting number one. At age 14, she was the youngest British female singer to ever obtain a number one slot. Her parents were too poor to own a record player and she had to go round to play her new record at a neighbour's house.[35]

'Don't Treat Me Like A Child' made Helen the most sought after teenager in 1961. 'It was probably the first protest song', she explains 'because its theme was the cry of teenagers at the time'. She played at the London Palladium during the school holidays and her headmistress allowed her half days off during term time to do broadcasts.[36] David Robson recalls how at his Jewish boarding school it was one of the few moments of ethnic glory when a Jewish girl had a record in the hit parade and everyone was summoned into the hall to be told the news. The disc played to them on the school radiogram was husky little Helen singing 'Don't Treat Me Like a Child'.[37] Her rich powerful voice made her the idol of teenagers and coupled with a lively refreshing personality added to first class entertainment. She was a born artist.[38]

Jonathan Miller considers that Helen made an important contribution to the world of entertainment. Her voice set its mark upon the 1960s. 'Her song 'Don't Treat Me Like a Child' proved to be an uncannily close, epigrammatic expression of teenage bewilderment. The lyrics are a revealing mixture of cynicism and romance and Helen sang them with a laconic force which immediately captured the attention of her young audience. Her voice is strong and confident; insolent almost in its mature control of tone. It seems somehow to express the shrewd, sarcastic independence of modern youth. At first sight it is rather surprising to find such a relaxed mastery of technique in anyone so young although I think it is just another expression of the freedom and self-confidence of the teenager of the 1960s. For the first time the teenager has developed an independent, almost an alien culture, in the midst of adult society. The young no longer see themselves as embryo adults, biding their time until their legal majority. Long before they get legal responsibility they have grasped a cultural, and above all economic power which sets them up as a powerful pressure group of their own'.[39]

A performer at the age of 14 was a novelty. There was no one else filling this role and it filled a gap. However, the novelty was bound at some point to wear off. A few years later her days of great fame were over.[40] With new singers and groups appearing in the charts each week it was hardly surprising that some artists slipped into the background. Helen was one such example. A pop star overnight and then, almost overnight again, nothing.[41] With the new wave of beat music and newer female singers such as Dusty Springfield, Cilla Black, Sandie Shaw and Lulu, Helen appeared old fashioned and emblematic of the pre-Beatles era.[42] However, non-appearance in the charts did not necessarily mean goodbye to show business. As her pop career declined, she turned to cabaret appearances, touring the working men's clubs in the north of England. She branched out as a performer in musical theatre and jazz. She played the role of Nancy in Lionel Bart's musical *Oliver!* and appeared in a British television soap opera *Albion Market* (1985-1986). Between 1984 and 2001, she toured extensively with British jazz trumpeter Humphrey Lyttelton and his band whilst still performing her own jazz and pop concerts.

During her pop career and until the mid-1980s Helen showed an affiliation with her Jewish roots and the Jewish community. Her first husband was theatrical impresario Duncan Weldon whose family were prominent in the Southport Jewish community.[43] Her second marriage was to Maurice Gundlash whom she had known from her Clapton Jewish Youth Club days. They both attended a Jewish Marriage Education Council marriage preparation course at the Lea Bridge Road synagogue. The course consisted of seven evenings of talks which covered the spiritual, physical, emotional, financial and everyday aspects of married life. For Helen it was the religious aspect of the course that she found the most illuminating.[44] After her marriage she lit the Sabbath candles and would make the Passover meal.[45] She was actively involved in Radom, a Jewish welfare society that raised money for various causes. She toured Israel in 1963 where she was a great success and sang a number of Hebrew songs and entertained at an army base.[46] She made many appearances at Jewish events that included a charity performance with American comedian Jackie Mason for the Manchester Benevolent Society (1963), a coffee morning for Hull Judeans (1964), a rally at the Hammersmith Odeon for the Association of Jewish Ex-servicemen and Women (1967), the Jewish Blind Society fair in Southport (1968), a gala concert to raise funds for Magen David Adom ambulance service (1973), a celebrity concert for Liverpool National Fund

(1974), the Board of Deputies 220th anniversary reception (1981), the Manchester Jewish Social Services fundraiser (1983), a cabaret for the British Friends of Israel Disabled (1983), a fundraiser for Middlesex New Synagogue (1984) and a Jewish Welfare Board bazaar (1987).

Helen's life changed dramatically after her teenage years of fame. Although she made a lot of money in her teens, she lost most of it 'in one fell swoop' after investing in her second husband's fashion business. She no longer felt the privileges of wealth, her second marriage had ended and she was back home living with her widowed mother. 'The clubs were a hard grind. Not going on before midnight, eating chips on the motorway, *shlepping* around for digs in drab towns. That's no life.'[47] By 1987 she had reached a low ebb in her life. She had appeared in the musical *Seesaw* at Northampton Royal Theatre but after the show finished there was no interest to take it elsewhere as Helen had expected and her diary was relatively empty. 'There was a big gap in my life'. It was at this time that she visited her music producer friend Bob Cranham who was a Christian. He had no idea of the crisis she was going through and she felt jealous as he spoke of the security of his faith. She wanted that security and purpose. 'I was directionless, rudderless'. He gave her the book *Betrayed* by Stan Telchin, a 50-year-old successful Jewish man whose 21-year-old daughter announced that she had accepted Jesus as her Messiah. Her father was in a state of shock and set out to prove his daughter wrong by studying the scriptures, Talmudic writings and talking to rabbis. After several months he too was a believer together with his wife and other daughter.[48]

Helen started to think about Jesus. 'I lay on my bed one night and asked "Jesus, if you really are the Messiah, show me". After that, everywhere I went I bumped into things connected with Jesus'. Stan Telchin's book quoted Messianic prophecies from the Old Testament that she was not aware of such as Isaiah 9: 6 'unto us a child is born, unto us a son is given' and Isaiah 53 where the chapter speaks about the one who is to come and take upon himself our sins and our punishment. 'On 26 August 1987 at 10.30pm I went round to Bob's house and prayed to receive Jesus as my lord and saviour.'[49]

Helen charts her journey from being raised in a warm, musical traditional Jewish family in the heart of a large Jewish community in the East End of London. 'Our extended family, although not a very orthodox group, was nevertheless totally Jewish in identity and heritage. I suppose I believed in God from my earliest days. I took his existence for granted'. She had separate religious education classes and assemblies at school with the other Jewish children and as a consequence had never heard of the New

Testament or Jesus until she was around six years old and a non-Jewish girl accused her in the playground of killing Jesus Christ.

During her years of fame she did not give much thought to spiritual matters. It was only in the late 1960s when everyone was searching for the 'meaning of life' that she began to visit mediums and clairvoyants and read books about Buddhism and psychic phenomena. 'I incorporated a smorgasbord of 'isms which today would be called New Age. I associated everything I believed in with God'. For quite a number of years she was comforted by what she had discovered. It seemed to fill a void in her life until she became 40. 'For the first time in my life I had nothing to believe in. Inside I was empty. Looking back I can see this was God's hand'. She wondered whether, as she had become a follower of Jesus, would she still be Jewish. Stan Telchin assured her that she would be fulfilling her Jewishness by believing in Jesus, the Messiah of Israel and that she would be coming back to the God of Abraham, Isaac and Jacob. 'What he said was true. The very reason that God created the Jewish nation was to point to the Messiah. This is the purpose of every Jew. I am fulfilling that very purpose by receiving Jesus as the Messiah, Lord and Saviour'.[50]

Her conversion caused concern in the Jewish community. Rabbi Shmuel Argus, director of Operation Judaism that works to combat missionaries was concerned that someone of Helen's stature would give a major boost to Christian missionaries working amongst Jews. Rabbi Arye Forta said that Helen's conversion to Christianity had highlighted the dangers of the Messianic approach.[51] Helen responded that Forta's words 'conversion' and 'Christianity' were inaccurate and calculated to stir up animosity towards herself and other Messianic Jews. 'I have not "converted" to a new religion, neither have I stopped being a Jew. On the contrary, through belief in Yeshua as the Messiah in its original context, I am returning to the God of Abraham, Isaac and Jacob. I know more about why I am Jewish, I feel more Jewish and I identify with my people more than ever. I am still a dedicated fundraiser for Jewish causes. I became a believer not through missionaries but through carefully reading the Scriptures'. She suggests that instead of writing sensationally about her, the issue of whether or not Jesus is the Messiah should be addressed.[52]

Helen now performs with her group Manna at Gospel outreach evenings. She leads people in worship, sings 'Walking Back to Happiness' and gives her whole testimony with four or five tracks from the gospel albums. 'And then I give them the gospel – the why of it – why Jesus came to die. And then I challenge the audience. It's very old fashioned: sin, heaven, hell – nothing wishy washy. But it's also about God's love'. She now no longer reads anything apart from the Bible. 'I'm happy when I'm rejoicing in the Lord, when I'm peaceful, when I'm singing and worshipping the Lord in songs. It's lovely to sing to the Lord. There's nothing better than the great old hymns sung in the Spirit. Since becoming a believer I'm more Jewish than ever I was before. I'm more familiar with the Scriptures. I understand more about God's relationship with us. I know why I'm a Jew, where my roots are. Most important of all I have a relationship with God. I don't just believe in him as some vague, faraway being as I did when I was a child'.[53]

Helen was the Amy Whitehouse of her day whose rich jazzy voice belied her youth.[54] However, the advent of the Beatles helped to undermine the singer's career. She was perceived as belonging to an outmoded era. In the early 1970s pop started to splinter into different styles, each with its own loyal audience. Concerts were large scale, showy occasions and the artist or band wore outrageously flashy costumes. One of the bands to evolve during this period was British R & B band Vinegar Joe with their lead singer Elkie Brooks.[55] 'Brooks was raunch'n'roll personified – a thigh thrusting hybrid of Janis Joplin and Tina Turner'.[56] She gained her biggest success in the late 1970s and 1980s. Known for her powerful husky voice, she was often referred to as the 'British queen of the blues'. By the 1990s she was established as one of Britain's leading singers.[57]

Elkie Brooks (1945 –)

British pop-jazz-blues crooner Elkie Brooks (born Elaine Bookbinder) dominated British radio in the late 1970s with a series of hit singles that established her as one of the biggest selling female album artist in the history of the British pop charts. Born in Manchester, she grew up in a musical family and left school at the age of 15 to join a dance band in London. She eventually made the jump to radio as well as numerous appearances with legendary jazz bandleader Humphrey Lyttelton before embarking on a career in pop music. She joined the blues-rock band Dada in 1970 which would eventually find success through a name change to Vinegar Joe where she gained a reputation as a hair flailing wild woman.[58] After the band disbanded in 1974 Brooks began a solo career with songs such as 'Rich Man's Woman', 'Two Days Away', 'Shooting Star' and 'Pearl's a Singer' as well as frequent sold out tours and numerous silver, gold and platinum recordings which would go on to cement her reputation.[59]

Elkie was born on 25 February 1945 in Broughton Park, Manchester to Marjorie Violet 'Vi' and Kalman Charles 'Charlie' Bookbinder. Her paternal grandparents Franklyn Bookbinder and Minnie Wientroube came with their parents to Britain from Gdańsk, Poland around the turn of the twentieth century. In 1911 Franklyn met and married Minnie and shortly after opened his first bakery Bookbinder & Goldstone in Cheetham Hill, Manchester. He was very successful and subsequently moved the business to new premises in Bury Old Road, Prestwich where it became Bookbinder & Son. Elkie's mother Vi came from a Catholic background although Elkie never discovered this fact until after her mother died. Vi lost her father in the First World War and she lived with her mother and step-father, whom she disliked, in Fleetwood, near Blackpool. When she left school she moved to Cheetham Hill to work with a local Jewish family which was where she met her husband and they married at the local registry office in 1937. She subsequently converted to Judaism and they were married in a religious ceremony at the United Synagogue, Leamington Road, Blackpool. It appears that everybody knew that Vi had not been born Jewish apart from Elkie and her brothers Ray and Tony. 'It must have been a bit of a scandal at the time'. Elkie never met her mother's brother and sister but she believes he might have been a monk and her aunt a trapeze artist in a circus. Her mother had a picture of this glamorous lady in a black sequinned leotard and large cross around her neck in her bedroom but when asked would not divulge any more about her. Elkie later found out that the sister visited her mother once but was whisked in and out of the house quickly so as not to attract attention from the neighbours. Elkie's childhood was to all intents and purposes very comfortable and her struggles and suffering were to come much later in her life.[60]

Elkie began to sing at an early age. It all began when she was about five with the rabbi getting her to sing a few of her favourite songs at various festivals. From there she went on to sing at her brother Ray's barmitzvah and was subsequently asked to perform at her parents' friends functions. 'I started to take it seriously when I was about 11 and would be invited to weddings and barmitzvahs and where I'd ask the band if they knew any songs of the day and just get up and sing'.[61] It was a Jewish connection that put her on the road to becoming a professional singer as she spotted an advertisement in the local Jewish newspaper, the *Jewish Telegraph*. The music promoter and agent Don Arden was holding auditions at the Palace Theatre, Manchester for shows he was taking around the country. She went alone, unbeknown to her family, and was the last person to be auditioned. She passed her audition, performed that night and Arden asked her parents if they would allow her to go on tour. She was just 15.[62] Her parents were not opposed to her going on tour. She explains that in those days parents in the north were quite naïve and knew nothing about the music business. Had they been more worldly they probably would not have let her go, especially when she went abroad, touring the airbases in Germany.[63]

Arden made her change her name to Elaine Mansfield as Bookbinder sounded too Jewish. 'It was quite common for people to try and conceal their Jewishness in order to succeed in public life'. Arden had done the same. He was born Harry Levy and brought up in a strict Jewish family in Manchester's Cheetham Hill. [64] Arden saw her as a kind of Mancunian answer to Brenda Lee,[65] although her voice had yet to develop the husky tones she would later be known for. She headed to London where she performed with the Eric Delaney Band that played up tempo dance music and with jazz musician Humphrey Lyttelton. It was at this time that 'Elkie Brooks' was born. Someone had told her that Elkie was Yiddish for Elaine and she considered that Brooks was a shortened version of Bookbinder.[66] In 1964 she landed a recording contract with Decca and was sent on tour to Germany. Elkie gained further live experience by appearing on pop package tours alongside groups such as The Animals and in late 1964 she supported the Beatles on tour, with the Yardbirds and Freddie and the Dreamers. The following years saw her performing in cabaret in a succession of northern clubs. In 1970 she met the guitarist Peter Gage. The pair married and formed the rock fusion band Dada. When Robert Palmer joined them they renamed themselves Vinegar Joe and achieved a certain notoriety for the sexual chemistry they displayed in their live performances.[67]

'Our music was often described as "an hour of get up and boogie". We had a very lively exciting and vibrant feeling which was what the audience liked. This energy also had an effect on me and I started to get a reputation for my over exuberant performances'. She explains that she underwent a bit of a personality change during her time with Vinegar Joe. 'Gone was the nice but naïve little Jewish girl from Prestwich who was terrified of Don Arden and sang what she was given'. In her place was a raunchy rock 'n roll artist who would abuse her audiences if they were not getting into her music sufficiently. One of the music papers once said 'if Elkie Brooks is on stage and the audience aren't giving enough of a response she'll tell 'em to get off their f'ing arses and start boogying'. She now regrets behaving in that way but that was how she was then. She also worked on her new image and bought stage outfits including a bikini type top which had Elk embroidered on the front in diamantés.[68]

In 1974 Vinegar Joe split up and Elkie went solo. The cover of her 1975 debut album *Rich Man's Woman* featured her naked, her modesty covered by a feather boa. In 1977 she gained real success, scoring an international hit with 'Pearl's A Singer'. Further successes followed, including 'Sunshine after the Rain'. 'Lilac Wine' and 'Don't Cry Out Loud'. In 1978 she married her second husband Trevor Jordan. Three years later her album *Pearls* became one of the biggest selling LPs by a British female artist, spending 79 weeks on the UK charts and selling over a million copies. In 1982 the single 'Fool If You Think It's Over' gave her another top 20 hit while 'No More the Fool' issued in 1986 proved her last top five success. She continues to record and perform to this day.[69]

She was a controversial singer. Her picture appeared on the cover of the music magazine *Melody Maker* as the face of 1973, where they described her as a hard biting lady from Salford and that Vinegar Joe looked like becoming the working-class heroes of 1973.[70] This was a far cry from Elkie's conventional background living in a heavily Jewish populated area of Manchester. Her education began at Broughton Jewish Preparatory School and from there to Sedgley Park County Primary which was a school right in the heart of Prestwich where 99 per cent of the children were Jewish. Her paternal grandmother lived with the family and was very religious. This naturally had an effect on the family when she was living with them but the next Bookbinder generation were not religious. Their synagogue visits were saved mostly for festivals such as Passover or Yom Kippur.[71]

Elkie excelled at her Hebrew classes that she attended after school and received a certificate from the rabbi for her efforts; she could read very quickly from the Jewish prayer book. Her father worked hard in the Bookbinder bakery and was an upstanding pillar of the Jewish community. Elkie admits that 'he was kosher on the surface'. Despite his strict Jewish upbringing he loved bacon, as did her brothers, and he would go to great lengths to get bacon from an area where he was not known. He worked very hard and the only day he would be home in time to eat with the family was on Friday night. She loved the Friday night meal where she was allowed to have the Palwin sweet wine, the chopped liver that she adored, the chicken soup with *kreplach* or sometimes matzah balls, a dish which she still makes today. 'While there were undoubtedly big question marks over my parents' commitment to the Jewish faith, I on the other hand, at the age of eight, was very determined to do the right thing and maintain the links to my family's heritage.'[72]

Elkie appears not to have had a problem with her Jewishness. Her autobiography *Finding My Voice* is a wealth of Jewish minutiae about her childhood, a veritable cornucopia of *kneidlach* and *kreplach*[73] and references to the Friday night kiddush (blessing over wine) and singing in the synagogue. Her manager convinced her to have a nose job in 1966 'to remove the Jewish bump' although she admits she came to regret that decision.[74] She always refers to herself as Jewish. When worrying about her son learning to fly hang-gliders she said 'You can't stop a mother worrying about her son, especially when she is Jewish'.[75] If there were times in her 'wild days' that she distanced herself from her Jewish background, she now has second thoughts. She admits that whenever she sings she always tries hard to do what her singing teacher Rabbi Berkowitz told her in lessons she had with him. She didn't listen to his advice for many years and now has learnt the error of her ways and does what he taught her and the correct way to project her voice on certain notes. He also tried to give her confidence and helped her to think differently about herself. She lost contact with him when she became famous 'and in my misguided wisdom tried to distance myself from my Jewish roots, his teaching has, without doubt, left an indelible mark on my life, a fact borne out by the visions I often have of him as I am about to go on stage'.[76]

Elkie was a mainstay of British radio in the 1970s and 1980s. She is still touring and belting out rock, blues and jazz with her soulful husky voice. She confesses that she has had lots of down times but it has made her stronger and she would not have written certain of her songs if she had not gone through such experiences. Looking back over her career she admits that she would have done things differently and that she should have read some of the fine print in some of her contracts. She still considers herself 'a rocker' and the second half of her latest show comprises raunchy material. 'You can take the girl out of rock'n'roll but you can't take the rock'n'roll out of the girl'. In the past there were late nights and indulgence – she had a fondness for brandy and the occasional line of cocaine.

In the late 1990s she received an unexpected tax bill of £250,000 and this necessitated the sale of her five-bedroom bungalow in Woody Bay, Devon. For a time the family lived in a mobile home on a caravan site. She now lives in Woolacombe, Devon where her husband has a fruit farm with thousands of willow and poplar trees. Her second husband is also not Jewish and she does not visit the synagogues in Exeter or Plymouth. 'I'm a bit of an atheist. But I'm proud of my roots'. When asked where she thinks she fits in with the pantheon of great British female performers, she answers: 'They call me the Queen of the Blues'.[77]

Other new sounds that emerged in the 1970s in Britain were punk rock and ska/2-Tone. The punk explosion when it came, like the coming of rock and roll and the arrival of the Beatles, changed pop music. Punk music rejected the perceived excesses of mainstream 1970s rock and produced short, fast paced songs with hard edged melodies and often shouted political anti-establishment lyrics. It put into words the feelings of ordinary young people. The lyrics expressed disgust with the society they were part of.[78] Ska music, a precursor to reggae, originally came to Britain with West Indian immigrants in the 1950s and in 1979 enjoyed a revival in the hands of groups on a small independent record label called 2-Tone whose lyrics were closer to punk. The most prominent female singer of the 2-Tone movement was Pauline Black.

Pauliine Black (1953 –)

Pauline Black was described as the queen of the British musical genre ska in the late 1970s, the only woman in a movement dominated by men. She was lead singer of the multi-racial band The Selecter which was one of the bands credited with starting the ska revival movement and rose to prominence against the backdrop of the riots that swept the country in 1981. The Coventry-based band had hits with *On My Radio* and *Three Minute Hero* and sold more than 500,000 copies of their debut album *Too Much Pressure* (1980). Pauline made records about prejudice as black youths fought police on the streets. As a mixed race woman she knew about racism. And then in 1981 she found out she was Jewish.[79]

Black was brought up as Pauline Vickers by a white working-class family in Essex. She had been adopted by Arthur, a mechanic, and his wife Ivy, who were middle-aged and already had four sons. At the age of four she was told that she was adopted and that her father was from Nigeria. Her mother, who came from Dagenham, was only 16 when she became pregnant. She had given birth to Pauline in a mother and baby home and then given her up. A few years later Black found papers in a drawer bearing her mother's name, Eileen Magnus, and an adoption certificate with her birth name Belinda Magnus.[80]

It was a difficult childhood. Racism was ingrained in British society in the 1950s. In white working-class Romford no one, including her own family, had a good word to say about black people. Her brothers and other family members were openly racist in front of her. An aunt gave her a golliwog as a present. Her mother's nephew, who read gas meters, would regale everyone with stories about what he saw in people's homes. 'You should see the way some of those darkies live'. It seems somewhat strange that Pauline's mother was given a black child to adopt considering there was so much antipathy in the family towards black people. The initial decision to adopt a child into the family had been made after her mother developed Bell's Palsy, a partial facial paralysis. This affected her looks and confidence; her health began to deteriorate and she became more reclusive. The family doctor suggested that she should have another child to take her mind off her situation. As she had already had a hysterectomy, adoption was the only option. Her mother was desperate for a girl after four boys. 'So much so they didn't care what colour it came in', Black explains.[81]

In effect Black was brought up as though she was white and taught to fear black people. Later, when she began to describe herself as black instead of coloured she was shouted down by her mother. When she grew an afro in defiance, her mother screamed at her that she looked like 'a golliwog'. She explains that 'you just didn't talk about black people in those days. To my family black people were "over there"'. It was only when independence and the civil rights movement in America came in the 1960s that I started to get a sense that not everyone thought like that'. She experienced racism when she tried to join the Brownies and waited outside the church while her mother was told in no uncertain terms that Black would not be permitted to join as 'we're not going to take one of them'.[82]

Black considers that adoption is like having a total blood transfusion. 'It may save your life in the short term but if it is not a perfect match rejection issues may appear much later'. She admits that she was loved but 'grew up feeling like a cuckoo in someone else's nest'. Despite the undercurrent of racism that pervaded British society at the time she made friends easily with her white schoolmates. There were no other black people at any of the schools she attended.[83]

Black just watched and waited for the day she could leave the area. She would listen to the radio in her room and music became her salvation. 'It was my conduit. It was the only way I was able to explore notions of blackness. And then Motown came along and I started to see black people on the television on programmes such as *Ready Steady Go!*'.[84]

She moved to Coventry in 1971 to study a combined science course at Lancaster Polytechnic (now Coventry University). 'I liked the idea that Coventry was in the middle of England. I wanted to be in the middle of things. I was tired of being an outsider so I thought if I placed myself at the centre geographically then the rest, whatever that was, would follow'.[85] She did not complete the course but went on to train as a radiographer at the city's Walsgrave Hospital and worked for the NHS for five years. During this time she would sing in a local pub. Someone heard her sing and introduced her to the members of The Selecter. The band was a part black, mixed race seven-piece band with one white person and Black became the female singer. When she joined the band in 1979 she changed her name by deed poll to Pauline Black in order to conceal her involvement from her employer, choosing the name 'Black' partly in reaction to her upbringing. Her adoptive family had always referred to her as 'coloured' rather than black.[86]

The Selecter, together with the bands The Specials and Madness, are credited with starting the ska revival and 2-Tone movement that fused traditional Jamaican ska music with elements of punk rock and new wave. Ska music combined Jamaican folk music and calypso with American rhythm and blues. In the early 1960s ska was the dominant music genre of Jamaica and was popular with skinheads[87] and British mods,[88] whose two-tone Tonic suits[89] gave the movement its name.

The 2-Tone movement was a sub-culture of different youth tribes. Punks, rude boys and rude girls were trying on Jamaican immigrants' old clothes or listening to their music. They were drawn to it because the lyrics discussed racism, economic equality and sexism. In 1979 those words were not in the popular vernacular. Black says that 2-Tone was the precursor to what is today called multiculturalism. 'We were aware as young people that there were injustices based on skin colour and gender'.[90] White and black youths danced together. The movement was created against a backdrop of high unemployment, deindustrialisation, strikes and a rising far-right movement and sought to promote a message against the racism and sexism so prevalent at the time. Black explains that 'we did it through music and through our style of dress, and black people and white people playing in a band just demonstrated that it was possible for people to get on and find common goals politically and socially'.[91] She maintains that the 2-Tone movement probably would not have happened in Coventry in the 1970s if it had not been like a miniature Detroit. This was where the cars were made and where immigrant labour came to work. People from the West Indies worked alongside white people in the car factories, listening to each other's music.[92] Despite this, racial tensions were high and jobs were scarce. Black recalls that it was a time when one could be pulled over by the police if you were black. She was picked up by the police after they told her some black girls had been seen shoplifting. Tensions like these were reflected in The Selecter's music. 'The Selecter was an angry band but we were angry for a reason'.[93]

Black adopted the Rude Boy look that originated in 1960s Jamaican street culture and feminised it.[94] She considers that she was probably the first rude girl.[95] I was a bit of a feminist so I'd just wear the same gear as the boys'.[96] She wore slim-line black trousers with socks showing and a trilby hat. Shirts were tucked in and buttoned up to the neck and were sometimes adorned with a ribbon or a man's tie. The two-tone check was often added to an outfit, either as a headband or worn as the print of the shirt. It was a uniquely androgynous look in a music scene renowned for its testosterone that made her an icon at the time. She was part of a new wave in punk, rock and reggae, alongside singers Debbie Harry and Chrissie Hynde, who did not care what anyone, especially men, thought of them. 'It was about being a feminised rude boy. I didn't want to go on stage in dresses and skirts. I wanted an upfront image and I preferred wearing trousers. It was great that no other woman was doing it because there was no blueprint. I could do what the hell I liked'. When she first started to perform live, critics were confused. Who was this boyish lead singer, swaggering around the stage, venting aggression and belting out songs in a wild theatrical soprano? She loved getting mistaken for a boy. She considered that 'a spot of androgyny was not a bad thing. Black women were often forced into the exotic fake bouffant look'.[97] She inspired a whole generation of women who did not want to conform to the pretty style and colours of the early 1980s.

The Selecter released a number of hit singles and went on the legendary 2-Tone tour with The Specials, Madness and Dexy's Midnight Runners, playing to 1,500 people a night. An acrimonious split came in 1982. 'We were almost evangelical in our desire to get out there and change things' as she refers to the years when National Front skinheads would pitch up at gigs and lead 'Sieg Heil' chants at the front of the stage. Behind the scenes there were disagreements on which direction the music should go, whether it be towards a more white, rock direction or a more black reggae one.

After the band split up Black worked as an actress and television presenter and appeared in such dramas as *The Vice, The Bill* and *Hollyoaks*, co-starred with Christopher Lee in the horror film *Funny Man* (1994) and narrated the BBC4 documentary *Soul Britannia* (2007) that examined the dynamic impact of black American and Caribbean sounds on British music and society. She won the 1991 Time Out Award for Best Actress for her portrayal of Billie Holliday in the play *All or Nothing At All*. The Selecter reformed in 1991 and still continue to tour worldwide. Her life is explored in *Pauline Black: A 2-Tone Story* which premiered at the 2024 London Film Festival.

With a successful career to her name, Black was unprepared for an incident that occurred in 1996. She had bought a black Prada jacket on Sloane Street, London and then went to Selfridges department store. Whilst there she paused to admire her new jacket in the ladies' room. A white woman watching her asked her why she did not do something useful and make sure the toilets were furnished with toilet paper on a regular basis.

Black was horrified and outraged that the woman thought the only reason a black person could be there was as a cleaner. The moment marked a turning point.[98] 'It was as if my identity had been shattered into tiny pieces'. A small voice in her head told her to find her birth parents.[99]

Black never gave up thinking about her mother throughout her musical career. 'It was something I had fantasised about. When I was on *Top of the Pops* I used to think: Ooh, I wonder if my real mum is watching, I wonder what she might think or if she might recognise me'.[100] Black waited for eight years after her adoptive mother's death before she started her search and eventually found her mother who was living in Australia. She had married an Irishman and had a son and daughter. Previously the notion of family had not meant much to Black or her husband. They had known that they did not want children even from the early days of their relationship. 'We were both illegitimate and each of us happily regarded being a bastard as a badge of honour. But lately I noticed that my badge had lost its shine'.[101] Her birth father died a year before she traced him; it transpired that he was Prince Gordon Olodosu Adele from the Yoruba tribe who had come to London to study engineering.

Black met with her mother and discovered that her maternal great grandparents had emigrated from Greece where they had been traders and probably arrived in England in the mid-nineteenth century.[102] The revelation of these Jewish roots brought back memories of her childhood. 'At school there was a young Jewish boy that I grew up with. We used to get on really well together. He didn't go to school assembly and I was the only black kid at the school so that marked us out. Maybe there was some understanding between us'.

Having grown up in Romford in the 1960s, surrounded by only white people, Black had always felt an outsider. She watched the television series *All My Yesterdays* with its newsreel footage of the Nazis and the Holocaust and she began to recognise a pattern to the oppression experienced by minority groups. 'I began to discover what had happened during the Second World War and I equated that with what I saw black people were going through in places like South Africa. As I grew up I started to realise what racism was about'. To discover that she was Jewish years later only sharpened that realisation. 'It's a bit like having two helpings of something that maybe gives you indigestion'.[103]

Black is an example of someone who does not fit the image of the stereotypical British Jew and there are many who for a variety of reasons do not conform and can feel alienated. Yet her background is an illustration of how central Jews are to the multicultural reality that there is in Britain.

Rabbi Sybil Sheridan comments that many people are not aware that there are a variety of Jewish groups and not just the accepted one that is considered Anglo-Jewry. 'We are used to seeing a sliver of Judaism as if it was the whole of Judaism'.[104]

It was racial alienation that partly led Black to be part of The Selecter. It was a search for an identity as she did not know other black people. Through music she found people of a like mind who had something to say politically about the racism that pervaded this country at the end of the 1970s and early 1980s. 'That was what I felt I could do something with, and write songs for, and perform on stage'. Learning about her Jewish roots was certainly a defining moment. 'It's very important for me to know the truth of my identity. Without that, you're always wondering certain things, and so yes, it was complete closure'. Finding out about her roots had helped her self-esteem.[105] She also discovered she had inherited the performing gene from her mother's side of the family. Her cousins had sung and toured with D'Oyly Carte Opera while her grandfather was a music hall artiste.[106]

Black and The Selecter celebrated their 40th anniversary in the music business in 2019 and are still going strong. They first came together to fight racism, sexism, economic inequality and homophobia; 2-Tone was the musical embodiment of multiculturalism. Black still believes that a hybrid mix of ska/reggae/punk and rock with a dash of calypso and forthright musical content gives a voice to disaffected people everywhere and that the band is at home anywhere it plays. 'We embrace the subcultures and they embrace us'.[107] Coventry was the UK 2021 City of Culture and Black's contribution and importance on the music scene and the rise of 2-Tone in the city was celebrated at events and an exhibition on 2-Tone during the year. Black, who become part of the local heritage, donated a number of items to the exhibition, including her trilby hat and a 1980s Selecter T-shirt from the US, an example of how 2-Tone gained worldwide popularity. Black had said it would allow people to see the narrative they were putting out into the world and how that was impacting on all the things that were going on now, like Black Lives Matter. 'We did it through music, and through our style of dress, and black people and white people playing in a band just demonstrated that it was possible for people to get on and find common goals politically and socially'. She had wanted young people to come and see the history we lived through and how that still resonates today.[108]

One singer that had a love of ska, 2-Tone and reggae was Amy Winehouse. Recording Amy's song *Back to Black* on a single in 2011 was a way for the older British female musician to pay respect to the younger one. 'Amy was one of the best in the world. She could take any song and make it her own. I think that in the future her songs will be like Gershwin standards, interpreted by lots of different musicians'.[109] Black considered that Amy was the most talented person on the planet.[110]

Pauline and Amy illustrate the interaction between the Jewish and black worlds. Amy derived great influence from jazz and black singers and musicians. She heard the music of Ella Fitzgerald and Thelonious Monk from an early age. Amy said she learnt to sing from Dinah Washington and Sarah Vaughan was 'one of her favourite singers of all time'. Commenting on her musical evolution from childhood, 'It goes jazz, soul, Motown, then hip-hop'. She also listened to gospel singers such as Mahalia Jackson and Aretha Franklin'.[111]

Amy Winehouse (1983-2011)

Amy Winehouse was blessed with an incredible voice – a once in a century phenomenal voice.[112] The popular jazz singer shot to stardom in 2003 after her first studio album *Frank* was released and that won her a raft of nominations and awards. Amy was immediately distinctive both in terms of music – in an era dominated by girl and boy bands hers was an incredible, authentic and big selling jazz voice carrying the most original lyrics out — and style, with her winged eyeliner, beehive hair and growing collection of tattoos. More than *Frank* it was *Back to Black* that solidified her place firmly comfortably alongside but also outside jazz and into popular culture and mainstream mass consciousness. Singles 'Rehab', 'Back to Black' and 'You Know I'm No Good' were among those that made her huge. What ensued for the singer was a life under the spotlight plagued by paparazzi clashes, pressure from tabloids and fame shadowed by ultimately destructive behaviours. Alongside all of this was *that* voice. It always came back to that utterly unmatched, rare and modern yet powerfully nostalgic jazz voice.[113]

Amy held her audiences in thrall to her wild child image: a diminutive girl with a hugely granular voice, gothic eyeliner and a tumult of hair. Later that striking look was enhanced with a retro beehive which she said reflected her increasingly turbulent life.[114] Music was in Amy's life blood. She grew up listening to her father's jazz records and soon she was performing in local Jewish groups. She attended stage schools from the age of eight including the Brit School in Croydon and the Sylvia Young Theatre School where her beautiful voice was noticed as well as her feisty and tempestuous nature. She impressed teachers with her intelligence and talent but was rebellious and found it hard to concentrate on academic work.

Sylvia Young herself was captivated by Amy and her talents, so much so that she helped promote Amy's career after she had left the school.[115]

At 16 she had a tattoo and turned to cannabis, shrugging her shoulders at parental dismay. Her then boyfriend Tyler James sent a cassette of her voice to a record company with the result that songwriter Felix Howard collaborated with her on her first album *Frank* which was released in October 2003 when she was 20. She was hailed by critics and earnt two BRIT[116] nominations. It was at this time that she met Blake Fielder-Civil. A change in her music came after their complex relationship broke up as she poured her torment into what became her hit album *Back to Black*, released in 2006. This spawned the concerts and TV appearances by striking changes in style and looks. The new, thinner, wilder Winehouse with tattoos and voluminous hair suggested something at best fragile, unguarded, at worst crazed and spooky. But her lyrics became edgier, more passionate, at times incomprehensible and the performer even more fascinating.[117]

Back to Black's first single 'Rehab' expressed her despair. 'They tried to make me go to rehab, I said no, no, no.' She scored a top 10 hit with this song which stayed in the charts for 57 weeks. It made her the first British singer to win five Grammy awards, selling 10 million copies. What appealed was her naked integrity – visceral, raw, upbeat – and a contrast from the squeaky clean and anodyne pop world. She embraced every musical genre. She sang in pop's darkest key. She was also a titan of soul music. She was the music industry's first conceptual artist, a chanteuse reminiscent of Edith Piaf and Billie Holiday, both emblems of personal anguish. Amy's admirers have also credited her with paving the way for unconventional women to have mainstream pop success.

But for Amy herself a series of breakdowns following her tempestuous love life resulted in drug overdose and several abortive visits to the Priory for rehab, plus trouble with the police. She married Fielder-Civil in May 2007 but with both heavily dependent on drugs they divorced in 2009. Many blamed him for giving her the first hit of heroin to which she became immediately addicted. Amy went to St Lucia to avoid the London drug scene but turned to alcohol.[118] In 2011, just five years after she had become a global star upon the release of *Back to Black* she was found dead in her London flat, having succumbed to alcohol poisoning exacerbated by bulimia. She was 27.

Amy was a nice Jewish girl from Southgate who was keen to shake off her middle-class roots.[119] She was descended from Jewish immigrants of Eastern European origin on both her parents' sides. Amy's great-great grandfather Harris Weinhause (later anglicised to Winehouse) came from

Minsk, Belarus in 1891 and lived in Booth Street, Spitalfields with his family. He was a tailor and one of his sons ran a barber shop in Commercial Street. Amy's grandfather Alec grew up living above the salon and became a black cab driver. In 1948 he married Cynthia Gordon from Albert Gardens, Stepney, who prior to her marriage had dated jazz musician Ronnie Scott. After living for a time in Stoke Newington they moved to Southgate in the late 1950s, a suburb of north London, with a sizeable Jewish population. Their son Mitch, Amy's father, was born in 1950 but considered himself an East Ender, such were the family's connections to the area. He would go there most weeks to join the extended family at Albert Gardens for Friday night dinners. He worked for most of his life as a black cab driver as his father before him.[120] Mitch considered himself a true East Ender and recalls how Amy and Alex were fascinated by the area and he would take them there regularly.[121] Amy's mother Janis had Eastern European roots. Her mother Esther Richman was the youngest of three girls and their immigrant mother had arrived in London penniless after leaving her husband in Newcastle. Janis's father Eddie worked as a tailor and had grown up in Norwood Jewish orphanage.[122]

The family were not particularly religious but they observed the major Jewish life events. Both Amy and her brother Alex went to Jewish nurseries and Sunday Hebrew classes. The family celebrated Passover and enjoyed Friday night dinners to which Amy would sometimes bring friends. In the documentary film *Amy,* her first manager Nick Shymansky told the *Los Angeles Jewish Journal* how he met Amy when she was 16 and he was a 19-year-old aspiring music manager. They hit it off, in part because of their shared Jewish heritage. 'Amy had a really strong Jewishness about her,' Shymansky recalled. 'It was her humour and her whole get up. She and her friends were those loud, mouthy, confident Jewish girls. I used to go to Friday night dinners at her grandmother's place and when she and a friend got their first flat, you'd go in and they'd offer you chicken soup and kneidlach. Neither of us were particularly religious but we were very culturally Jewish'. In a home video in the film Amy tells Shymansky that she was 'your favourite Jewish girl apart from your mum'.[123]

In 2013 there was an exhibition at the Jewish Museum, London entitled *Amy Winehouse: A Family Portrait* which shows Amy and her family as a close, boisterous Jewish clique. The exhibition included Amy's childhood treasures, her record collection, photographs of loved ones and some of her distinctive outfits. Her brother Alex, who co-curated the exhibition, described it as 'a snapshot of a girl who was, to her deepest core, simply a little Jewish kid from north London with a big talent who, more than anything else, wanted to be true to her heritage'. The exhibition was one of dozens of private pictures, clothes and personal effects that belonged to Amy. Jewish items are interspersed throughout the exhibition, reflecting the way in which the Winehouse family's Jewish identity was totally integral to their lives.[124] Their parents divorced when Amy was nine years old but brought them up with an appreciation of the faith's rituals and rites of passage. Both he and Amy felt culturally Jewish.

The exhibition included a copy of Claudia Roden's book on Jewish food which Alex bought Amy for her birthday in 2002 because she wanted to make chicken soup. There is a photo of Amy sitting on a faded blue sofa in her grandmother's house, dressed in the uniform of her youth group, the Jewish Lads' and Girls' Brigade. Just two days before her death, Amy summoned her father Mitch to sift through a battered black suitcase full of family photographs. The photos themselves could have belonged to almost any Diaspora Jewish family. There is Amy pictured standing by her brother at his barmitzvah and her parents in evening dress at anther Jewish celebration.

How Jewish was she? Amy's dramatic eye make-up and iconic beehive were not the singer's only fashion statements. She was frequently seen wearing a thick gold Star of David pendant around her neck.[125] In a *Jewish Chronicle* review about her Jewishness, they considered her to be 78% Jewish. 'Her alcohol consumption suggests she could not be Jewish. Her face suggests otherwise'. Points in her favour were that she was brought up in a Jewish area and the daughter of a black cab driver; she loves her grandma, likes to make roast chicken on a Friday night and looks forward to matzah and Edam sandwiches after a night out. Points against were her predilection for getting drunk; prominent tattoos and that she did not know the lyrics of the Hebrew celebration song 'Hava Nagila' when asked.[126]

She was a study in contrasts. Amy declined to give an interview with the *Jewish Chronicle* because she did not want to be associated with the newspaper or the Jewish community. Paul Lester found that strange as there was at that time talk of her compiling an album of Jewish songs with record producer Mark Ronson.[127] When prodded to comment on her bad girl ways, she tended to bring up her Jewishness herself, offering it as a reassuring counterpoint to the rest of her image.[128] She called herself 'the Jewish lioness' on her Twitter page.[129] Although she tweeted sporadically she became known for her spat with Jewish music producer Mark Ronson when she said 'Ronson. You're dead to me; one album I write and you take half the credit – make a career of it? I don't think so BRUV'. She later backtracked writing 'Ronson I love you that make it better. You know I love you. It's a Jew thing'.[130] She was clearly not religious. 'Being Jewish to me is about being together as a real family. It's not about lighting candles and saying a brocha' (prayer). Her brother said that she expressed her Jewish identity through mothering her friends, making them chicken soup and reeling off Yiddish phrases and insults.[131] She had wanted her husband Blake Civil-Fielder to convert to Judaism before they got married although in the end they had a £60 wedding in Miami and even her family did not know in advance about the wedding.[132]

'The media were obsessed with her music, that she was a crack smoking train wreck and that she was Jewish. Both the media and Winehouse herself have joyfully portrayed her Jewish identity as a bizarre contrast with her bad girl image. The Jewish community, ever eager to claim a celeb for the team, managed to boast and sneer about her at the same time. 'Winehouse is the proud antithesis of the nice Jewish girl'.[133] Comments included: 'A slight 20 year old Jewish girl from north London'.[134] 'The beehived, heavily tattooed Winehouse might be a wee Jewish girl from north London but she can snarl and walk like Etta James or Eartha Kitt'.[135] 'Those who have only heard her voice express shock upon seeing the body that produces it: the sultry, crackly, world weary howl that sounds like the ghost of Sarah Vaughan comes from a pint size Jewish girl from north London'.[136] 'Winehouse has an exceptional voice that's even more striking when you catch a glimpse of its source: a wispy, heavily tattooed young Jewish woman with a mile high beehive for a hairdo and a gothic level of mascara caked onto her face. It almost doesn't compute'.[137]

When reporting Amy's funeral the media had a fascination with the Hebrew prayers, the sitting *shiva* and many of the obituaries referred to Amy's shiny Star of David necklace and showed poignant pictures of her dressed up as a child for the Jewish festival of Purim. Anthony Clavane considered that Amy was not defined by her religion but both she and the public were comfortable with the image of a working-class, north London Jewish girl made good. Amy's emergence reflected a new respect, and a more open attitude towards Anglo-Jewish dual identity. The London Jewish Museum's exhibition *Entertaining The Nation* in 2011 told the story of three phases of Jewish integration. The first generation of entertainers, viewed at best as exotic outsiders or at worst dangerous aliens, were cast as Shylocks, Svengalis and Fagins. The second generation, in their desperation to escape the ghetto, became more English than the English. In the third phase of integration artists such as Winehouse and actors such as Sasha Baron Cohen not only take pride in their ethnic heritage but are considered to be edgy Jews – Jews with attitude. Theirs is a more confident integration, one based on accepting difference.[138]

Amy's pushed her 'edginess' to the extreme. 'She was a frail little girl on a course of self-destruction'.[139] In a few short years she changed from fabulous Jewish princess to a frightening hulk of her former self.[140] Her parents, although divorced, worked together as to how to deal with their daughter's multiple addictions. Her father Mitch explained that they got advice from the most eminent experts in the field when the problems began and advice varied from adopting tough love to being there and pretending that it is not happening. ' We had to find a happy medium. Amy is so family oriented, how could we wipe her out of our lives and tell her we didn't want to see her'. He believed that the death of his mother with whom Amy had a very intensely close relationship could have been the catalyst for her descent and it did not help that it was at a time when she was vulnerable as she was not coping with the fame her first album brought her and was having self-image problems.[141] In 2007 when she was in and out of rehab and forced to pull out of various events in the continued effort to protect her well-being, her mother blamed her daughter's health on the pressures of the music industry. She lacked the maturity needed to cope with fame and it was as if her whole life was turned into a stage performance.[142]

Amy died tragically on 23 July 2011. Her mother did not believe any of the endless speculation that Amy wanted to die. 'There was no doubt that she battled with who she was and what she had become but she dreamed that one day she'd have children and there was a large part of Amy that had a zest for life and people. But she was a girl who kicked against authority, a person who always took things that bit further than everyone else around her'. She also considered that if Amy had been older and more mature when she met success, would things have been different and that it all happened too fast and she was too young.[143]

A private funeral took place on 26 July 2011. The Jewish ceremony at Edgwarebury cemetery in north London was attended by 150 friends and family. The service was conducted by Rabbi Frank Hellene who told those present that a person's life is measured in deeds not years and in the end what was left was her brilliant legacy. Her body was then cremated in Golders Green.[144] Amy had wanted to be cremated, as had her grandmother, so that their ashes could be together. The family observed three nights of shiva at Southgate Progressive Synagogue, where Amy's mother was a member. Rabbi Daniel Rich led the service on the first night at what he called 'Amy's shul, where Alex celebrated his barmitzvah and Amy was brought up'.[145]

Fans built a shrine of cards and other artefacts outside Amy's home in the days after her death. Among the things left were Jewish memorial candles, bottles of alcohol, cigarettes and sketched tributes. It made a moving tribute for the love that was felt for Amy. Addressing the fans and reporters that were present her father referred to the Amy who had existed beyond the music and notoriety. He talked about the sweet, caring and loving woman known to those closest to her. 'Amy was about one thing and that was love' and how her whole life was devoted to her family, friends and fans and that is the Amy that must be remembered as well as remembering her enormous talent and majestic musical legacy.[146]

In style terms she redefined what was expected of a pop star. Instead of being primped and packaged as a teen market popstrel, she had a towering beehive, heavy eyeliner and a fondness for leopard print and tattoos. Karl Lagerfield claimed her as his new muse in 2007 and sent beehived models down the Chanel catwalk. Vogue France dedicated a whole fashion story to her look and hundreds of girls bought a version of her style on the high street.[147] She was also rebellious, volatile and wild. She was mesmerising: the dual narratives of musical brilliance and wayward hedonism meant she was always discussed widely. At the height of her fame she would simultaneously have her love life plastered over the front page of a tabloid newspapers, be photographed in a celebrity weekly staggering home from a bar, have the intricacies of her musical influence discussed in a music weekly and be heralded as a cultural icon in broadsheet supplements. She was one of the most gifted, sincere and talked about artists ever to emerge from the UK's music scene. She sold millions of records, won numerous top awards and earned the respect, fascination and devotion of people across the globe. The tragic death of Amy Winehouse robbed the world of a unique musical talent.[148]

Jessie Ware (1984 –   )

The most successful British Jewish female performer since Amy Winehouse is singer songwriter Jessie Ware. Over the past decade her sensuous gauzy vocals have become part of the fabric of British pop music and *Table Manners*, the immensely popular podcast she co-hosts with her mother Lennie, has turned her into somewhat of a national treasure.[149]

Born on 15 October 1984, Ware was raised in Clapham, London and is the daughter of Helena Keell (known as Lennie), a social worker and counsellor and John Ware,[150] a journalist and investigative reporter. Lennie is Jewish and grew up in Manchester where her family lived in the

Orthodox enclave of Broughton Park but were members of Manchester Reform Synagogue (Jackson's Row). Her father Alfred Morley Keell was of Russian Jewish origin and from Belfast, Northern Ireland. Her mother, who converted to Judaism, was from Birmingham. Lennie was the first in her family to go to university and she says she went into social work to avoid going into M & S management which her mother had wanted her to do.[151] Lennie and her husband divorced when Jessie was ten. Her other children are actress Hannah Ware and Alex, a doctor.

Ware was encouraged to sing at an early age. Her mother loved that she could sing as it was said that when her father sang in synagogue in Ireland he made everyone cry. Her mother was supportive in her early musical career and Ware considers her to be her 'hero'. She was raised as Jewish in a secular household. 'So Jewish we put up our Christmas tree in November'.[152] Ware recalls that 'like most Jewish homes ours was loud and emotional. And that was just when we were deciding what to eat'. She added that home life was brilliantly chaotic and her mother made sure that her children always experienced new things.[153] Ware was estranged from her father for some years.

Educated at the private school Alleyn's in Dulwich, Ware became friends with Felix White[154] and Jack Penate[155], both of whom would become prominent musicians. She then studied at the University of Sussex where she graduated with a degree in English literature. She began her working career in journalism, starting at the *Jewish Chronicle* where she cut her teeth as a web reporter. Her stories included an interview with teenagers from Sderot, Israel and a report on non-Jewish emergency personnel travelling to Auschwitz on an educational trip.[156] She also had a stint at sports journalism at the *Daily Mirror* and worked behind the scenes at the television company Love Productions.

Ware was due to start law school when Jack Penate asked if she would do the backing vocals on his tour. He was unable to pay her but it gave her the opportunity of having six weeks in America. Her mother gave encouragement and told her to live her life, defer her place and take the opportunity.[157] She went on tour and then collaborated with a host of indie[158] and rap performers. She became swept up in a wave of new British alt-soul singers including Adele, Florence and the Machine and Paloma Faith as her sound started to evolve. Somehow Ware was the glue between all these scenes: indie, club and pop.[159] Her efforts earned her a record deal of her own and she became one of the fastest rising names in music.[160]

In 2012 she released her debut album *Devotion* which peaked at number five on the UK Albums chart and was shortlisted for the Mercury

Music Prize for Album of the Year. It was an album of downtempo R&B (rhythm and blues) and her voice was reminiscent of the singers Sade or Witney Houston from the 1980s at her most melancholic.[161] It produced the single 'Wildest Moments' which was used by the BBC over a montage of Andy Murray at Wimbledon.

On the back of *Devotion* she received two BRIT[162] nominations for British Breakthrough Act and British female solo artist and became the new queen of UK soul. Her work draws on R&B, garage and electronica while her voice prompts comparisons to Adele and Florence Welch. It is a measure of her success and standing that her second album *Tough Love* (2014) included collaborations with Brit Boy wonder Ed Sheeran and Miguel, one of America's foremost R&B singer-song writers and producers. Ware and Miguel co-penned a track called 'Kind of… Sometimes… Maybe' and the idea was to evoke soul's classic era.[163] The album featured 'Say You Love Me', a belt it out power ballad that became a popular selection on British singing competitions such as *The X Factor* and *The Voice*.[164]

Her third album *Glasshouse* (2017) was a vulnerable exploration of motherhood, love and the creeping pressures of adulthood. One review commented that her versatile voice could whisper and soar against a musical palette drawing from soul, R&B, jazz and pop.[165] Her fourth record *What's Your Pleasure* (2020) was a contrast. It was recorded during lockdown and Ware wanted the sophistication that disco offered as well as the melodrama. She explained that 'It's a time where people should be able to listen to music that can help them fantasise and move away from reality'.[166] *New Musical Express* commented that although her initial tunes were rooted in soul, R&B and sophisticated pop, in this album she rediscovers her dancefloor strut on a record filled with euphoric disco, funk and groove with heady '80s sounds. 'She has moved away from the wistful melancholy that permeated her last record and takes to the dance floor'.[167] She was nominated for the British Female Solo Artist for the 2021 BRIT awards.

As an offshoot to her musical career, Ware became a UNICEF UK ambassador and travelled with them to Bangladesh, Cameroon and North Macedonia to see their work and to help children who have fled violence. In 2014 she joined the charity group Band Aid 30 along with other British and Irish pop acts recording the latest version of 'Do They Know It's Christmas' to raise money for the 2014 Ebola crisis in West Africa. She was also part of the line-up for the 'Artists for Grenfell' charity single which was released to raise money for the families of the victims of the Grenfell Tower fire in June 2017 and for the London Community Foundation.

At the start of her career Ware announced that 'all I wanted was to be in a position when the *Jewish Chronicle* would write about me. It made my month when it put my video on its website home page. I had been working on the website so I thought that was wicked'.[168] She was proud of her Jewish roots and said they were a big part of her identity.[169]

When appearing at the Glastonbury Festival in 2013 she even tried to bring a little Jewishness to bear on the crowds by getting them to say 'mazeltov' to a musician friend of hers whose wife had given birth the day before. 'All you could see were bemused expressions as 35,000 festival goers tried to work out what a 'mazeltov' was and whether you could buy one at any of the food stands. Jessie might come across as a demure soul diva on record but as a character she is down-to-earth Jewish London personified'.[170]

In 2014 Ware married personal trainer Sam Burrows, her childhood sweetheart, on the Greek island of Skopelos. She recalled that they had a 'Jew-ish' ceremony. It was a civil ceremony but they married under a *chupah* (wedding canopy), had seven blessings recited by friends, stamped on the glass and took part in some Jewish dancing. Ware found the ceremony moving. Her *aufruf*[171] had been at her local synagogue in Wimbledon. 'It was important for me and my family to have some Jewish aspects'. She was especially pleased with the way that Rabbi Sylvia Rothschild made Burrows, who is not Jewish, feel included. 'Instead of people thinking you're marrying out of the community they should think of it as marrying into our Jewish community. That's a much more positive way of looking at it. They were very welcoming and generous towards Sam'.[172] They now have two children.

Ware became the first patron of Apples and Honey, the pioneering nursery on the site of the Jewish residential home Nightingale House which brings intergenerational activities into the home's daily programme. She said having grown up in Clapham she was aware of the home at which family members had volunteered.[173]

Ware received antisemitic abuse on Twitter – 'X' after she had performed live on Channel 4. She had sent a tweet to her 28,000 followers on the social network site praising DJ A-Trak (real name Alain Macklovich) who is also Jewish and performed on the show. A tweeter identifying himself as 'John Sin' and using the Twitter handle @fortherub replied: 'Cor a conk like that bet your (sic) deluded like those other ***** at the JC (*Jewish Chronicle*). Other Twitter users came to the singer's defence telling Sin that he was 'revolting' and would be reported for racism. Following the abuse Jessie tweeted: 'Pretty shocked by my first encounter with an antisemitic twitter troll last night. I won't stand for it'. She said it was the first time she had encountered direct antisemitism. 'It's upsetting and moronic but I will never sit back and take it'.[174]

A wider public are now exposed to Ware's background due to the podcast *Table Manners*. The original idea was to gather a group of Ware's interesting friends for dinner and to record them all chatting, eating and gossiping. Her mother Lennie would cook and Ware would steer the conversation. The blueprint for *Table Manners* came from the Ware family's Jewish Friday night dinners when Ware would bring too many friends home and Lennie would happily over cater, with everyone oversharing, overeating and having a grand time.[175] On Friday nights Lennie cooked food she had eaten as a child: chopped liver, chicken soup with carrots and matzo balls and roast chicken. 'I'm not very Orthodox but it was fun'.[176]

By the time *Table Manners* went on line in late 2017 it had evolved into a one guest per show format with Ware and her mother sharing hosting duties. Each week guests from the world of music, culture and politics drop by to eat and chat.[177] It became a comedic double act with the brand of loving sparring that only a mother-daughter duo can provide. Listeners frequently tell them that their banter reminds them of their relationship with their own mothers.[178]

Both women cook and interrogate their guests with blasts of candid curiosity. The comedian Alan Carr spilled the beans about his wedding (chief celebrant singer Adele), singer Sam Smith admitted he always thought Mexico was in central Europe and London mayor Sadiq Kahn broke the Ramadan Fast with the Wares.[179] Mother and daughter make no attempt to hide their Jewish origins. Nigella Lawson was a guest and they discussed her Jewish background. They asked her what ingredient she put in her chicken soup and whether she bothered with making matza balls. Nigella described her mother's recipe and said it was an act of devotion for her as her mother had died young.[180] They made chopped liver and latkes[181] for hip hop musician Loyle Carner. Although this book is on public performance, the interior and private space of the Friday night dinner meal has become mainstream to a non-Jewish audience through this podcast and also the television sitcom *Friday Night Dinner*.[182]

The series has produced 11 sessions, clocked millions of listeners and was nominated for a British podcast award. There is also the cookbook *Table Manners* which contains over 100 recipes divided into categories: Effortless, a Bit More Effort, Summertime, Desserts and Baking, Chrismukkah and Jewish-ish Food. Ware's next book *Omelette: Food, Love, Chaos and Other Conversations* was published in June 2021 and blends food writing and memoir.

Ware's success and fame in the music world made it easier to launch the podcast. She considers how fortunate she has been. 'I think it is so funny that I have been allowed to get away with being called "a bit of r&b" seeing I am this white Jewish girl from south London. Amy Winehouse opened for us Jews to get away with the soul and r&b thing'.[183]

Conclusion

Although some of the singers featured above are no longer remembered, they were trailblazers in their time. Alma Cogan with her novelty songs heralded in the 1950s and Helen Shapiro was the youngest ever teenage star and symbolised the new era of the 1960s. In addition to their music, they were fashion icons. Alma was known for her fabulous frocks which lit up a rather dull and dour postwar Britain. Helen Shapiro and her beehive hair, a style that defined the early 1960s when American First Lady Jacqueline Kennedy wore her hair in this style, was her trademark look. Elkie Brooks with her slinky dresses cut to the thigh was the epitome of the 'rock chick' when the link between sex and selling records was becoming more explicit.[184] Pauline Black adopted the feminised rude boy style, a uniquely androgynous look that was part of the punk scene at the time. Amy Winehouse became a modern-day style icon with her signature beehive, heavy winged eyeliner, skin-tight, thigh-skimming dresses and skirts. 'With her cocktail dress displaying her tattoos, her hair piled into a beehive and her panda eyes, she looked like a classic lost chanteuse from New York in the late 1950s with a modern twist'.[185]

Despite their different styles, the majority came from middle-class suburban homes and were open about their Jewish backgrounds. Alma wore a Star of David and showed pride in her Jewishness and Amy, despite her unconventionality and outrageous behaviour, also wore a Star of David and called herself a 'Jewish lioness' on her Twitter page. All those featured contributed greatly to the music of their particular decade with Amy becoming a pioneer for the twenty-first century. 'She paved the way for other female stars with not only her talent but also her unique style and demeanour, making her arguably one of the most influential and greatest artists of all time. Like Amy, they could be whoever they wanted to be and still be successful'.[186]

1. Sarah Bernhardt

(Wikimedia Commons)

2. Miriam Karlin OBE

(Lewis Morley Archive, Board of Trustees of the Science Museum, London).

3. Fenella Fielding OBE

(Wikimedia Commons)

4. Claire Bloom CBE

(Wikimedia Commons)

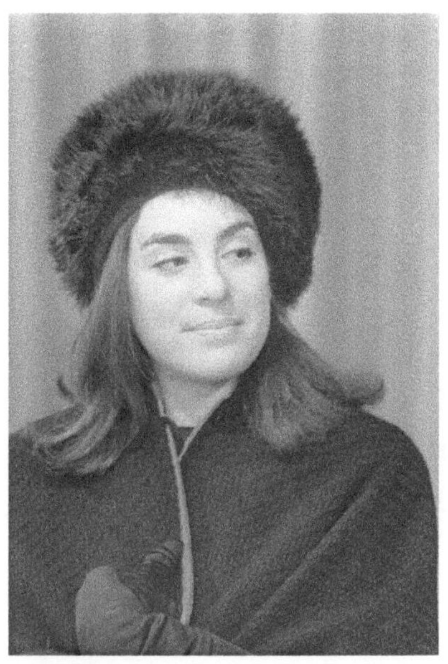

5. Eleanor Bron

(Wikimedia Commons)

6. Miriam Margolyes OBE

(Wikimedia Commons)

7. Maureen Lipman DBE
(Wikimedia Commons)

8. Tracy-Ann Oberman
(Wikimedia Commons)

9. Sophie Okonedo CBE

(Wikimedia Commons)

10. Grace Aguilar

(Wikimedia Commons)

11. Amy Levy

(Wikimedia Commons)

12. Naomi Jacob

Courtesy of Tony and Thomas Atcheson)

13. Bernice Rubens

(Stephen Hyde, via National Portrait Gallery)

14. Anita Brookner CBE

(Mark Gerson via National Portrait Gallery)

15. Linda Grant

(Charlie Hopkinson)

16. Naomi Alderman

(Annabel Moeller)

17. Charlotte Mendelson

(Sophie Davidson)

18. Alma Cogan

(Wikimedia Commons)

19. Helen Shapiro

(Wikimedia Commons)

20. Elkie Brooks

(Wikimedia Commons)

21. Pauline Black OBE DL

(Wikimedia Commons)

22. Amy Winehouse

(Wikimedia Commons)

23. Jessie Ware

(Wikimedia Commons)

24. Myra Hess DBE

(Courtesy of the Royal Academy of Music)

25. Fanny Waterman DBE

(Simon Wilkinson/SWpix.com)

26. Natalie Clein OBE

(Neda Navaee)

27. Abraham da Costa, Catherine da Costa's son

(Jewish Museum, London)

28. Painting by Rebecca Solomon

(Wikimedia Commons)

29. Rachel Lichtenstein

(Courtesy of Rachel Lichtenstein)

30. Hannah Gluckstein

(Wikimedia Commons)

31. Dorothy Levitt

(Wikimedia Commons)

32. Sheila van Damm

(Lewis Morley Archive, Board of Trustees of the Science Museum London)

33. Angela Buxton

(Michelle Wayne)

34. Lady Judith Montefiore

(Wikimedia Commons)

35. Claudia Roden

(Wikimedia Commons)

36. Nigella Lawson

(Wikimedia Commons)

4

Classical Musicians

Prior to the twentieth century female classical musicians had a struggle to be accepted in a professional capacity as it was considered immodest for women to perform in public; women's roles in music was meant for their private lives inside their homes. The private sphere of the home allowed women to perform in classical music as singers and pianists and British Jewish women conformed to that pattern, especially as they linked the piano as a totally respectable piece of Victorian and later domestic furniture. It is therefore not surprising that two of these case studies that moved from the domestic to public sphere were pianists. In the freer sphere of the immigrant world women were singers and instrumentalists but the focus here is on the British born.

The piano was thought to be the most appropriate instrument for female musicians. Unlike other instruments that you could take out of the house, it was stationed in the home.[1] The success of the piano as an instrument of choice in Britain was due in part to the prevailing social conditions. The start of the nineteenth century saw the beginnings of the consumer society with the steady rise of the affluent middle class, many of whom were anxious to display their wealth and social position.[2] The piano symbolised respectability, achievement and status.[3] As the century progressed the popularity of the piano spread down through society so that 'even among the small traders and artisans precious time and money was diverted to secure, at least for the daughters, piano sheet music, teachers and a musical education'.[4]

To satisfy the increasing demand for piano skills there was an expansion in the number of music teachers. As the appeal of learning an instrument increased the number of teachers rose. As playing the piano was largely a female activity, for many Victorian women piano teaching offered a relatively secure way to earn a living and by the 1860s, 60 per cent of all piano teachers in London were female.[5] Their pupils were generally from their own or similar social class. Music became a respectable source of income, most often on a temporary, pre-marital basis.[6] By the end of the nineteenth century women piano teachers were to be found amongst the working classes as cheap pianos were now available and many people aspired to buy one.[7]

It was only in the second half of the nineteenth century that music teachers and conservatoires began to train young women interested in pursuing music on a professional level. By the turn of the twentieth century there were professional women musicians working in Britain as singers, instrumentalists, composers and writers of music. Yet many of these women were fighting against a mainstream belief that as women it was appropriate, or even possible, for them to play in a professional symphony orchestra or compose a symphony.[8] The Society of Women Musicians was founded in 1911 to provide a space for women to meet and discuss musical matters and help with the business aspects of a musical career as well as giving concerts. The first concert was held in 1912 in Queen's Hall, London and regular concerts followed that featured premieres from women composers.

Although the contributions of women musicians to symphony orchestras has been extensive many had to overcome barriers, such as acceptance as full members and resentment from male musicians, in the path of professional achievement.[9] Despite these obstacles Myra Hess, who was a past president of the Society, managed to make her name on the international music scene. Fanny Waterman, one of the later generation of women musicians who played various roles in the organisation, continued to campaign for the rights of women musicians as well as organising concerts and meetings.

They were both to become icons in the musical world and although neither were religious, were proud of their Jewish identity. Hess attributed her success to her self-discipline with regard to her work which was a result of her strict Jewish upbringing.[10] Waterman wore her Jewish roots on her sleeve.[11]

Myra Hess (1890-1965)

Myra Hess secured a special place as a musical heroine in wartime Britain by abandoning her international concert career and giving daily lunchtime concerts in the National Gallery during the Blitz. In 1941 she was awarded the Dame Commander of the British Empire in recognition of her wartime service.

Julia Myra Hess was born on 25 February 1890 in West Hampstead, London to Frederick Solomon Hess, a textile merchant, and his wife Lizzie (Jacobs). Hess's paternal grandfather Samuel Hess (1824-1905) came from Alsace and set up his own textile firm in the East End in 1847. He married

English-born Alice Cantor and moved into an elegant home in Islington. He was an Orthodox Jew and regularly attended Dalston synagogue where he was a warden. Myra's father was the oldest of seven children and joined his father in the expanding family firm which manufactured accoutrements of uniforms for clients that included the London Police, St. John Ambulance and the Beefeaters. In 1884 he married Lizzie Jacobs at Bayswater Synagogue.[12] Lizzie was the daughter of John Jacobs, a wealthy shopkeeper and money lender who lived at Warrington Crescent, Paddington.[13]

Hess grew up in an affluent home and started piano lessons at a very early age. She attended the Trinity College of Music and became the youngest pupil to receive the Trinity College Certificate. At the age of 12, she won a scholarship to the Royal Academy of Music where she met her mentor Tobias Matthay who was to be instrumental in developing her talent.[14] She had a difficult time in launching her career and had to make all the initial arrangements for concerts by herself, a challenge she had not faced before. It was around this time that her family fortunes changed and her father had to declare himself bankrupt as a result of bad investments and Hess supported herself by teaching.[15]

She made her formal debut in 1907 at the age of 17 when she played Beethoven's Fourth Piano Concerto and Saint-Saens's Fourth Piano Concerto with the New Symphony Orchestra under the baton of Thomas Beecham at Queen's Hall, at that time London's most prestigious concert hall (it was destroyed during the Blitz). Hess's international career took off following this debut. In 1908 she played the first of what would eventually number 90 concerts with the Proms. By 1920 she was performing nearly 100 concerts a year in Britain and Europe. She made her American concert debut in 1922 to huge acclaim and remained a favourite of American audiences until the end of her life.[16] Her repertory ranged from Baroque to Romantic music and included in earlier days many contemporary works. She played all Mozart's 21 concertos, Beethoven's 5 and the two by Brahms besides other favourites such as Schumann and Grieg.[17] In 1936 she was awarded a CBE (Commander of the Order of the British Empire) as she was already considered a national treasure and this was before her remarkable war work for which she achieved great fame.

Just before the outbreak of the Second World War Hess took the risky decision to break her contract for a seven-month tour of America and Australia that was due to start in November 1939. She returned to London where she set up daily chamber concerts at the National Gallery in order to boost morale for Londoners during the Blitz (1940-1941). Historian Patrick Bade commented that if one person could be deemed to represent the musical life of London during the war, it would have to be Myra Hess.[18] Hess had always felt that classical concerts were available almost exclusively for a privileged section of the community and she wondered how she could reach the many thousands of potential music lovers outside the limited world of concert goers. She longed to throw open the doors to the very best music, at a price all could afford.[19] The National Gallery concerts gave her that opportunity.

Hess believed that the arts played a powerful spiritual role in the health of the nation at the best of times and would play an even greater role in wartime. The outbreak of war created a cultural black out in London as theatres, cinemas, concert halls and museums closed, including the National Gallery. Bombing raids were a serious threat and the Home Office was keen to avoid the mass casualties that would ensue if public venues were targeted. The National Gallery closed on 23 August 1939, the evacuation of its pictures having already begun. Every day containers of paintings left London for secret safe destinations in Gloucestershire and Wales.

With the pictures evacuated, Director Kenneth Clark waited for notification that the Gallery would be requisitioned for administrative purposes, saddened by its inability to offer Londoners comfort when they needed it. A few weeks after the outbreak of war he was visited by Hess who shared his dismay.[20] She had written to the BBC on 16 September 1939 to complain that 'since the outbreak of war the whole world has been listening to England and the entire nation has been waiting in vain for programmes of good music befitting the dignity and seriousness of the present situation'. On receiving no reply Hess took matters into her own hands and approached Clark with her proposition.[21]

Hess proposed using the Gallery as a venue for music. There had been a precedent in 1922 when fundraising concerts had been performed there. Clark began by winning the blessing of the Gallery's trustees for the project and then convinced the Home Office and Ministry of Works to grant the concerts dispensation from the ban on public gatherings. It was agreed that the concerts would take place daily at 1pm with a repeat performance at 5pm on Tuesdays and Thursdays. An admission fee of one shilling would be charged for the midday concert and two shillings for the afternoon programme. Chairs were rented and Steinway and Sons delivered a grand piano. For the first of the concerts the Home Office gave permission that 200 could attend. Hess had to put together a production practically overnight. She had to raise operating funds, line up performers and programmes, prepare the venue that included building the stage, installing seats and lights.

The queue that stretched around Trafalgar Square on 10 October 1939 gave Hess and her team the first hint that the concerts were going to be more popular than expected. As the opening event had been organised very quickly there had been little time for advertising and Hess decided to give the first performance on her own rather than expose a group of musicians to the embarrassment of a small audience. She expected 100 of the people she knew just to turn up to support her.[22]

By 12.20pm the queue for the concert reached all the way down the side of Trafalgar Square and around the corner. Over 1,000 heard Hess play the first concert with many hundreds more turned away. Clark described the people who were hungrier for music than their lunches. 'There were all sorts. Young and old, smart and shabby, Tommies in uniform with their tin hats strapped on, old ladies with ear trumpets, music students, civil servants, office boys, busy public men, all sorts had come'.[23]

The extraordinary symbolic value of these concerts quickly became apparent and members of the royal family began to regularly attend as well, sitting with members of the public. In 1945 Queen Elizabeth the Queen Mother remembered her attendance at the concerts as being among the happiest hours she had known during the war.[24] For the musicians as well as their audience the concerts provided relief from the news that reached Britain from Europe in the early months of the war. It was one of the most potent symbols representing the spirit of war-torn Britain.

The concerts ran Monday to Friday, for six and a half years without fail. If London was being bombed the concert was moved to the basement. In all there were 1,968 concerts seen by 824,152 people. Every artist was paid five guineas no matter what their standing or fame. It was calculated that over 1,500 musicians took part over the six years, including 13 orchestras and 15 choirs. Hess herself performed in 146 concerts. She refused all invitations to return to the States to perform whilst the concerts took place. Before the war Hess was renowned for performing works by Austro-German composers such as Bach, Beethoven, Mozart, Schumann and Brahms. She continued to schedule their works in her wartime performances demonstrating her belief that enjoyment of music could be separated from politics.[25] Besides giving pleasure to thousands of people the concerts raised through the ticket fees, £15,000 for the Musicians Benevolent Fund.

Hess gave other war time concerts in London. When the Lyric Theatre, Hammersmith reopened in 1944 Hess gave the opening concert. Charles Landstone, an assistant director of Coma, the forerunner to the Arts Council, recalled how she had hardly seated herself at the piano when the buzz was heard of a flying bomb. A terrific nearby explosion followed, the audience swayed and the scenery dock doors were blown in on to the stage. Hess gave one short glance over her shoulder and then went on playing. Any panic in the audience was immediately quelled.[26]

Hess appeared in 14 wartime Prom concerts, played for Queen Elizabeth whilst she was having her portrait painted by Augustus John and travelled to Bletchley Park to entertain code breakers. She showed a strong support of the armed forces, performing with the uniformed orchestra of the Central Band of HM Royal Air Force as part of the 1942 propaganda film *Listen to Britain* produced by the British Government's Ministry of Information to support the Allied war effort. It was a documentary, public information film and morale booster. The film presented the sounds of Britain at war from bird songs mingled with the roar of planes over wheat fields to Hess performing at the National Gallery and was a clear clarion call to local and international audiences to fight and save Britain from the onslaught of war.[27] This classic film constructed Britishness at the time and Hess's inclusion reflected her iconic status. Hess also climbed on to the wings of a B36 bomber aircraft in Trafalgar Square to make a public appeal for war savings. Her performances were filmed by two camera crews, widening the reach of her concert series beyond London.[28]

The success of the National Gallery concerts made Hess an international star, encouraging people such as conductor Arturo Toscanini to invite her to perform a Beethoven concerto with him and his orchestra during her first post-war tour of America. Hess toured extensively and packed concert halls on both sides of the Atlantic. By the early 1960s increasing bouts of ill health forced her to give up concert playing but she continued with her teaching. Her proteges included Steven Kovacevich, Clive Lythgoe, and the twin duo pianists Richard and John Contiguglia whom she prepared for their professional debut at the Wigmore Hall in 1962. Her last public performance was at London's Royal Festival Hall on 31 October 1961 when she played Mozart A Major Concerto under Sir Adrian Boult. The Royal Philharmonic Society awarded her its gold medal and she received honorary doctorates from Cambridge, Durham, London, Manchester, Leeds and St. Andrews universities.

Hess had rather a mixed personality. Although she was a hardworking student and musician, she developed an outrageous sense of humour to go along with a rebellious streak. Her penchant for Rabelaisian stories, vulgar jokes and smoking in public would appear to be a reaction to a strict Orthodox Jewish upbringing.[29] She took pleasure in being vulgar, funny, raunchy and crude. She went out of her way to tweak the social mores of her time. She delighted in smoking in public at a time when nice Jewish girls and older female concert artists did not do so.[30]

Her parents had a rather idiosyncratic interpretation of traditional Jewish practice which included eating any meat as long as it was not pork or ham while at the same time not allowing travel on the Sabbath, including riding a bicycle. Hess's attitude to religion was complex. She rejected Orthodox Judaism but said she never forgot it and was proud of her Jewish ancestry. She considered that it was impossible for an artist to keep the orthodox faith strictly but she looked back on those religious times in her home as happy times. She had great self-discipline with regard to her work and she attributed this to her strict Jewish upbringing. 'That has always been my saving'.[31] Hess became increasingly drawn to Christianity through the teachings of the American Episcopalian Theodore Parker Ferris. Although she considered baptism she did not convert to Christianity believing the act could be construed as desertion of her fellow Jews.[32] Harold Rosenthal writes that she never lost her Jewishness and it was her great spiritual beliefs that made her playing of Bach so memorable. When her mother died her agent sent her a large cross formed of white roses and Hess pulled every rose from it.

She did give her support to some Jewish causes and these included a concert at the Cambridge Theatre, London in support of the work of the Jewish National Fund and the Federation of Women Zionists.[33] She was a member of the arts group of the Friends of the Hebrew University[34] and president of the musical section of the Jewish Arts Society.[35]

She never married though both Jewish American violinist Mischa Elman and Jewish Russian born British pianist Benno Moiseiwitsch wanted to marry her.[36] She maintained close relationships with openly lesbian composers and musicians of the day such as Maude Valerie White and Irene Scharrer. With that said, little is known about the truth of Myra's sexuality. Most historians accept the fact of her 'intense relationships with women' and yet are reluctant to label her as a lesbian historical figure.[37]

Her friends and family remember her as a loyal and funny woman who always had time for others despite her unwavering commitment to her art. On stage she was a model of dignity and compassion. But once the performance was over she would relax, often treating her friends to an array of parlour tricks, She was much loved for her earthy sense of humour, her ear for accents and her range of impressions which included an imitation of Queen Victoria for which she wore a lace doily. Sir Paul Mason, former British ambassador to Holland, recalls when Hess played Chopin's Black Key Etude at an Embassy dinner party. He heard a guest whisper to his neighbour that he thought Hess was losing her technique, as at the time she was nearly 70. He was not to know that Hess was playing with an orange concealed in the palm of her right hand.[38]

Hess died on 25 November 1965. She had made her mark in a male dominated profession and her courage had mirrored the indomitable spirit of the British people during the Second World War. Among the women pianists of the world none held a higher place in public approval and affection than Hess.[39] She could open doors for the unsophisticated listener with her own much loved arrangement of Bach's *Jesu, Joy of Man's Desiring*, whose score is now in the British Library. The following incident illustrates how wide a public she reached. A man shared a train with a soldier whistling the above mentioned piece and he asked the soldier whether he enjoyed Bach's music. The soldier replied: 'That's not Bach. That's Myra Hess'.[40]

Novelist Amanda Craig considers Hess to be her most inspiring heroine. Her work introduced many people who had never heard classical music before to some of the greatest works ever composed. 'Her courage in playing through air raids and her indomitable strength as a pianist made me think of a flame in the dark that refused to be put out'.[41] Composer Vaughan Williams said that her perception of the need of music in war time sprang out of her profound understanding, as a great artist, of the need for music at all times.[42] The affection in which she was held everywhere was underlined on many occasions, such as when she had an emergency gall bladder operation in Chicago. All radio programmes were changed and her records were broadcast throughout the morning of the operation.[43]

Another pianist and teacher who believed in the power of music and brought joy to millions was Fanny Waterman. Although they shared a strong Jewish heritage she had grown up in a very different household to Hess who belonged to a wealthy and established Anglo-Jewry family whereas Waterman was the child of poor immigrant parents. They both shared the same tenacity to deal with any obstacles that came their way.

Fanny Waterman (1920-2020)

Dame Fanny Waterman was renowned across the musical globe as the founder of the Leeds International Piano Competition, one of the most coveted prizes in music. She was a pianist and teacher who lived all her long life in Leeds and wielded profound and extensive influence through the celebrated contest. It developed an unrivalled reputation for musical integrity over the decades, bringing to prominence artists including Murray

Perahia, Andras Schiff and more recently Frederico Colli and Eric Lu.[44] She became one of the most prominent personalities in the musical world and was piano teacher to millions through her iconic series of tuition piano lesson books which included 30 volumes and inspired generations of musicians.

Fanny was born in 1920 into a Russian Jewish family in Leeds. Her father Myer Waterman (the original name was Wasserman) was born in 1892 in Berdichev, Ukraine. He came to Britain in 1909 and worked as a jeweller in London's Hatton Garden which was one of the centres of the world's diamond trade. He married Mary Behrman, also of Russian Jewish origins and moved to Leeds where his older brothers Isaac and Nahman had set up a tailoring business and his sister Raisel was their seamstress. Myer set up his own business.

The Jewish community in Leeds is generally regarded to have been established in 1840 by wool and cloth merchants of German origin as Leeds was then an important wool manufacturing area. The railways had come to the town in 1834 which helped its rapid development as an industrial centre. A tailoring industry was established in the 1850s and began to attract immigrant workers. The 1891 census revealed that the Jewish population had increased to almost 8,000 with 72% involved in tailoring and the remainder in slipper making, cabinet making and hawking. The Leeds Jewish community was predominantly working class and peaked at some 22,000-25,000 by the late 1920s.[45]

Fanny's family observed the religious festivals and ate kosher food but her father had to work on the Sabbath. The family were poor. Fanny remembers going to the grocery shop with her mother who cried when she did not have enough money to pay the bill. They lived in a house without an indoor bathroom and shared a toilet with five neighbours. 'I didn't realise we were rock bottom'. Her parents loved music and even though they were unable to play an instrument they had an upright piano in the front room.[46]

Fanny recalls that she was a happy child who would dance around the table to the music of Henry Hall and the BBC Dance Orchestra. She started to play the piano at the age of four and would climb on the stool and play *Tiptoe Through the Tulips* and songs that she had heard on the radio. Her parents did all they could to nurture her talent and scraped together the little spare money that they had for piano lessons although her early piano lessons were farcical as the teacher, instead of concentrating on her pupil, spent her time cooking. Fanny constantly wanted to play. 'I remember being on a tram and kneeling on the seat and rippling my fingers on the seat in front as though I were playing. From an early age, I wanted to ripple the notes'.[47] She insisted that she was not a prodigy. 'Prodigies were people like Beethoven and Mozart. There is a difference between prodigy and gifted. I had talent. My parents did all they could to help'. As a result the family could not afford to move house and there were no luxuries.[48] Her parents took her to hear great musicians when they came to perform at Leeds Town Hall and she heard pianist Rachmaninoff and violinist Heifetz when she was eight years old. 'I remember the atmosphere as much as the playing. It was magical'.[49]

She went to Chapel Allerton High School for Girls. 'They let me play the piano for prayers every day for six years even though I was Jewish. Our headmistress used to give us homilies on making the best of our talents and those six years turned me as a young child into a perfectionist'. When she was 18 the music critic of the *Yorkshire Post* who had heard her play suggested that she should have lessons with Myra Hess. This shows that Hess had a reputation as a noteworthy teacher. He wrote to Hess but she said she was too busy to take Fanny on as a pupil herself but recommended her own legendary teacher Tobias Matthay[50] and she went to have lessons with him in London.[51] Her father could only afford for her to have an occasional half hour lesson with him.[52] In 1940 she won a scholarship to the Royal College of Music, studying with Cyril Smith and she graduated with a glittering testimonial: 'a brilliantly gifted pianist and musician who will be a source of inspiration to her pupils'.[53] She recalls how her time there had a great influence on her.[54] She won important prizes and awards and was invited to play at the Proms in 1942 with Sir Henry Wood conducting. This was a great honour for such a young student and she gave many more memorable recitals and was a frequent broadcaster.[55]

Her performances were curtailed when she was informed by the College's director George Dyson that there was a possibility that she could be called up into the Women's Land Army but she might be exempt if she was in a reserve profession such as teaching. She returned to Leeds and taught at her old school. Forty of her pupils sat for music exams and all received distinctions.[56]

In all probability Fanny could have had her own solo concert playing career rather than becoming a piano teacher. The decision was taken out of her hands when she met and married a London doctor Geoffrey de Keyser in 1944 at the Leeds Beth Hamedrash. Geoffrey, whose family originated from Lithuania and Latvia, had set up a practice in Leeds and was committed to his Yorkshire patients. Fanny was happy to stay in Leeds rather than move to London and decided to devote herself to teaching. She made a conscious decision that she would rather be happily married to a doctor than a successful concert pianist touring the world, living out of a suitcase and being at home with her two sons Robert and Paul, and she never regretted that decision. 'In life there is a left turning and a right turning and some people choose the wrong one. I think I was lucky. In the big things in life I always made the right and best decision'.[57]

Some of her pupils began to secure prestigious engagements at the Festival Hall and Edinburgh Festival and gradually the word spread that if your child had any talent, Fanny would tease it out. She said she would handpick the parents and not the students as however talented someone was unless they had fine teaching and parental support they would not be successful.[58] All her pupils were from Leeds. 'When they got older they considered me the local teacher and went to London to have lessons'. It would appear that Fanny decided at this point that she wanted to establish herself further and work on a grander scale.[59]

The inspiration to create the Leeds competition came to her one night in 1961 when she could not sleep. When she mentioned the idea to her husband he thought that it should be held in London but Fanny disagreed. She considered that London was too big and it would have been difficult to get the competitors from one end of the city to the other and there would be a problem getting volunteers. She developed the idea with Countess Marion Harewood whose children she had been teaching.[60] She had already teamed up with Marion to write a series of piano lesson books. Together they drummed up a corps of volunteers and a jury.[61] Marion and Fanny shared not only musicianship but a background of emigration.

Marion Harewood CBE (1926-2014) was married to George Lascalles, 7th Earl of Harewood. The daughter of musician Erwin Stein, who had worked closely with the composer Arnold Schoenberg, the family had fled Vienna in 1938 and came to London. Erwin Stein took a job with music publisher Boosey and Hawkes and was an early mentor of Benjamin Britten.

Marion studied at the Royal College of Music and became a noted concert pianist, known for her performances of Mozart and Schubert, Bach and Mahler. It was through Benjamin Britten, at the first of his festivals at Aldeburgh in Suffolk in 1948, that she met George VI's musical nephew George Lascalles, 11th in line to the throne and son of the King's sister Princess Mary and her husband Henry, the 6th Earl of Harewood. They married at St Mark's Church, Mayfair the following year.[62] She moved from London to the grand country estate of Harewood House near Leeds where she lived with her mother-in-law Princess Mary, the then Princess Royal. Initial relations were frosty with the Princess Royal reportedly remarking that her new daughter-in-law was 'not only Jewish… she doesn't hunt'. The

Steins were one of the most prominent Jewish families in inter-war Vienna. Laurence Brass, a former treasurer of the Board of Deputies, commented that although Marion doubtless preferred playing the piano to baking challah, she was fiercely proud of her Jewish heritage.[63] She gave up her concert career in favour of raising her family. Marion and Lascalles divorced in 1967 and she married Jeremy Thorpe, the Liberal Party leader in the 1970s.

The first Leeds competition was held in 1963. Funds were raised from banks, businesses, the City Council and the University of Leeds. From the start Fanny conceived of the competition, which is held every three years and became known as 'The Leeds', as a means to foster musical values that she had cultivated as a performer and teacher. The competition was an immediate success with 94 entrants from 23 countries,. Over the years the competition joined the ranks of the world's elite contests, including the Van Cliburn, Tchaikovsky and Chopin. Such competitions are major springboards for careers in music and one finalist who became a major artist was Andras Schiff.

It was during the third competition in 1969 that Fanny asserted herself after the Romanian pianist Radu Lupu came fourth in the second round which meant he would not advance to the finals. Deeply impressed by Lupu's playing, she insisted that the number of finalists be increased from three to five and vowed not to organise another competition unless he made the cut. She got her way and Lupu wound up winning and going on to a distinguished career.[64]

Murray Perahia, an American of Sephardi Jewish origin, won the competition in 1972. Fanny said that he was the perfect illustration of the importance of competitions for any young musician as there were very few great pianists who have had a career without winning a prize in a major competition. In spite of playing twice with the New York Philharmonic he could not get a foothold in Europe. Playing in Leeds gave him the chance he was looking for. Before the competition was over, the impresarios descended on Leeds and tried to sign him up. Nevertheless Fanny admitted that winning the Leeds does not bestow magic fairy dust. All it can do is offer the winner the opportunity to showcase his or her talent in the upscale concert engagements which form part of the prize package.[65]

The Leeds became big business, part of the international music circuit embraced by the civic leaders and receiving corporate sponsorship. It also relied on a huge army of volunteers who acted as drivers, stewards, programme sellers, messengers, interpreters and lenders of pianos for competitors to practise on.[66]

Fanny became known amongst her volunteers as 'Field Marshal Fanny' and much of the competition's success story can be traced directly to her mix of will power and charisma. She remained its chairman and artistic director until her retirement in 2015 at the age of 95. She served frequently on juries of piano competitions around the world and gave masterclasses worldwide.[67] She became Dame Commander of the Order of the British Empire in 2005 for her services to music.

Her magnificent eight bedroom Victorian house in Oakwood, a suburb of Leeds, was the venue for many lively musical soirees that over the years included guests such as composer Benjamin Britten, tenor Peter Pears and Prime Minister Edward Heath.[68] It was a far cry from her humble beginnings. She always expressed gratitude to the values she learnt from her parents. 'We were never well off but my parents gave me a priceless gift and that was never to value anything that money can buy but to value good health, talent, integrity, reliability'.[69] She continued this principle making no distinction between people on grounds of their wealth or background.

She came from an immigrant Jewish background and although she was not religiously observant she never lost her affection for Jewish culture.[70] She belonged to the United Hebrew Congregation in Leeds and the Blanche Dugdale WIZO group. As part of a traditional Jewish family Fanny wore her Jewish roots on her sleeve. She remarked that everyone knew that she was Jewish but she considered that music was her religion because it united everyone and there was no barrier of race, sex and age and that it was the biggest power in her life.[71]

Fanny was proud of what she had done for Leeds. She said that when friends went abroad and mentioned they were from Leeds, they were often asked whether that was where the competition was held. 'We have put Leeds on the map'.[72] The city recognised her contribution by awarding her the Freedom of the City of Leeds in 2004, the first person to be granted the Freedom since Nelson Mandela seven years previously and the only woman apart from the late Princess Mary. The award was made for her 'sheer determination and energy in establishing Leeds as home to one of the world's premier music competitions'.[73] Her motto in life was 'You don't stop working because you grow old. You grow old because you stop working'.[74] Fanny, who was still teaching in her 90s, considered that teaching was the greatest profession in the world. 'What greater pleasure is there in life than giving a young person a little direction in the direction of his stars?'[75]

Fanny died on 20 December 2020. Adam Gatehouse, artistic director of the Leeds competition, commented that from nothing she had created the world's most prestigious piano competition and chose to do so not in

London but in Leeds which at that time was a dark industrial city. The lives that she touched through the competition and her piano books were too numerous to mention.[76] Field Marshall Fanny was a force of nature.

When Myra Hess started her career it was still at a time when female musicians were struggling to be recognised in the musical profession. Her work with the Society of Women Musicians, which was continued by Fanny Waterman, ensured an easier path for future generations and for women such as cellist Natalie Clein.

Natalie Clein (1977 –)

Natalie Clein came to widespread attention at the age of 16 when she won the BBC Young Musician of the Year in 1994. She made her concert debut at the Proms in 1997 and in 1999 was invited as one of the first artists to join the BBC Radio 3 New Generation Artists Scheme. She is regarded as one of the finest talents of her generation.

Born in Poole in 1977, Natalie comes from a musical family. Her mother Chaya (Salamonson) is a professional violinist and her father Peter, a doctor who studied at Cambridge as an undergraduate and researcher is a passionate viola player.[77] His grandparents had come to Ireland from Lithuania and settled in Dublin for several generations before his family came to London where he was born and raised.[78] Natalie's mother was born in Holland at the beginning of the Second World War and she and her sister were taken in by different Christian families at the beginning of the war when her grandmother went into hiding. Her grandmother and grandfather, respectively an architect and an actress, were cared for by members of the Resistance in Amsterdam and later reunited with their children.[79] Chaya was a member of the Netherlands Chamber Orchestra and first came to London when she toured with the ensemble. She met her husband in London when she gave him music lessons at Morley College.[80] 'I am sure her experience had a bearing on the intensity of our childhood'. She considered Natalie and her sister to be very precious and Natalie felt very treasured.[81]

String playing was part of Natalie's life for as long as she can remember. Her parents played string quartets at home and she used to fall asleep on the sofa with the sounds of Schubert and Beethoven. She took up the cello aged six and rapidly proved that she was prodigiously talented. She found that the cello was exciting for her as it was different from the instruments that her parents played.[82] Her first public concert was when she was ten in a church hall in Dorset.[83] She knew from the age of 12 that she wanted to be a professional cellist. 'It became an extremely private world. It takes years of dedication and focus before you are happy on the stage.'[84]

After winning the 1994 Young Musician of the Year with her performance of Elgar's Cello Concerto at the Barbican, she was the first British winner of the Eurovision Competition for Young Musicians held in Warsaw that year. At the time she was described by *Strad* magazine as 'an assured and precocious musical talent'. She was awarded the Queen Elizabeth the Queen Mother Scholarship by the Royal College of Music and completed her studies with Heinrich Schiff in Vienna. A decade of triumphs followed, topped by a Classical Brit award for the most promising young performer of 2005. She is a regular chamber musician with the Belcea Quartet, Jerusalem Quartet and the Nash Ensemble and has performed with orchestras that include the Philharmonia, Halle, Bournemouth Symphony, BBC National Orchestra of Wales, Montreal Symphony and New Zealand Symphony. In 2015 she secured a four year appointment as Artist in Residence and Director of Musical Performance at Oxford University. She is also a professor at the Royal College of Music and artistic director of the Purbeck Chamber Music Festival in Dorset.

Natalie was brought up in Poole and is forever drawn back to her native Dorset.[85] Although there were few other Jewish families there, she enjoyed a culturally Jewish upbringing and would visit London every Passover to spend time with her paternal cousins.[86] Natalie's sister actress Louisa Clein[87] explains that because of their mother's experiences she was adamant that the two girls were not brought up to be seen as different.[88] Their upbringing was not very Jewish as such as being Jewish was not something you celebrated. 'But being the first generation afterwards I feel it is something very important because of the fact we survived and because it is such a big part of who we are.'[89]

Natalie considers that her Jewish background has been a source of creative inspiration. One recording of cello music had declared Jewish connections. The composers are twentieth century Swiss American Ernest Bloch whose *Scenes from a Jewish Life, Rhapsodie Hebraique* and *Schelomo* all feature.[90] Ernest Bloch's music draws deeply on Jewish traditions and folklore.[91] The spiritual connection intrigues Natalie. 'His music is like the Jewish soul, it speaks to me. The cello sounds like the cantor's voice.'[92] The recording also features the earlier German Romantic Max Bruch's *Kol Nidrei,* inspired by a text from the service for Yom Kippur. Natalie is intrigued by the fact that Bruch was not Jewish and born and raised a Christian. He simply took an interest in Judaic liturgy and music.[93] It is the cultural rather than religious aspects of this repertory that attracted her.

'I was born into a Jewish family that was completely non-religious but my background still means something to me. And being European Jewish, as Bloch was, involves a sense of division that can be a great source of creative energy. One of the things I've tried to do in the recording is to discover what it meant for Bloch not in terms of antisemitism or the Holocaust but simply trying to establish what was his specific voice as a composer'. When asked if this was another way of saying that it is helpful to be Jewish if you are playing a Jewish repertory, she explained that if she agreed with such a viewpoint, she would have a problem with everything else that she did as her last recording was Kodaly's Cello Concerto and she is not Hungarian. She did not think there were boundaries. Musicians have to be like actors; they get into role and find between the music and themselves something that resonates. The reason she did the Kodaly recording is that she was interested in the issues of nationalism and identity that were circulating at the turn of the nineteenth and twentieth centuries and the Bloch/Bruch recording was also about exploring identity.[94]

Her Jewish identity was evident when interviewed by the *Jewish Chronicle* about how she would spend her time during the Rosh Hashana festival. She said that she would sit and read through some prayers and take some time to think, eat apple and honey and would endeavour to get to a synagogue if her performance schedule allowed. She reflected that she always got a feeling of spiritual renewal at Rosh Hashana, an energising feeling that was really beautiful. 'I treasure the day. A new pathway has opened and it is a real gift to have that and the connection to my Jewish heritage'.[95] Her support for Jewish charities have included a concert in 2005 that raised funds for the Israel Sports Centre for the Disabled for the rehabilitation of children hurt in terror attacks and a concert for Jewish Care's Holocaust Survivors' Centre in 2008.

She performed at the Holocaust Memorial concert at the South Bank Centre in 2002. Such participation had a certain poignancy due to her mother's history. 'My mother's family was mentally devastated by the Holocaust'. The concert featured a selection of chamber music pieces for strings and piano written by Jewish composers who died in the concentration camps. She remarked that she felt very close to the music. The pieces were interspersed with extracts from the *Holocaust Trilogy* by her cousin playwright Julia Pascal[96]. With regard to her Jewish identity, she commented that 'it's not something I can analyse. It's just part of me'.[97]

Natalie and her sister took part in the 2020 BBC documentary *My Family, the Holocaust and Me* in which Robert Rinder, lawyer and television presenter, helps Jewish families discover the truth about what happened to their relatives during the Holocaust. They travelled to the Netherlands where they learnt about their grandmother's work in the Resistance and about their great aunt Els who taught contemporary dance. Els was sent to the transit prison camp Westerbok in 1943 as a punished inmate as it is believed that she refused to wear the yellow star. She was subsequently murdered in Sobibor. Natalie and Louisa, who were overcome with emotion during the filming, considered that it was a great privilege to have taken part as they knew very little about Els beforehand. They came away with a feeling of pride that they had come from that family.[98]

When Natalie visited Cologne for work she loved seeing the 'stumbling stones', the bronze Holocaust memorial squares on the pavement.[99] She found them strangely reassuring, a record of an inhabitant that lived where the stone was with the person's date of birth, date of arrest or expulsion and usually which concentration camp they died in. She considers Germany's ability to confront its past is one reason why she felt so comfortable there.[100] The Jewish Museum in Berlin is one of her favourite museums in the world as she considers it is a beautiful building where anything feels possible.[101]

In a similar vein to Fanny Waterman, she is passionate about teaching 'It helps me to understand how to do things better myself. It challenges technical and musical questions. I am constantly digging for more depth and meaning. This is what excites me'.[102] She wants her students to develop unique voices and to try and help them play in a way that reflects who they are and how they emotionally react to a score as well as how to understand it.[103]

Natalie does not consider classical music elitist. 'I want to inspire conversation. I want to challenge people'. She feels a burden of responsibility to help her audience understand and love the music as much as she does. 'I always talk about the pieces before I play them to give them a context. Some people will know a lot about the pieces but some people might be at a concert for the first time in their lives and I want to speak to both. The audience gives me energy. Some performers are happy to do their perfect piece behind a pane of glass. And they are usually incredible musicians but that is not me'.[104]

Natalie, who received an OBE for services to music in the 2021 honours list, is interested in all types of art forms and regularly works with contemporary composers. She has curated and been involved in cross disciplinary projects that have included the director Deborah Warner, the dancer Carlos Acosta and writer Jeanette Winterson which utilises Bach's *Goldberg Variations* in conjunction with Winterson's text. Her music continues to give great pleasure to classical music lovers with the description of her musical prowess as 'a graceful lyrical player with a sound like a fine spun silver thread'[105] and 'as close as you will get to musical champagne'.[106]

Conclusion

Myra Hess and Fanny Waterman were icons in the musical world, showing great stubbornness to overcome whatever obstacles were in their way. Hess was considered a trailblazer because of the numerous concerts she gave during the Nazi bombardments in London that became a great morale booster. She became a symbol of resistance facing the horrors of war. Waterman was a trailblazer to create an international competition in a city that did not even have a resident orchestra compared to London with its music conservatories and international concert hall. At the time of its inception there were few international competitions worldwide.

They came from different social backgrounds. Hess was third generation to be brought up in England and enjoyed the trappings of an affluent household whilst growing up whereas Waterman, daughter of immigrants, was brought up in poverty. Despite their reduced circumstances she wished that her parents could have been there when she, the child of poor Russian immigrants, was granted the Freedom of the City of Leeds in 2004.[107]

They both moved with ease in non-Jewish worlds as music overcame all social barriers. Hess was one of the earliest guests invited to the newly inaugurated Palace luncheons in the late 1950s.

Even before she started the Leeds competition, Waterman had a reputation as a great teacher and her social circle grew. It was at a tea party given by Lady Dorothy Parkinson, niece of Lord Halifax, the last Viceroy of India, that she met Princess Mary. She recalled that Lady Parkinson was truly classless and music was their bond.[108]

Neither were religiously observant but were proud of their Jewish identity. The same applies for Natalie Clein, although her connection as second generation British on her maternal side, is through Holocaust commemoration and she was brought up in a totally non-Jewish environment. She was able to embrace her passion and an acceptable career as a female professional musician due in great part to the groundwork carried out by Hess and Waterman.

5

Artists

Western art before the twentieth century was dominated by male artists. Women artists have historically struggled to have their work recognised. They were often hampered by societal expectation, a difficulty accessing artistic training and a lack of financial independence. Historically painting was viewed as a male profession and it was unusual for women to establish themselves as working painters.

The nineteenth century witnessed a marked increase in the number of professional female artists but opportunities remained limited and limiting. A variety of art schools catering for women were established, such as the Female School of Art and Design in 1842, but these schools were expensive and only accessible to the wealthier classes. While Victorian women certainly had greater access to formal training, there was a pressure to conform to traditional gender roles and live practical, domestic lives.

During the nineteenth century the British art world was dominated by the Royal Academy (RA) that was founded in 1768. Although two of the 34 named founders were women painters, it was not until 1922 that other female artists were included. A woman's place in society was perceived as passive and governed by emotion. In the 1850s the idea that women could be artists was hotly debated by English writer and art critic John Ruskin and others in various journals. Women were not considered as serious contributors to the field of art and had great difficulty in obtaining a public showing. Their education in the arts was limited and they had been excluded from the practice of drawing from the nude figure since the RA was founded. After much debate and petitioning, the RA agreed to provide life classes 'for the study of the partially draped figure' to female students but it was a further 10 years before women were admitted to these classes.[1]

In the early 1900s women began to enjoy comparable success with their male counterparts. The roots of this lay in the Victorian era when those born, raised and educated in the later decades of the 1800s were able to seize upon the huge changes in society, occurring during a time of burgeoning modernism, transformation and increasing emancipation.[2]

Jewish female artists had to overcome many obstacles to work professionally, one of which was the difficulty of obtaining art lessons. Even so, in 1906 over one-third of the paintings exhibited at the Jewish Art and Antiquities at the Whitechapel Art Gallery were by women and a year later 16 Jewish women exhibited at the summer Royal Academy Exhibition. This was in spite of the fact that Jewish women had to battle not only on account of their sex, but also because they were adopting careers for which there were few precedents in the Anglo-Jewish community, even among the men. Although a number of Jewish women worked as artists in the period 1850-1940, most came from wealthy backgrounds. The majority of women who painted professionally in the nineteenth century were close relatives of male painters and Jewish women were no exception.[3]

Catherine da Costa (1679-1756) was the first noteworthy female Anglo-Jewish artist. Her father Fernando Mendes came from the town of Trancoso in Portugal, which had a Jewish community surviving as crypto-Jews. Fernando moved from Portugal around 1660, first to France where he studied medicine and then to England in 1669. Jews had been expelled from England in 1290 but Oliver Cromwell allowed them to be readmitted in 1656. Fernando went into business with his very wealthy cousin Alvaro Rodrigues da Costa who was hugely successful trading inside the East India Company. Neither men could be seen to be Jewish if they were to succeed. Fernando was a Catholic and Alvaro became a Protestant. Fernando became doctor to both Charles II and his wife Catherine de Braganza and was provided with his own apartment in Somerset House, the Queen's royal palace in London. Catherine de Braganza came from a senior noble house in Portugal and lived there until she married King Charles II of England in 1662. An article of the marriage treaty was that Queen Catherine was allowed to practise her faith; her chapels in St James Palace and Somerset House were the only two places in London where Catholics could legally worship.

Fernando married Isabel Rodrigues Marques, daughter of a devout Jewish merchant. Their first child Catherine was born in Somerset House. Queen Catherine who could not have any children was delighted with the little girl and asked that she be called Catherine. Although she was baptised on the orders of the Queen, she was given the Jewish name of Rachel and she married her cousin Moses de Costa, a wealthy merchant, in a synagogue and was buried in Mile End Jewish cemetery. She studied painting under the miniaturist and court painter Bernard Lens III which led to her specialising in miniature portraits. Lens was the first British artist to replace vellum, the most common material for miniatures, with ivory.

Da Costa was well regarded as a painter and impressed the French writer and satirist Voltaire with her wit when he visited London in the 1720s. He recorded an exchange between her and a priest in his notebooks.

Madame Acosta said in my presence to a cleric hoping to convert her to Christianity:

'Was your God born Jewish?'

'Yes.'

'Did he die Jewish?'

'Yes.'

'Well then, become Jewish.'[4]

Most of her surviving works are portraits of family and friends.

Rebecca Solomon (1832-1886)

Among the first women from a Jewish background to make a prominent career as a painter in Britain is Rebecca Solomon who was born into a prosperous Jewish family in Bishopsgate, East London. Her father was Michael (Meyer) Solomon, a hat manufacturer and the first Jew to be honoured with the Freedom of the City of London. The Solomon family immigrated to England from the Low Countries in the eighteenth century. She was one of eight children and her brothers were the artists Abraham Solomon and Simeon Solomon[5]. They were encouraged by their mother Kate (Catherine) Levy who was an amateur miniature painter.

Although she was barred from a formal artistic education, she was affiliated with the Pre-Raphaelites, worked in the studios of John Everett Millais and Edward Burne-Jones and exhibited regularly at the RA summer exhibition between 1852 and 1869. She was deeply concerned with inequality in Victorian Britain and campaigned for social justice and was part of a group of 38 artists who petitioned the RA to open its schools to women where both her brothers studied.

Rebecca Solomon's success as a professional artist was remarkable in the mid-nineteenth century, a time when women artists were the exception rather than the rule. While her artistic style conformed to the most popular art of the time – scenes from everyday life known as genre paintings – she used the images to critique ethnic, gender and class prejudice in Victorian England.[6] In 2023 her painting *A Young Teacher* (1861) representing a young white girl reading a book to her black maid was acquired by the Tate and Museum of the Home for the national collection and will be held equally by both institutions. The work is characteristic of Solomon's interest in social issues and marginalized groups. The painting is a reflection on gender, race, religion and education in mid-nineteenth century London. As with many of her works it considers women who worked in better off households as professional carers. It modifies a traditional domestic scene between mother and child with the surrounding books emphasising the theme of learning. The woman at the centre of the image was modelled by Jamaican-born Fanny Eaton, whose mother was a former enslaved woman. She became a prominent muse for many Victorian artists and featured in some of the most iconic paintings of the Pre-Raphaelite period.[7]

Despite being a single Jewish woman, she earned her living working in John Everett Millais' studio as a painter of draperies and exhibited her oils and watercolours. She succeeded in many ways in breaking free of the restrictions and expectations that nineteenth century society imposed on her but ultimately and tragically she was affected by them. She struggled financially and died in an accident, run over by a hansom cab, amid rumours of alcoholism.[8]

Hannah Gluckstein (Gluck) (1895-1978)

Another artist born into a wealthy family was Gluck, the only daughter of Joseph Gluckstein, one of the founders of the British restaurant chain J. Lyons and Co. Her American mother Francesca Halle had musical aspirations but had been forced to give these up on her marriage to conform to the conventions of the family into which she had married. Gluck was determined to escape such a fate and seems to have been convinced that her parents wanted to prevent her becoming an artist although it appears more likely that they were upset by the fact that she refused to conceal that she was a lesbian. She had initially wanted to be a singer but changed her mind after viewing a photograph of a portrait by John Singer Sargent.[9] She had already won drawing prizes at school and her parents agreed that she could attend art school and they chose the St John's Wood School which was close to where they lived. She did not enjoy her studies there and felt restricted at home. After a painting trip to Cornwall where she was encouraged by other women artists, she left home in 1915. She had meagre resources and at this stage began to wear men's clothing and insisted on being known as Gluck. Despite this eccentric behaviour her family soon agreed to support her financially.[10] She was determined to live her own life and to establish herself as a professional artist. Criticism of the family's staid conventional views did not prevent her from accepting a substantial allowance.

Gluck is best known for her portraits and her flower paintings inspired by her liaison with the cookery and flower expert Constance Spry. An affair with an actress led to a series of works showing scenes from the London stage. These works particularly suited the spirit and fashions of the 1920s and 1930s. Her lovers also inspired some of her best portraits, none more so than Nesta Obermer, the love of her life.[11]

Gluck was one of the most mercurial and rebellious artists of her day. She was unapologetic in her work, her desires and her many battles with authority. She abandoned her birth name and requested that Gluck be reproduced with 'no prefix, suffix or quotes'. When the Fine Art Society printed her name as 'Miss Gluck', she threatened to resign and after her exhibition there in 1926 she was angry that critical attention focused more on her looks than on her paintings.

Her hair was habitually cut in an Eton crop and she dressed in androgynous and masculine clothes long after this had ceased to be fashionably avant-garde. The photographer Emil Otto Hoppe, who encouraged her to exhibit her work, wrote of her in *The Royal Magazine* in 1926 'to look at her face is to understand both her success as an artist and the fact that she dresses as a man. Originality, determination, strength of character and artistic insight are expressed in every line'.[12]

After considerable acclaim in the 1920s and 1930s, Gluck disappeared from the artistic scene, apparently dried up and forgotten. Towards the end of her life she enjoyed a new spurt of energy and in 1973 persuaded the Fine Art Society to hold an exhibition after a break of 35 years. It was a great success and critics hailed a lost English painter. Five years later Gluck was dead, assured of her small but permanent niche in twentieth century British art.[13]

Rachel Lichtenstein (1969 –)

Rachel Lichtenstein is an artist, writer and curator known for her books, multi-media projects and artworks that examine place, memory and Jewish identity. She trained as a sculptor and her artwork has been widely exhibited both in the UK and internationally. She currently combines writing and research with a post as Reader in the English and History departments at Manchester Metropolitan University where she co-directs the Centre for Place Writing. She has worked as an archivist and historian at Sandy's Road Synagogue, London and her publications include *Rodinsky's Room* (1999), *On Brick Lane* (2007), *Diamond Street: The Hidden World of Hatton Garden* (2012) and *Estuary: Out from London to the Sea* (2016).

Born in Westcliff, the daughter of a Hatton Garden jeweller, she studied sculpture at Sheffield University. Her grandfather's death in 1987 resulted in Lichtenstein becoming determined to safeguard her Jewish heritage. She first changed her surname by deed poll back to his, from the anglicised Laurence which her father and his brothers had adopted in the late 1960s. When she told her grandfather she was changing her name 'he beamed from ear to ear and told me how happy he was'. Lichtenstein, whose mother is not Jewish, grew up aware that she was 'partly Jewish' and her family celebrated the festivals until her grandfather died. 'Then it stopped. I think that had a huge effect on me. It was something mysterious and beautiful. I suppose growing up with these stories, being very aware that both my grandparents were from Poland, that they'd lost lots of family meant that my Jewish identity was connected to the Holocaust. I had this strong sense that if I didn't take my Jewish identity on board it would be lost, after they had been through so much. I wanted to find out more'.[14]

As a young art student she chose to work on projects connected with her roots, an idea which was then unfashionable. In 1991 she won a prize at an exhibition for young Jewish artists with a memorial to her grandfather for which she embedded in wax small possessions of his, such as his glasses and watch, thereby creating a beautiful and original *yahrzeit* (memorial) candle.[15]

She became fascinated with the history of the Jewish East End after moving there in the 1990s, tracing the footsteps of her grandparents Gedaliah and Malka, Polish Jewish immigrants who met and married in the area in the 1920s. She worked to preserve the Princelet Street Synagogue which had been in use from 1870 to 1964. When she first visited the Synagogue she expected to find a museum, archive and library and found instead a building with peeling paint, a brown door with no bell and no indication of what was inside. 'The experience of entering the synagogue was totally overwhelming. I knew I was meant to be there. I later found out that my grandparents had their first marital home and watchmaking shop in Princelet Street'.[16]

On that first visit she learnt about David Rodinsky, who had lived above the synagogue until his mysterious disappearance in 1969, the year she was born. He had become somewhat of a mystery ever since his locked room was opened in 1980 and found exactly as he had left it, with a half-finished cup of solidified tea beside the unmade bed and remains of a near-fossilised pan of porridge on the stove that testified to an abrupt departure. The scene was one of chaos and decay; books, newspapers, records and scraps of paper with jottings in many languages. Little was known about the man whose room contained more than 50 cases of books. Yet there were many indications that Rodinsky was a fine linguist with knowledge of more than 15 languages, some of which were no longer spoken.[17]

Lichtenstein managed to persuade the committee in charge of the building to allow her to become an unpaid artist in residence. Initially she was so overwhelmed by the atmosphere that she was unable to work and instead decided to catalogue Rodinsky's belongings, trying to create a picture of who he was. As some were difficult to describe, such as the Egyptian hieroglyphics on the back of a chocolate wrapper, she began to photograph them. At the same time she became intrigued about what happened to Rodinsky and the project inspired her to research her own origins in Poland as well as his. She subsequently wrote *Rodinsky's Room* in collaboration with Iain Sinclair[18] which reveals a sad tale of how his mother was marked by her experiences in the pogroms,how his sister ended her life in a psychiatric hospital and that he had probably died alone, in a Victorian asylum in Surrey, and was buried in a pauper's grave. She finished the book just before giving birth to a son, whom she named David in his memory.[19]

Lichtenstein has been involved in creating a memory map of the Jewish East End that was launched in 2020.[20] It is an online interactive map that allows users to explore former sites of Jewish memory in London's Jewish East End. On it are audio interviews, photographs and essays about more than 70 sites that consistently appear in people's recollections of the area. The project is a collaboration between Lichtenstein and researchers within three different research units at the Bartlett Faculty for the Built Environment at University College, London University of London.[21] It is a wonderful resource for people interested in exploring the memories and history of Jewish culture and a great testament to Lichtenstein's endeavours to keep the area's rich history alive.

Jewish women, like all women, faced many obstacles in entering the male-dominated art world. From the Renaissance to the nineteenth century, only a few exceptional women artists ever achieved recognition or fame, often only because a male relative who was an established painter had given them training. Even those who acquired the necessary instruction were generally limited to a narrow range of 'women's' subjects: portraiture (usually of other women), flower painting or still lifes, and paintings of domestic scenes and subjects. Denied full membership in the influential royal academies, women struggled to make themselves seen in the world of fine art. Rebecca Solomon and Hannah Gluckstein benefitted from the revolutionary new art movements that arose in the late nineteenth century, which offered new opportunities to women artists. Despite the fact that British Jewish women remain under-represented in the contemporary art world, Rachel Lichtenstein's career demonstrates the strides that Jewish women artists have made in the twentieth and twentieth-first centuries.

6

Sport

One area of British life not usually associated with the Jewish community is sports and recreation. Despite the recognition given to individual athletes such as Harold Abrahams,[1] the idea of Jewish involvement and interest in sport ran counter to perceptions of British and other Jews. Jews were thought of as doctors, lawyers and businessmen but not as athletes. A misconception has long existed that Jews excel in intellectual pursuits and not the physical. The stereotype has historical roots. In Greek and Roman times, sports were associated with idol worship and Jewish texts from the post-biblical and Talmudic periods are critical of sporting activities.[2]

Throughout British history stereotypes and perceptions of Jews focused on their physical weakness as evidenced by Shakespeare's Shylock and Dickens' Fagin, emphasising especially the idea of the effeminate but dangerous Jewish male. This viewpoint was shared across Western society. Yet in Britain, from the period of mass immigration in the 1880s, there was an increased Jewish involvement in sports at both elite and amateur levels including sporting heroes in the boxing world like Daniel Mendoza.[3] Jews also participated as businessmen, administrators and sports spectators[4] such as the involvement of wealthy Jewish families as race goers and stable owners. During the first half of the twentieth century, Britain produced British, European, Empire and World Champions and football played a major role in shaping British-Jewish identity with its 'anglicising' influence. All these sports were male dominated.

The participation of Jews in British sport was not without difficulties. Sport was an arena for social, non-organised expressions of antisemitism from the 1890s onwards. Antisemitic sport propaganda emerged in the 1930s among right wing organisations such as the British Union of Fascists, which derided the Jews' supposed lack of sportsmanship and condemned Jewish managerial control over sports generally. These ideas reinforced notions of Jews as 'the other' and 'different' which remained after the post-war period. Middle-class sports clubs discriminated against Jews by enacting subtle but pervasive exclusionary measures and Jewish applicants often met with rejection. In 1958 Frank Davis, a local Liberal councillor accused Conservatives of tolerating the blackballing of Jews at the Finchley Golf Club, London. Alan Cohen, the then Liberal leader of Finchley Council arranged for two or three Jewish members with a good handicap to apply and they were rejected. Shirley Porter, together with her friend Freda Gold, extended the campaign across north London by applying to ten golf clubs and they were turned down each time, fobbed off with lame excuses such as there were no vacancies or the ladies' section had become suddenly filled. The Council then had the evidence and told the golf clubs in the area that their licences would not be renewed if they continued their discrimination.[5]

Jews entering into the middle-classes also faced considerable discrimination in their other leisure choices. Clubs, such as a large motoring club in Middlesbrough introduced a quota for Jewish membership. During the period from the 1890s through to the 1960s there were numerous examples of Jews being openly or secretly discriminated against and finding their entrance into tennis, badminton and squash organisations blocked due to antisemitic membership policies,[6] forcing many Jews to form their own institutions.[7] The Sunderland Jewish Badminton Club was founded in 1954 due to antisemitism in local clubs and Jews in Birmingham playing squash were forced to create their own establishment, the Wingate Club, because they could not gain entry to local clubs due to their ethnicity.[8]

Sections of non-Jewish society felt threatened by the presence of Jews in their social strata and responded by outright banning or enacting exclusionary measures to keep Jews out of their milieu. Jews may have achieved social mobility but they still faced sporting discrimination as they carried the stigma of perceived difference.[9] Given this background, it is impressive that the three Jewish women featured in this chapter made headline news in their sporting fields: Dorothy Levitt and Sheila van Damm, who were pioneers in female motor racing and Angela Buxton in the world of tennis.

Dorothy Levitt (1882-1922)

In the early twentieth century the opportunities for handling a racing car were few and far between which meant that the chance of a woman getting behind a wheel was practically non-existent.[10] They had to fight prejudice and bias in a sport dominated by men. For many years women drivers had to face claims that they would spoil the macho image of the sport; that they would be unable to handle powerful cars safely at speed; that they had neither the stamina nor the physique to withstand the rigours imposed on drivers during races and that they would be a danger to themselves and to other drivers if they were allowed to take part. Even when the first purpose built motor-racing track in the world opened in Britain at Brookland, Surrey in 1907, women were banned from racing there and it was nearly 20 years before the racecourse authorities allowed them to race against men. Overcoming such prejudice demanded a special breed of woman who set about proving their critics wrong by winning races and breaking records.[11] One such woman was Dorothy Levitt.

Dorothy Levitt (1882-1922), born Elizabeth Levi, was the first British woman racing driver, who taught Queen Alexandria and the Royal Princesses how to drive. In 1905 she established the record for the longest drive achieved by a lady driver by driving a De Dion-Bouton from London to Liverpool and back over two days. The press referred to her as the Fastest Girl on Earth and the Champion Lady Motorist of the World. 'She astonished the most daring drivers by her iron nerve and courage'.[12]

Levitt was the daughter of Jacob Levi, a prosperous jeweller, tea dealer and commission agent of Colvestone Crescent, Hackney and Julia Raphael, daughter of a hotelier and retired diamond merchant. A family of Sephardic descent, who came to England in the 1760s, their surname had been changed to Levitt by the time of the 1901 census. (This could have been to make the name less obviously Jewish). During her career, her Jewish origins appear not to have been mentioned directly but her appearance was remarked upon and inferred that she was not a typical English rose. She was described as 'a long-legged beauty with unusually wide eyes which gave her a rather mysterious Oriental look,'[13] 'attractive with long eyes reminding one of the East"[14] and having a look that was 'partly French, partly Irish with a soupcon of American. Yet she is wholly English. A charming winning face'.[15]

Levitt had gone to the Napier Motor Company as a temporary secretary in 1902. Whilst there she caught the eye of Selwyn Edge, the company's managing director, who was one of a small band of British racing enthusiasts who had been competing successfully in Europe. He had been impressed by the considerable amount of publicity Camille du Gast[16] was creating for French cars and felt that an English woman driver, with similar beauty and talent, should be able to do the same for British cars and his company's cars in particular. He chose Levitt because she was strikingly attractive, had a good personality and was keen to be a racing driver.[17] He sent Levitt, who was apparently also his lover, to Paris for six months to learn from his friend Adolphe Clement-Bayard who manufactured cars. She returned as a skilled driver and able car mechanic.[18]

On 3 October 1903 Levitt became the first Englishwoman to win an automobile race, the Southport Speed Trials, clocking a time of approximately 59 mph. The following year she participated in the Hereford 1000 Mile Trial, posing after the race with her Pomeranian dog Dodo who barked at all the other competitors, all male. In 1905 she completed the longest drive achieved by a female driver and hit a speed of 80 mph at the Brighton Sweepstakes. She had a remarkable flair for getting maximum publicity with eye-catching motoring outfits made especially for her. Over the following years she became a well-known figure both on the racing circuit and the gossip columns.[19] She mixed at the highest social levels and her appearances were reported in advance in the court circulars of the *Times*.

Levitt encouraged women to get behind the wheel. She lectured and her book *The Woman and the Car: A Chatty Little Handbook for all Women Who Motor or Who Want to Motor* (1909) recommended that women should 'carry a little hand mirror in a convenient place when driving' so they may 'hold the mirror aloft from time to time in order to see behind while driving in traffic', thus inventing the rear view mirror before it was introduced by manufacturers in 1914. She also advised her readers who planned 'to drive alone in the highways and byways' to carry a small revolver, adding that 'I have an automatic Colt and find it easy to handle'.

Levitt disappeared from public view after 1910. She never married and little is known of her life after she stopped racing other than she took flying lessons. She died on 17 May 1922, aged 40, at her home in Marylebone, London. An inquest concluded that she died of 'misadventure' caused by morphine poisoning while suffering from heart disease and the measles.[20] She expressed a wish to be buried overlooking the sea and she is buried in the Jewish cemetery in Meadowview. Levitt was exceptional for her time. Apart from popularising the sport among women, she was the first woman to become a successful works team driver and the first British woman to receive international recognition.[21]

For many years after Levitt's death, it was still difficult for women in the motor racing world. While the motoring industry were happy for women to buy cars, the idea that they might become professional drivers was a different matter. Manufacturers frequently used the slogan 'So Simple That Even A Woman Can Drive It' throughout the early decades of the twentieth century in an attempt to reassure hesitant men and apprehensive women. There were anti-women driver and 'wife at the wheel' jokes during the 1950s and 1960s in magazines targeted to a male audience. Even in the 1980s comedian Jasper Carrott quipped about his mother-in-law: 'She's driven for more than 50 years and she's never had an accident. She's seen thousands'.[22]Despite the fact that the number of women drivers increased tremendously as the car industry expanded, 'they were still considered objects of curiosity and had to do a great deal of extra work over and above men to become adroit motorists'.[23]

One woman who succeeded and was an heir to Levitt was Sheila van Damm. An outstanding rally driver, she was one of the few women to race cars successfully during the 1950s.[24]

Sheila van Damm (1922-1987)

Sheila van Damm was notable in two respects. A director of London's famous Windmill Theatre and a pioneer rally driver, she was was the first British woman to win an Alpine Rally cup in 1953 and won the ladies' section in the 1954 European Touring Car Championship. She was considered 'probably the world's fastest racing driver' and had the spirit and determination that took her to the top in racing.[25]

Born on 17 January 1922 to Vivian van Damm and Natalie Lyons, she was the youngest of three daughters. She came from a comfortable middle-class Jewish background whose families lived in the suburbs and central London. Her paternal grandfather George van Damm was a lawyer of Dutch Jewish origins and had been elected to the Common Council of the City of London for Lime Street Ward in 1908[26] and lived in Christchurch Avenue, Brondesbury, London. Her maternal grandfather was Isaac N. Lyons of 1 Hyde Park Street, London, the brother of Sir Joseph Nathaniel Lyons.[27]

Vivian van Damm had left school at 14 to work in a garage and was a mechanic for Clement Talbot in the early days of automobiles before managing West End cinemas. By the time his daughter was born he was general manager of the Tivoli Cinema in The Strand and they lived in a large comfortable house in Paddington and would rent fabulous country houses in the summer. They had a butler, cook, nanny and housemaids.[28] In 1931 he was just about to sign a lucrative contract with Sidney Bernstein who wanted him to manage his Granada cinemas when he was introduced to Laura Henderson, owner of The Windmill Theatre. In 1930 the recently widowed Mrs Laura Henderson bought the old Palais de Luxe cinema and fitted it out as a tiny one-tier theatre, renamed the Windmill. It was not profitable and she hired Vivian van Damm to change its fortunes and when she died in 1944 she left him the theatre lease in her will. Van Damm came up with the idea of 'Revudeville', a programme of continuous variety with 18 entertainment acts. They added the daring dimension of nudity to create the illusion of the Folies Bergere and the Moulin Rouge.

To get around the Lord Chamberlain's censorship laws,[29] Vivian exploited a legal loophole that nude statues could not be banned on moral grounds and this led to the legendary 'Windmill Girls'. The girls had to remain motionless, the Lord Chamberlain's ruling being 'if you move, it's rude'. It was argued that since nude statues cannot be banned neither can living statues or *tableaux vivants*. Sheila explained that it was not the den of iniquity that people expected it to be. 'Our fan dance was usually such a masterpiece of timing that it could have been performed at a vicarage fete with scarcely a tut of embarrassment'.[30]

Vivian's flair for public relations created the legend of the theatre 'that never closed'. Newspapers carried pictures of plucky Windmill girls in tin hats on fire watching duties and stories of show girls giving V-signs to German bombers. Indeed, except for a 12-day period in 1939, when all London theatres were ordered closed, the Windmill remained open throughout the Blitz. It became famous for its claim 'we never close' and achieved iconic status in war time memory. During the war The Windmill did up to six shows a day. Servicemen thronged to the theatre, high spirited and noisy. Even men's lives had depended upon knowing about the theatre. Nazis who got through into British lines pretending to be shot down Allied airmen were sometimes asked a trick question: 'What's the title of the play at the Windmill?' A supposed RAF man who thought the Windmill Theatre put on plays was immediately under heavy suspicion.[31]

Van Damm began working at the theatre aged 16, a few months before the outbreak of the Second World War. As the Blitz began and men went off to war opportunities for women increased and within a short time she was head of publicity until she was conscripted.[32] When her father died in 1960 she took over. 'The Windmill was the background of my life'.[33] She continued its revue format supporting young comedians including Alfred Marks, Michael Bentine, Peter Sellers, Tony Hancock, Harry Secombe and Bruce Forsyth. The theatre was the 'nursery' for unknown comedians who later blossomed into international stardom.[34] She was proud of those that started their careers there and went on to become famous. In respect of Alfred Marks, she commented that Jews made the best comedians because of their enormous heart and the wonderful warmth and kindness that is a Jewish characteristic.[35] The van Damms always felt the comics provided a much needed injection of mirth and humanity after the rather antiseptic displays of female flesh.[36]

Van Damm was by all accounts extremely protective of the girls who were segregated backstage from the rest of the company. Barry Cryer,[37] one of the young stand-up comedians who cut his teeth at the Windmill, recalls her as a very extrovert character with sparkling eyes and a bright smile. She was known to one and all as 'Miss Sheila' and had no difficulty stamping her authority on an establishment that was renowned, despite the risqué fare on offer, for its probity and professionalism.[38] She ran the Windmill in a no-nonsense manner. The girls on arrival were an average age of 17 and she discouraged them from staying out late, going to pubs in the area and boyfriends were not allowed backstage. The family atmosphere was reflected in its welfare policy.[39] She was a large matronly figure who spoke in an upper class English accent with great confidence that was probably a reflection of the background that she came from.

She energetically presided over the Windmill for a further four years before relinquishing the battle against the advancing tide of strip shows and permissive cinema in the Soho area which forced the theatre to close in 1964. By the early 1960s Soho's adult entertainment industry was offering a lot more than naked tableaux and the Windmill began to look decidedly old fashioned.[40] Its closure marked 'the end of an era famous in its heyday as the age of stage door Johnnies drinking champagne out of chorus girls' slippers.'[41] The show had run for longer than any other worldwide and its 60,000 performances had been watched by more than 10 million people.

Van Damm ran the theatre alongside a driving career which had started during the war when she became a driver for senior staff at RAF Stanmore and periodically took parties of Windmill girls on morale-boosting tours around the airfields in the south of England. She was a driver in the women's Auxiliary Air Force and in the course of her service gained a pilot's licence. She gave up flying when rally driving took up the majority of her time.

It was her father who gave her a start in competition motoring when he entered her into the *Daily Express* car rally in November 1950. This was her first rally and a publicity stunt for the theatre. She drove a Sunbeam Talbot that her father had persuaded the British car manufacturer Rootes Group to enter with the words 'Windmill Girl' on the side of the car. It was the first such race in Britain since the war and involved driving a thousand miles in 48 hours. Navigated by her sister Nona, she claimed third place in the ladies' section, a performance which so impressed the Rootes team manager that he invited her to join an all-woman crew in the 1951 Monte Carlo rally. Her first major success was in the 1952 Motor Cycling Club rally, when she won the ladies' prize in a Sunbeam Talbot. She soon afterwards entered the record books, outpacing her teammate Stirling Moss,[42] to set a class record for 2 to 3-litre cars, driving the prototype Sunbeam Alpine sports car at an average of 120mph at Jabekke in Belgium.[43]

Described as a 'fresh faced woman possessed of an infectious sense of fun', she had an ebullient and outgoing personality which masked a fearsomely competitive and determined approach to her sport. The 1953 Alpine race, one of Europe's toughest events, saw her co-driving with Anne Hall. She won not only the Coupe des Dames, which had not been won by a woman since 1939, but also one of the coveted Coupes des Alpes. She competed in the 1954 Dutch Tulip Rally, a performance that saw her winning outright the ten-lap race around the Zandvoort circuit. Winning a further ladies award in the 1954 Viking Rally in Norway successfully clinched the Ladies European championship for van Damm and Hall, a feat they were to repeat in 1955. It entitled her to the epithet 'fastest woman in Europe'.[44] She had a record of finishing every event which she started in her five-year career.

Her considerable success is reflected in the statement 'her achievements in motor rallies during the last few years have been remarkable for a member of either sex'.[45] There was a lot of prejudice against women in the motor racing world. Stirling Moss, widely regarded as one of the greatest Formula 1 drivers of all time, claimed that the average woman was not a good driver as she has little sense of anticipation. 'I'm as good as the next man', said van Damm. Her message to women was that they should not be bullied into thinking that they were not as good as men and that they only had themselves to blame if this attitude continued.[46] She wrote regular articles on how women could drive as well as men, was among well-known motoring personalities appearing in ABC's late night television summer programme for motorists (1958), spoke on the BBC about making roads safer for children (1959) and was vice president of the Careful Drivers Club of Great Britain that used some of its member subscriptions to help children who were victims of road accidents. Her success is also noteworthy in that she succeeded in a field known for its exclusivity and links to British fascism.[47]

She retired from racing in 1955 after her father became ill so she could take a more active role in the theatre and 'take the strain off his shoulders'.[48] When the theatre closed, she moved to Sussex with her sister Nona and ran a small farm. Her commitment to her family was evident throughout her life and was the reason that she stepped away from a spectacular racing career to help out her father at the theatre. She added that 'the successful running of the theatre will eventually rest on me and I have not only to think of myself and my future but also that of my mother and the family as well'.[49]

In respect of her Jewishness she paid tribute to the close and happy Jewish family life in which she was reared. Her father was generous to charities including many Jewish institutions, as was his father George van

Damm who was a contributor as early as 1905 to the Jewish Board of Guardians.[50] Vivian was a member of Hampstead Synagogue, where his marriage took place in 1914, and George was one of the founder members.[51] In 1959 Sheila became the first chairperson of the newly formed women's group of the Friends of the Hebrew University.[52] However, in her autobiography *No Excuses*[53] she does not refer to her Jewishness. It would appear that she did not follow religious observance as she said her favourite light meal was bacon and eggs.[54] In later years she consulted spiritualists and believed in the afterlife. She died from cancer on 23 August 1987. There was no funeral as she 'had not wanted a fuss'.[55]

Van Damm's competence and great abilities were highlighted in a Martini advert: 'Choose a career for this carefree lady. The stage? The services? Champion driver? Author? Pilot? Business woman? Right you are, every time! Yes… it is Sheila van Damm. Learns to drive in the WAAF; graduates to international rallies; twice ladies European champion; publishes her life story; holds a pilot's 'A Licence'; directs London's non-stop review six shows a day at the Windmill. Pause for breath. If we drop in for a chat at her home or the theatre she'll welcome us with a glass of Martini. Which seems to prove she's a connoisseur as well'.[56]

Levitt and van Damm excelled at a time when it was unusual for women to make their mark in this sport. Their Jewishness was not openly referred to and therefore did not appear to be a hindrance, perhaps because of their personalities, abilities or their novelty in a male-dominated sport. Class might also have been a factor as both seem to have adapted to the expectations of Englishness very successfully and easily. However, their experience was not shared by Jews in other sports, as the case of the tennis star Angela Buxton demonstrates. Though also born into a prosperous middle-class family and given the support necessary to pursue tennis, Buxton was challenged by both racism and antisemitism that affected the course of her career.

Angela Buxton (1934-2020)

Tennis legend Angela Buxton, regarded as one of the greatest Jewish tennis players of all time, fought antisemitism during her career and broke racial barriers in the 1950s by forging a friendship and formidable tennis partnership with Althea Gibson, the black American trailblazer from Harlem who also faced discrimination. Together they won the women's doubles title at both the French championships and Wimbledon in 1956. Buxton was proud to team with Althea when others refused and helped raise money for Gibson when she fell on hard times. The World Tennis Association commented that she spent her life standing up to discrimination and injustice and the Lawn Tennis Association called her 'a champion for inclusion on and off the court'.[57] Buxton had her most successful tennis year in 1956 and was ranked fifth in the world after she won the women's doubles title and reached the singles final at Wimbledon, the first Briton to contest the singles finals in 17 years.[58] After suffering a serious hand condition, tenosynovitis, Buxton was forced to retire at the age of 22 following the 1957 season. She went on to mentor young players and write about tennis. Her books included *Tackle Lawn Tennis This Way* (1958), *Starting Tennis* (1975) and *Winning Tennis Double Tactics* (1980).

Buxton was born in Liverpool on 16 August 1934 to Harry Buxton and Violet Greenberg. The family came from Russia and the surname had probably been Bakstansky but had been anglicised to Buxton.[59] Harry was originally a salesman from a working-class Orthodox Jewish family from Leeds but he won a fortune at the casino in Nice in the late 1920s. Smart and ambitious, he briefly traded in the stock market, dealt in jewellery and then found a niche in the entertainment industry. He bought cinemas in Manchester and all over the north of England and became an entertainment mogul. Bruce Schoenfeld comments that 'Harry was the embodiment of the cartoonish Jew. He was the loudest man in the room everywhere he went. He was ostentatious and made money easily. After the war he bought a white, chauffeur-driven Rolls Royce that had belonged to Queen Wilhelmina of Holland and still had her crest on the door'. Harry and Violet were not a suitable match but her father urged her to marry him as she was already 24 when he proposed.[60] Sandy Harwitt points out that Buxton was a child of privilege who would be raised to go after whatever goals she set for herself with her father as a successful entrepreneur and her mother who never felt the necessity to conform to the typical life envisioned for women at that time.[61]

Harry sent his wife and two children to South Africa in 1940 to escape the bombing and perhaps mend a ruptured marriage while he stayed behind to run his business. He was a restless soul and maintained suites at the Grosvenor Park Hotel, London and the Hotel de Paris, Monte Carlo. Buxton spent the war years in Johannesburg with her mother and brother Gordon and went to a convent school where she was one of the few Jewish girls. It was there at eight years old that she was introduced to tennis which was a compulsory subject. She was selected as the girl 'who stood out' which resulted in a free lesson once a week from the South African national tennis coach.[62]

The family returned to England from South Africa in 1946 and moved with Harry to Sussex. Harry had purchased the rights for the Bognor Regis pier that had been destroyed, built a new pier and music hall and started booking some of the top acts in England. The marriage did not last and Violet and the children went to north Wales to be with her parents who had evacuated there from Liverpool during the war. Buxton was sent to the boarding school Gloddeath Hall where she continued to play tennis. A coach saw that she had promise and convinced her mother that she should take part in a series of tournaments that were held every summer in Southport. Due to the war England had not fielded a national tennis team for seven years. The national coach Dan Maskell travelled around the country looking for potential stars. Buxton, probably due to her success in Southport, was invited to 'a sifting' in Colwyn Bay, Wales where she, together with the other hopefuls, hit briefly with Maskell. Some months later she was invited with several dozen others to a grand sifting in Wimbledon but at this point she was not successful. Harry decided she should move in 1950 with her mother to London as the city afforded more opportunity for tennis instruction than anywhere else in England. They lived in Rossmore Court near Baker Street and Buxton went to a small private school, Queens House in Hampstead and started to have lessons at the Cumberland Club which was at the time the best tennis club in London.[63]

In 1952 Buxton played her first Wimbledon. She lost in the first round and was very aware that aspects of her game were in need of improvement. Buxton told her father that the best players came from California and he agreed to send her there to get out from underneath the British tennis infrastructure and for her to have an advantage on her domestic rivals. She and her mother rented an apartment overlooking the Los Angeles Tennis Club where she started to play. She applied for membership but was turned down because she was Jewish. She subsequently practised at the public courts where her instructor was Bill Tilden, who had been the No 1 tennis player in the world in the 1920s before going to jail for sexually abusing teenage boys. Despite his downfall Tilden remained friends with many Hollywood stars and had access to Charlie Chaplin's tennis courts where he would take Buxton for practice and she started to play in tournaments throughout southern California.[64]

Back in England in 1953, Buxton felt she was ready to be a contender. Unfortunately, she suffered a humiliating loss to Doris Hart, the reigning Wimbledon champion, at the Bournemouth hardcourt championships. Disheartened she believed she had been wasting her father's money by pursuing tennis and decided that she would become a dress designer. Nevertheless she did not totally abandon tennis and in October 1953 decided to conclude her tennis career in Israel by playing at the Maccabiah Games, an illustration of her strong Jewish identity, where she won a singles gold medal and gold in the doubles. Her success gave her the impetus to refocus on the sport. She contacted Jimmy Jones, a tennis professional and sportswriter, who had previously offered to train her. Almost immediately she went from being on the fringes of the sport in England to being invited onto the 1954 and 1955 Wightman Cup team, an annual tennis competition between women from the United Kingdom and United States and in 1955 reached the Wimbledon singles quarterfinals.[65]

Her greatest glory was when she won the women's doubles with Althea Gibson in 1956. In the segregated world of 1950s tennis they forged a remarkable friendship as champion doubles partners. They were both outsiders in the starched white world of elite 1950s tennis, superb players but excluded from tournaments and shunned on the circuit because of their heritage. Althea had been born in a sharecropper's shack in South Carolina and grew up in Harlem. For all of Buxton's prowess on the court – she was ranked in the women's top 10 in the mid-1950s – she is remembered for the long-lasting support and encouragement she gave to Althea.[66]

Buxton's first experience of racism was when she was a young girl in South Africa. Buxton became friendly with a black girl her age, the daughter of servants who lived next door; friends and neighbours strongly disapproved of the friendship and it had to end. Buxton was crestfallen. It had never occurred to her that skin colour might have anything to do with the friendship.[67] In a similar incident, Violet Buxton was approached by a young black woman looking for some cleaning work. A few days later she appeared with her six-month-old daughter desperately seeking a place to stay. Violet offered her a job and place to sleep until the landlord threatened to evict them all. Violet just accepted it. 'We are guests of the country. We need to keep our heads down and noses clean'. The incident stayed in Buxton's mind.[68]

It was the reaction to the treatment of black people in South Africa that was to become a major influence in her life. She developed an affinity with black people and found it hard to understand the policy of racial segregation. While playing on the tournament circuit in India in 1955 she met Gibson whom President Eisenhower had sent on a goodwill tour. Gibson was so discouraged by the barriers that she faced as the only black person in the top echelons of tennis that she was ready to give up the game. 'When I came on the scene the other players wouldn't speak to Althea much less play with her simply because she was black. She was completely isolated. I was too, because I was Jewish'.[69] It was Buxton's coach who suggested they form a doubles partnership. They were a formidable team.[70] Buxton's daughter Rebecca Silk explains, 'Althea was talented and marginalised. The reason my mother was attracted to her was because she was talented. Colour did not matter. She was not a campaigner. She saw something was wrong and was going to talk about it. She was colour blind'.[71] When Gibson fell on hard times and was suicidal Buxton wrote a letter to *Tennis Week* magazine describing Gibson's plight and asked for contributions. Money poured in from around the world and enabled her to go on living. In honour of her support, Buxton was inducted into the Black Tennis Hall of Fame in 2015. Katrina Adams, past president of the United States Tennis Association said Buxton had supported Gibson 'when no one else would in a racist era of our sport in the 1950s'.[72]

It is not surprising that Buxton had great empathy for Gibson's position as during her life she experienced racial discrimination. Her first episode occurred in South Africa. Her mother was in the common bathroom shared by several flats arranging her hair. When a man asked whether she was finished yet, he then remarked, 'you Jews are all the same. You think you own the world'. Violet Buxton hit him twice with her comb.[73] Throughout her career Buxton faced antisemitism from both the tennis community and the British tennis establishment. When she attempted to join the prestigious Cumberland Lawn Tennis Club in north-west London she received her first taste of sporting antisemitism. She had several lessons and kept asking her coach about membership. Eventually he turned round and requested that she stop asking him as she would never be able to join as she was Jewish'.[74]

On another occasion Buxton's mother received a phone call from the club notifying her that her daughter had been removed from an upcoming junior county tournament. 'Oh Mrs Buxton I'm very sorry to tell you but your daughter has been disqualified, so don't bother to come. We've heard on the grapevine that she doesn't really have Middlesex qualifications'. Violet Buxton took no notice and Angela went on to win the title. After her rejection from the Cumberland Club in 1949, she made it her personal mission to return there and win the Middlesex Junior Championships staged there annually. 'I made a point of going back to win their bloody tournament – twice – just to rub their noses in it — and they never gave me a cup of tea. Not even that'.[75]

The hostility continued wherever she went. After her move to California in 1952 her application for membership was rejected from the

Los Angeles Tennis Club, renowned at the time for its discrimination against potential members from minority backgrounds. Back in England, she wrote to Sir Simon Marks, owner of Marks & Spencer, asking to use his private indoor court. 'I am a young Jewish girl and I've got ideas to become a tennis champion'. She figured that she had little chance of persuading him unless he knew that she was Jewish too and by inference did not have access to the best clubs. She practised there during the years 1954-55 and the months of training there were to prove invaluable. It was about the only time that Buxton can recall her religion actually aiding her tennis rather than hindering it.

Buxton entered the women's Easter tournament at the Argyle Club, Southport in 1955 where Jews were allowed in for the odd appearance. She found herself without a hitting partner and asked if the club could provide one. They asked Derek Dutton, a club member and journalist, who although was a reasonable player was not one that would have been expected to hit with the fourth ranked woman in Britain. Years later Dutton learned that he had been asked only because none of the other club members would step out with a Jew.[76] In later years it was alleged that decisions taken by the Lawn Tennis Association during the 1950s not to pair her with several female British players in the international Wightman Cup tournament were driven by the fact that she was Jewish.[77] Buxton recalls that as she rose up the rankings the British girls on the international scene would ignore her. 'Playing out in Mexico they never once invited me to join them for a meal'.[78]

Another incident concerned the Wimbledon ball that was to be held the night before the finals day when Buxton would be competing for both the doubles and singles. Violet Buxton wanted to attend the ball with her daughter who was facing the biggest matches of her life. When they turned up to order their tickets they were told the ball had sold out. Violet, detecting antisemitism, was furious and threatened to keep her daughter at home on the finals day for both the women's singles and doubles, effectively stymying the entire championship. The pair stormed out before the ticket manager, realising how catastrophic Buxton's nonattendance would be, came after them in a panic, apologising and saying that she had managed to find two tickets.[79]

Even after her impressive showings in singles and doubles competitions during 1956 her success failed to translate into public honours as one might have expected. Buxton faced rebuffs from both the Lawn Tennis Writers Association and the All England Lawn Tennis Club (AELTC). The former, which gave an annual award to the individuals they consider made the greatest contribution to British tennis, preferred to leave the 1956 award vacant rather than give it to Buxton. The AELTC were equally reluctant to honour one of their most successful post-war players. While winning the Wimbledon singles championship was the only way to guarantee automatic membership to the club, the offer of honorary membership had become an established custom for British players who achieved notable success. Buxton's achievements more than qualified her but she believed that antisemitism among the club committee prevented her membership application ever being accepted.[80] Although she applied for membership to the All England Lawn Tennis Club in 1958 she never received a reply. 'I can only assume it is because I am a Jew'.[81] Despite facing significant prejudice Buxton showed a determination which enabled her to carve out a highly successful career. Indirectly she believed that her sporting success provided a retort to the antisemitism that she encountered. Although Buxton claimed that she was anything but a 'crusader' for Jewish rights, she admitted many years later that antisemitism had made her more determined. 'It did have a tremendous impact on my tennis and my life but the impact was to strengthen my resolve. I was always proud of the fact that I was Jewish'.[82] Although Buxton herself noted her disappointment over the indifferent response she received from the tennis establishment after her 1956 Wimbledon victory, she felt pleased to have gone a long way to realising her sporting ambitions in the face of racial prejudice. There was, however, not much publicity about her win. She remembered there was only one very small headline 'Minorities Win' in very small type lest anyone should see it.[83]

Although not a religious Jew, Judaism had always featured in Buxton's life. Her parents, like those of Judge Rose Heilbron, the first woman judge to sit at the Old Bailey, married at Princes Road Synagogue, Liverpool. In 1959 she married Donald Silk whom she had met at a meeting of the Marylebone Jewish Society. Silk was a member of the Law, Parliamentary and General Purposes Committee of the Jewish Board of Deputies, executive member of the World Jewish Congress and became chairman of the Zionist Federation of Great Britain. They had two sons and a daughter and she kept a conventional Jewish home in Winnington Road, Hampstead Garden Suburb. After the 1967 Six Day War Buxton volunteered to work on Kibbutz Amiad for six months with her children, all of whom were under seven years old. When they returned to England she and Silk divorced and she joined forces with her former coach Jimmy Jones, who was not Jewish, both professionally and personally. Judaism still held an importance for her. She had a book filled with the names and addresses of people to whom she would send Jewish New Year cards and she always lit candles on a Friday night. She belonged to the West London Reform Synagogue and was buried on her 86th birthday in an Orthodox cemetery in Manchester next to her son and brother.[84]

Buxton founded the Angela Buxton Centre in Hampstead Garden Suburb, London which specialised in the advanced development of tennis in the 1970s and 1980s. Rebecca Silk commented that she did so much to encourage young people into the game. Many of her pupils at the Centre became tennis coaches including former speaker of the House of Commons John Bercow who paid his way through university coaching tennis and she helped talented children obtain tennis scholarships to university.[85] She would take promising stars to Florida academies believing that exposure to the international game was vital to their development.[86] Buxton was one of the original founders of the Israel Tennis Centres and was inducted into the Jewish Sports Hall of Fame, Israel in 1981 for her outstanding contribution to tennis coaching and New York's National Jewish Sports Hall of Fame on Long Island, N.Y. in 2014. She was a coach to the Israel Lawn Tennis Association and appealed to readers of the *Jewish Chronicle* to donate their old racquets and balls that were no longer needed to the Association.[87]

Buxton made a huge impact during her life. She received an award at Liverpool Town Hall in 2004 to recognise her success in overcoming prejudice. The Lord Mayor said, 'Angela is not only a tennis champion but a champion of equal rights, overcoming the prejudice surrounding her faith to become one of Merseyside's greatest tennis players.'[88] When Sir Geoffrey Cass, chief executive of Cambridge University Press and President of the Lawn Tennis Association, was asked why there were not more British tennis champions, he replied 'we need more people like Angela Buxton'.[89]

Conclusion

In striving to compete at the highest levels in their chosen sporting fields, Dorothy Levitt, Sheila van Damm and Angela Buxton each contended with various challenges, including gender, class, ethnicity and racism. All three came from comfortably off, even prosperous families who supported their career choices, but faced outsider status as Jews within the British middle-class, subject to the exclusionary rules that existed in sporting clubs in the early and mid-twentieth century. All sports were dominated by men in this period, and Levitt and van Damm, whose Jewishness posed few impediments to their sporting pursuits, faced the additional hurdle of competing in motor sports, which was an exclusively male domain. For

Buxton, in contrast, gender presented fewer obstacles, but the dual barriers of antisemitism and racism were fixtures throughout her career.

Families and middle-class status played an important supporting role in the rise of these three female athletes. It was considered that for women to have access to motor racing in the early years a few essential conditions had to be met: a certain amount of wealth and a sturdy disposition.[90] Sheila van Damm certainly had these qualities and Levitt, though from a less wealthy background, was able to parlay a secretarial position into a racing career - something that would likely not have been possible had she been born into the working-class. Coming from backgrounds of economic privilege, both van Damm and Buxton had fathers who were larger than life characters and great entrepreneurs that supported their careers.

Gender presented challenges for all women athletes in this period, even in sports such as tennis, though once established in their careers, Levitt and van Damm found it could also be an asset in a sport that had no previous female participants. Levitt's career originated as a publicity stunt when motoring was in its infancy and she was viewed as an exotic novelty during the short time that she raced cars. Though she competed at the highest levels, broke many records and was admired for her daring, courage and nerve, she was arguably more celebrated for her beauty, style and flair than for her sporting prowess. By the time van Damm came on the motoring scene, mid-century attitudes about women and domesticity extended to widespread misogyny about women and driving, as the comments of Stirling Moss demonstrated. During her short career, van Damm competed largely on the ladies' circuit, though she proved she could win at any level, and she fought hard against the stereotypes of women drivers. For Buxton, as Robert Lake pointed out, despite tennis offering greater opportunities for women to participate and gain public admiration for their talents than most other sports, women remained limited in other ways. They were marginalized, their performances often trivialised and deemed less important than the male players. Their identities were constructed as wives and mothers first rather than athletes.[91]

Finally, attitudes about Jewish ethnicity and racism impacted these female sporting figures' careers in various ways. Levitt and van Damm faced no apparent discrimination perhaps because they were such rare and remarkable characters that their Jewishness posed no threat. But Levitt's exotic 'Oriental' looks were much commented on (in contrast to a typical 'English Rose' beauty) and van Damm succeeded in Formula 1 racing, which has long had strong ties to Nazism and British fascism. In contrast, Buxton competed in one of the sports associated with the middle-classes, where she encountered overt antisemitism and racism that affected the course of her career. Nouveau riche Jews were an affront to British middle-class status and Buxton was shunned by both Britain's and America's tennis establishments at various points in her sporting life. In addition, she encountered explicit racism during her wartime sojourn in South Africa and in her tennis partnership with Althea Gibson.

In the twentieth century, Levitt, van Damm and Buxton would have faced many challenges as female sporting figures even if they had not been Jewish. But their individual grit, determination, prowess and courage, along with their fortunate socio-economic status and supportive families enabled them to take up sports that had previously excluded or side-lined women as second-class competitors and they managed to compete at the highest levels, gaining international fame and respect for their talent and pioneering achievements.

7

Cookery and the World of Food

Although recipe books existed for centuries, often collections gathered together in a haphazard manner from older books and oddments from family and friends, the nineteenth century brought increasing precision in recipe writing particularly in the form of *Mrs Beeton's Book of Household Management* (1861) which included specific ingredients. Recipes were published in women's magazines and this market expanded after the First World War. Middle-class women had to think more about cookery as domestic servants were fewer and rationing during and after the Second World War resulted in magazines and books educating the population how to make the most of the food available. Radio and television took an increased interest in the subject. A trend towards more cosmopolitan and adventurous recipes developed and by the 1980s a sense of excitement about food was apparent in both print and electronic media and television cookery programmes became popular.[1]

Food habits over the past 150 years have shown a strong tendency to be nationalistic. For much of the twentieth century, favourite items such as roast beef, lamb with mint sauce, fruit cake and mince pies were invoked under the banner of 'tradition'. There was a preference for 'meat and two veg' and white bread, and until well into the 1950s plainness in food was seen as a virtue. The uniformity and blandness characteristic of much early twentieth century British cooking as well as a perception that food should be cheap may have been an inheritance from the poverty of the nineteenth century when few people could afford more than the basic foods. Food as a source of pleasure and creativity was largely unconsidered until after Second World War. Since the 1960s, it has gained a much higher profile as influential writers and chefs had an impact on post-war eating habits and both cooking and eating out have become leisure pursuits. A growth in advertising, in food and cookery as a subject for printed and electronic media, and the expansion in the number and range of places to eat out have played a part in the increasing interest in food. Foreign travel became a possibility for many in the 1970s and 1980s, introducing them to the eating habits of Mediterranean countries. Migrants also brought new ideas and there was the adoption of curries and other 'foreign foods' as popular dishes.[2]

The traditionally bland British palate, coupled with an attitude of frugality and restraint, seems far removed from traditional Jewish food and cooking in which taste and flavour is everything and more is definitely better. These factors, combined with the particular dietary requirements of the Jewish faith, gave rise to a number of Jewish cookbooks, the first of which appeared over a decade before Mrs Beeton's. Its author, Judith Montefiore, reigned as the sole Jewish cookbook author until the early twentieth century, when Florence Greenberg and Evelyn Rose took up the mantle, advancing beyond the pages of recipe books to work as food journalists. It was not until Nigella Lawson appeared on the food scene in the late twentieth century, however, that a Jewish woman became internationally popular as a food writer and personality in the world of cooking. The Jewish women's cookbook authors who preceded her had identified primarily as Jewish cooks writing for Jewish audiences, as epitomised by Judith Montefiore, whose book fused Jewish cookery with the sensibilities of upper middle-class Victorian dining and entertaining.

Judith Montefiore (1784-1862)

The publication of the first Anglo-Jewish cookery book *The Jewish Manual* (Practical Information in Jewish and Modern Cookery with a Collection of Valuable Recipes and Hints Relating to the Toilette) was published anonymously by 'a lady' in 1846. It was later attributed to Judith Montefiore, the wife of the Jewish philanthropist Moses Montefiore. *The Jewish Manual* aimed to make available 'the receipts peculiar to the Jewish people', addressing both the 'Jewish housekeeper' and also 'those ladies who are not of the Hebrew persuasion'. Jane Gerson comments that ironically the first self-defined attempt by an Anglo-Jewish woman to distinguish an identity for Jewish cookery in Britain has largely been regarded as 'not Jewish enough' by twentieth century commentators.[3] Adam Raphael comments that it set out a number of 'receipts' consistent with the religion but few you would recognise as Jewish food today. There were plenty of French or English recipes and from Spain and Portugal but few from Eastern Europe.[4]

The choice of recipes reflected Montefiore's background and cultural influences. She was born into an Ashkenazi family who had emigrated from Holland during the 1770s and married Moses Montefiore, a member of a distinguished Sephardi family, in 1812. Sephardi dishes feature dominantly in the book although some show a fusion style of cooking, such as kugel,[5] the Ashkenazi pudding. In Montefiore's version the kugel is a sweet English pudding made of bread crumbs and brown sugar seasoned with nutmeg, ginger, cloves and allspice. A *Jewish Chronicle* reviewer wrote in 1846 that the book 'supplies a desideratum of which the accomplished hostess who desires to give a hospitable and agreeable entertainment will not be slow to avail herself'. Gerson comments that the words 'accomplished hostess' indicates that the book was being marketed for a well-to-do Anglo-Jewish household. The transformation of one of the dishes commonplace in the late twentieth century Jewish kitchen, lokshen pudding (sweet pudding made with noodles) is representative of this general approach. The anglicised Yiddish title 'a luction' is given an alternative name 'a Rachael' and French terminology is introduced with the first instruction being 'make a thin *nouilles* (noodle) paste'. Gerson points out that the renaming of a common Jewish dish and subtle use of a language suffused with significance for class and status deliberately constructs a Jewish culinary identity as superior, keen to disguise any vulgar origins. '*The Jewish Manual* represents an act of cultural ennoblement, conferring Jewish food identity with the attributes necessary to be esteemed in well-to-do Victorian society. It cautions aspiring Jewish households to eschew vulgar and coarse practices at the table while asserting a discreet culinary superiority, derived from continental influences, to command respect in non-Jewish society'. The ultimate status recipe in the book was bola d'amour, a Sephardi sweet. In a British context the recipe was marked out as exotic and superior with its romantic name and a fabulous concoction requiring twenty eggs spun into threads with white sugar and shaped into a pyramid with layers of marzipan and citron.[6]

The distinctive thread of Anglo-Jewish culinary tradition established by Montefiore did not definitively emerge again until the twentieth century. The dishes brought by immigrants from Eastern Europe at the end of the nineteenth century did not initially influence the existing Anglo-Jewish cuisine. Efforts were made to teach them English cooking, and cookery books were published for the Jewish working-class that featured cheap English dishes.[7] The publication of Florence Greenberg's *Jewish Cookery* in 1947 was a landmark in Anglo-Jewish culinary history and became the definitive Anglo-Jewish cookery book in the post-war period.

Florence Greenberg (1882-1980)

Food historian Polly Russell comments that If you are British, over the age of 40 and have never heard of Florence Greenberg's *Jewish Cookery*, it is safe to assume you were not brought up in a Jewish household. Greenberg, cookery writer for the *Jewish Chronicle* (1920-1962), was the Delia Smith of the Anglo-Jewish community.[8] Entire generations of British Jewish brides reared families on the principles of cooking introduced by Greenberg. The volume was an immediate hit. Within the first 20 pages Greenberg explained the workings of a kitchen, food values, basic principles of koshering meat and chicken, food for toddlers and even a slimming diet. It was a kosher version of an English cookbook with some traditional recipes.[9] She became known 'Anglo-Jewry's Mrs Beeton'.[10]

Florence Greenberg grew up in a Jewish home which she described as 'a typical middle-class Victorian household'. Her father Alexander Oppenheimer originated from Germany and her mother Eliza Pool came from a family who were members of London's Sephardi synagogue Bevis Marks. Greenberg helped her mother run the home but she longed to be a nurse and eventually, aged 29, persuaded her father to let her train, despite his misgivings about women nursing men. She was a nursing sister in the First World War, going to Gallipoli, Egypt and Palestine, where she served with such distinction that she was mentioned in dispatches.[11]

Once home, she married Leopold Greenberg, the editor of the *Jewish Chronicle*. He encouraged her to write a column for the newspaper as she had excellent cooking skills. In September 1920 the 'Jewish cookery' column was launched and continued until Greenberg retired in 1962.[12] Her training as a nurse was an important influence in her approach to cookery, which was orientated by a concern for health. Although her background had certain features in common with Montefiore, the domestic life experienced by her readers was different, as many middle-class households were less prosperous after the First World War and there was also a lack of certain staple food products. Greenberg was sensitive to the situation and gave recipes that would suit a wide range of households, including housewives cooking for themselves and she offered sensible economic advice. The column proved popular with readers and there was soon a demand for a cookery book. *The Jewish Chronicle Cook Book* was published in 1934.[13]

The work was a break with tradition and attempted to influence modern Jewish dietary habits. She omitted some of the traditional Jewish recipes as she considered they were not wholesome and there was little time for the modern woman to prepare them. She did not include potato *latkes* (potato pancakes) or *cholent* (Sabbath stew made with meat and dry beans). The traditional recipes that were included were mostly given with English, not Yiddish names, such as beetroot soup instead of borscht. Promotional extracts from the *Jewish Chronicle* stressed that it was 'equally applicable to cooking for non-Jewish tables and suitable for all kitchens'.[14]

As an English-born middle-class woman and a trained nurse, Greenberg absorbed the attitudes of the nutritional experts of her day and excluded the supposed ill effects of the heavy greasy food of much of immigrant Jewish cooking. In excluding the recipe for cholent, an important dish for those that need to keep the Sabbath, the issue was not only one of health but of anglicisation and class differences in the community.[15]

During the Second World War, the Ministry of Food recruited Greenberg to advise Jewish women on how to eke out their rations. She gave talks across the country and for the BBC's daily government sponsored food programme *The Kitchen Front*. Through these appearances she became a familiar name to housewives in Britain. Although a famous cookery writer within Anglo-Jewish circles she never referred openly to her Jewish identity and its influence on her cookery in her radio broadcasts.[16]

Her next book *Jewish Cookery* was published in 1947, reprinted 13 times (1947-1977) and transcribed into Braille. This time there was a new emphasis on exotic flavour and traditional Jewish dishes, described as 'continental', were included. There was greater use of Yiddish terminology and the inclusion of these dishes indicated that immigrant food was now being accepted as part of Anglo-Jewish cuisine.[17] Following in Greenberg's footsteps was Evelyn Rose, a prolific cookbook author whose career also included print and broadcast journalism, introducing Jewish food and cookery to a wider British audience on both television and radio.

Evelyn Rose (1925-2003)

Following in Greenberg's footsteps was Evelyn Rose (1925-2003) who can be credited with the most concerted effort to develop a modern, post-war identity for Anglo-Jewish cookery. Unlike Greenberg, who confined herself to testing and writing recipes without literary pretensions, Rose was a food writer and a prolific journalist.[18] She was the leading Anglo-Jewish cookery writer of her generation and there are few Jewish homes in Britain without at least one of her cookbooks. Her first was the newlywed's bible, *The Jewish Home* (1969) and her most influential work was the *Complete International Jewish Cookbook* (1976) which aspired to provide a manual for the Jewish household in the late twentieth century. *The First Time Cookbook* (1982) was aimed at young people leaving the family home. Her singular accomplishment was to meld contemporary cooking with Jewish dietary laws.[19] Paul Levy considered that she was probably the first professional Jewish cookery writer in Britain. Greenberg produced a single definitive cookery book that only required periodic updating while Rose published new books every few years. She always endeavoured to ally traditional Jewish cookery with an innovative approach.[20]

Outside the Jewish world, Rose was the first woman commissioner at the Meat and Livestock Commission and was awarded an MBE for her work in 1989. Born in Manchester and educated at Manchester School for Girls she lived in the city all her life, except for four years from 1940 when she moved to Seattle. Her school there offered a home economics course and this started her on her career. On her return to Britain, although she had a university place to study psychology, she instead attended the Manchester College of Housecraft, where she specialised in demonstration techniques. Her television work started in the 1950s when she wrote to the BBC suggesting a course in Jewish cookery and she made cheese blintzes for the first programme.[21] In contrast to Greenberg's suppression of her Jewish identity in the British media, Rose produced a series on Jewish cookery for the BBC programme *About the Home* (1954) in which Ashkenazi food and Yiddish names were featured prominently. She showed her audience how to make cheese blintzes, *holishkes* (stuffed cabbage) potato latkes, potato kugel and plava (sponge cake).[22]

She was a regular on Radio 4's *Woman's Hour* and wrote for *Decanter*, the wine magazine. She had various corporate clients for whom she wrote recipes and demonstrated products, such as Cadbury's Smash (dried instant mashed potato). She travelled widely, picking up ideas wherever she went. Her daughter Judi, also a cook, comments that she was a real entrepreneur in the days when women were staying at home. Her daughter points out that she was ahead of the curve with aubergine and avocados from Israel in the 1970s. 'But it was her recipe for gefilte fish Provençale, inspired by a trip there, that showed she reinvented Jewish cooking to be fresh, vibrant and healthier'.[23] She wrote the cookery column for the *Jewish Chronicle* for 40 years. The archive of all her work is in London's Guildhall Library, which houses the largest collection of food, drink and cookery books in Britain.

Unlike Greenberg, Rose was keen to promote once frowned upon East European dishes adapted for modern housewives in their new suburban kitchens. Recipes were adjusted to meet the requirements of new technology in the kitchen and new ingredients. There was' blender borsch' and 'refrigerator kuchen' and she adopted the American approach to making cheesecake, modernising the *haimishe* (homemade, comfort food) recipe.[24] There were *haimishe* recipes with a modern twist, adapted to a modern and affluent setting. The middle-class fashion for promoting *haimishe* dishes did not refer to the poverty and hardship of Jewish immigrant memoirs.[25]

No less important than the reinvention of traditional Ashkenazi food was a new promotion of Sephardi food. Complementing her advocacy of traditional East European Jewish dishes she also embraced modern Sephardi cookery. This was not a rediscovery of the old Spanish and Portuguese dishes from *The Jewish Manual,* which were still partly represented in Greenberg's work but rather it reflected the availability in Britain of new produce from the Mediterranean as well as the stimulus of new recipes brought by post-war Jewish immigrants to Britain.[26]

The Victorian era gave rise to a unique Anglo-Jewish cuisine, rooted in the British experience. In their cross-fertilisation of Sephardi, Ashkenazi and English elements, Anglo-Jewry delineated a culinary identity that found its clearest expression in Montefiore's *The Jewish Manual*. This provided the foundations for Greenberg's mid-twentieth century output, which she updated and adapted but did not necessarily change. In the post-war period there were different expectations about food. Rose tried to draw together tradition and innovation, 'the woman of worth' in the Jewish home and modern careerism, unfamiliar Sephardi ingredients and flavours with traditional Ashkenazi dishes.[27]

Up until the time of Evelyn Rose, Jewish cookery writers were aiming for a largely Jewish readership. Afterwards there was a more universal approach with writers such as Claudia Roden,[28] who followed a global food trend by introducing people to the food of the Middle East. Her seminal book *Middle Eastern Food* (1968) brought colour, spice and a raft of new flavours to many a bland English kitchen and *The Book of Jewish Food* (1996) traces the story of Jewish cooking through over 800 recipes and stories that she has collected from around the world. She relates that smoked salmon became the prime Jewish delicacy in Britain at the turn of the twentieth century and was eaten by Jews in the East End of London long before the English middle classes discovered it. Bagels, smoked salmon's traditional accompaniment, have now also been fully integrated into the mainstream.[29] Even the fish in the great British dish of fish and chips was almost certainly first fried by Portuguese Jews in the East End of London. But if, on the whole, Jewish cooking has failed to impress a wider audience, Jews have made an indelible mark on food in Britain. In the 1940s and early 1950s every sizeable town in Britain had Lyons corner house tea rooms. Two families were behind the Lyons empire, the Salmons and the

Glucksteins, the ancestors of Nigella Lawson, one of Britain's most popular cookery writers.[30]

Nigella Lawson (1960 –)

Nigella Lawson, one of the nation's most celebrated and beloved cooks, began her career as a book reviewer, restaurant critic and journalist. She started writing cookery books in 1998 with the bestseller *How To Eat* that inspired a new generation of amateur cooks. It was both a collection of opinions on everything including not cooking when hosting a weekend lunch and a pragmatic manual for feeding oneself and others without suffering for it. After that first career changing cookbook, the others that have followed and the corresponding television programmes she has hosted have made her a global food personality.[31]

British food writer Bee Wilson described *How to Eat* as revolutionary. It was the first book to make the case that home cooking did not need to apologise for not being restaurant cooking. 'Suddenly there was someone saying that a comforting bowl of stew could be better than some cheffy creation designed to impress. This attitude has remained a constant in Nigella's career, the idea that food should be a joy as much for the cook as the eater, that recipes are malleable, that status anxiety and guilt and stress are enemies of one of life's greatest gifts: appetite.'[32] Nigella was ahead of her time in respect of ingredients such as tahini and kale. The recipes are precise, timings and ratios can be depended on. The new addiction to baking was sparked by Nigella and her cupcakes. Wilson considers that she brought a new spirit of informality to much of British cookery writing. No one has ever described food in quite the same way. In describing a dish of sage and onion puy lentils topped with cod wrapped in Parma ham, she writes: 'This looks wonderful - the pebbly, oil-wet khaki-blackness of the lentils like a cobbled street underneath the cat's-tongue-pink slabs of ham-wrapped fish'. *How to Eat* marked the end of the reign of the chefs and a start of a new era.[33]

Nigella Lawson's mother Vanessa Salmon was born into the Lyons coffee house dynasty. Vanessa grew up in Kensington and Chelsea, London and had a privileged childhood surrounded by power and money. She was a notorious society beauty who had trained as a ballet dancer before her marriage aged 19. The family originally sold tobacco under the name Salmon and Gluckstein and claimed to be the largest in Europe at their launch in 1873. One of the founding fathers was her great-great-grandfather Barnett Salmon whose surname was originally Solomon. On the 1841 census it is listed that his father Aaron Solomon was a clothes dealer in the

East End. Barnett started work as a travelling tobacco salesman and married Helena Gluckstein in 1863 and went into business with his father-in-law Samuel Gluckstein. The Gluckstein's came from Rheinberg in present day Germany, one of a small number of Jewish families in the town. Samuel's father Lehmann was a well-respected teacher who left for England in the 1840s. Samuel's early years, like Barnett's, were humble and in the East End. His wife, Ann Joseph, was born Hannah Samuels in 1819 in Amsterdam. Her father was Coenraad Sammes, an apprentice shoemaker. Coenraad had been accused of theft and had been tried, convicted and sentenced to 18 months imprisonment in 1830. He never served his sentence but fled to England He changed his name to Coleman Joseph and Hannah became Ann.[34]

It was on the back of the success as a tobacco company that the Lyons company was born in 1889. To ensure that none of his family were every threatened with poverty Barnett set up a family fund but equally insisted that none of the women were allowed to work. At his death the trust fund for his wife was worth £34 million in today's money. Nigella's grandfather Felix Salmon was instrumental in running the company and shaping its direction towards the famous Lyons corner house tearooms.[35] The business also included restaurants, hotels and supermarkets and traded until the late 1970s.

Nigella's father was Nigel Lawson, a former Conservative Chancellor of the Exchequer in Margaret Thatcher's government. Nigel Lawson grew up in Hampstead in a non-Orthodox Jewish family. His father Ralph Lawson was a successful tea broker in the city and his grandfather, who became a British citizen in 1911, was from Latvia. The family name was originally Leibson and was changed to Lawson in 1925. Nigel's mother Joan Elizabeth (Davis) was from a prosperous family of stockbrokers. Nigel did not consider that acknowledging his background was a good career move and he failed to mention his Jewishness as he climbed the ranks and it was not mentioned in his memoirs. Upon becoming editor of the *Spectator*, the *Jewish Chronicle* asked him if he would like to send a message to its readers and he declined.[36]

Nigella's early years were privileged but melancholy despite growing up in a household with three siblings. She had a difficult relationship with her mother and there was a frosty relationship between her parents who subsequently divorced. She mixed in upper-class social circles and went to five different schools as she was reluctant to conform. It was only when she went to Goldophin and Latymer School that she began to take her studies seriously.[37] She studied medieval and modern languages at Lady Margaret

Hall, Oxford University and after graduation started work as a book reviewer and restaurant critic for the *Spectator*.

Nigella was one of the few members of her generation who really knew about food. She was 25 when she spotted a gap for a restaurant review column in the *Spectator* which would propel her to food stardom. While Nigella was wooing a rich and powerful and largely Tory readership at the *Spectator*, her confidence was growing. The Wapping strike of 1986 offered Nigella her next career move. It was a time of great change in Fleet Street as Murdoch had taken on the printing unions and moved his papers from Fleet Street to the new plant at Wapping. The National Union of Journalists sided with the printers and ordered the strike so it was down to individual choice as to who crossed the picket line. Nigella was one of the people who did. She became deputy literary editor of the *Sunday Times* in 1986.[38]

It was at the *Sunday Times* that she met writer John Diamond and they married in 1992. They made an endearing couple: he the naughty East End Jewish boy and she the quiet society beauty.[39] He was her first Jewish boyfriend although they came from different backgrounds. Diamond was born in 1953, the son of a biochemist and a fashion designer with strong left-wing political leanings. He grew up in Hackney and was particularly proud of his secular Jewish upbringing.[40] When Diamond was diagnosed with throat cancer and lost his voice, Nigella became his translator to the world and at the point when he could no longer swallow food he suggested that she write a cookery book, coming up with a title of classic simplicity, *How to Eat*. She says that although it sounded strange it was about clutching on to life. Diamond died in 2001, leaving her with two small children, and two years later she married art collector Charles Saatchi.[41] The marriage ended in a brutally public manner in 2013 when Saatchi was photographed grabbing her by her throat and holding her nose outside the London restaurant Scott's.

Nigella had helped her mother Vanessa in the kitchen from a young age. She was very close to her maternal grandmother and would write to her every week from school, sending recipes cut out of newspapers and magazines. She was only 25 when her mother died and *How to Eat* was written not just to memorialise her food but to continue a conversation with her.[42] Her mother was an extravagant, instinctive cook who raised her children in the kitchen. As well as Lancashire hotpot and boiled chicken with egg and lemon sauce, Vanessa cooked comparatively outlandish meals for that time – moussaka, taramasalata and spaghetti with olive oil and garlic, which was then considered quite fancy because of its Mediterranean origin.[43]

How to Eat was written mainly in narrative form, the recipes told like stories. Her voice is intimate and chatty; in the midst of how to make soft and crispy duck, she talked about the intimacy of cooking with other people, memories of doing so with her sister Thomasina, who had died young from breast cancer. It marked a step away from technical, chef-written cookbooks and toward a philosophy of cooking that was about pleasing oneself rather than flexing culinary muscles to impress others. 'Never worry about what your guests will think of you. Just think of the food. What will taste good?'[44]

The book inspired a new generation of amateur cooks. It explained the pleasures and principles of good food to a world of food lovers with 350 simple recipes designed to give readers the skills of their grandmothers. Tips on how to make homemade mayonnaise, stock and pastry dough, ideas about what to do with leftovers, what to freeze and even low fat menus made people believe that they could produce a Sunday lunch or children's supper without resorting to a single packet. 'She persuaded a new generation how to cook and changed the way we eat. The food press salivated at the intelligent prose and choice of recipes.'[45] Bee Wilson comments that when she first read the words 'strangely it can take enormous confidence to trust your own palate, follow your instincts' it felt like angel trumpets going off in her head. Since a child, she had been an obsessive reader of cookbooks but had never encountered a voice like Nigella's before. Unlike chef Raymond Blanc, Nigella did not make her feel that she ought to pay homage to authentic French food traditions. Nor was Lawson implying, as earlier recipe writers had done, that it was her duty as a woman to master a certain number of dishes and serve them on a certain kind of crockery. All Nigella asked of her readers was to discover what they loved to eat and then learn how to cook it. 'The book offered an original voice which worked its way into your head and made you feel braver in the kitchen. She did not tell her readers, as Elizabeth David[46] did, the correct way to do something but the way it happened to give her the most pleasure for the least amount of hassle.[47]

Nigella went from strength to strength, hosting her own TV cooking series *Nigella Bites* on Channel 4 in 1999 and her second book *How to be a Domestic Goddess*, published the following year, cemented her glamorous flirtatious public persona. Other cookery programmes followed in the UK and the States such as *Nigella Feasts, Nigella Express, Forever Summer with Nigella, Nigella Kitchen* and *Simply Nigella*. The series were accompanied by bestselling and award-winning cookery books. She also launched a range of kitchen items and an iPhone app and became a household name around the world.

Although Nigella has never promoted Jewish cooking per se, her writing and television shows reveal a love of abundance and plenty which are clearly genetic. She learned to cook in her mother's and grandmother's kitchens and the apogee of her cuisine is a flavour packed roast chicken. She has said that roast chicken is the fundamental unit of cooking.[48] Her love of cooking comes from her childhood. At a time when it was not appropriate to talk about food, her family was imbued with the Jewish passion for discussing food and lots of it. Nigella recalls 'there was always enough food – sometimes too much. Although we were not an observant family my mother would always cook cabbage with caraway seeds the Jewish way'.[49]

Her upbringing was without religious Jewish content, a fact reflected in her cooking. While she enjoys cooking bowls of chicken soup she will often make the *kneidels*[50] with butter.[51] The family loved the Christmas tradition and cooked turkey and ham. Her advice on how to survive Christmas is to 'freeze bacon rashers and sliced bread in pairs so that you're never more than three minutes from a bacon sandwich'.[52] She has also said that 'it might sound blasphemous to say that my Jewish-mother leanings are best satisfied by the roasting of a whole shoulder of pork but I'm afraid I've found this to be the case'.[53]

Although she has celebrated Christmas all her life, she did not experience her first Passover meal until she met Diamond and it would appear that she had nothing to do with her Jewishness before then. Yet at one level she does acknowledge her Jewish identity and that is through food. In her book *Feast* (2004), that is about celebratory eating, recipes for Passover, Rosh Hashana and Chanukah are included and show that although she is not an expert on *kashrut* (Jewish dietary laws) she knows a great deal about the history and nature of Jewish cuisine.[54] Nigella appears to be clutching her culture to her chest when she writes fondly 'I can't think of any other faith that would lead one so directly to the deep fat fryer but then few religions express themselves so emphatically with food'.

The first time she had been in a synagogue was when Diamond's grandmother died. 'I think that the fact that I married someone Jewish may be a sign that I wanted it to be more significant'. It is the culture rather than the religion that seems to have flicked her Jewish switch and it was in *Feast* that she finally came out as a Jew.[55]

It has been noted that she is pretty much the only person apart from Princess Diana who can be referred to by first name alone to universal recognition. *How to Eat* was a novel and more personable form of food writing in Britain that blended friendly meditations on cooking habits with fool-proof unintimidating recipes. It became a sensation. Since then she has become a household name and published twelve cookbooks. 'From your grandparents watching afternoon telly in the deepest corners of the shire to an agenda-setting young chef from central London, everyone loves Nigella. Despite her silver-spoon upbringing and her starry enigmatic charisma – as well as her infamous ability to make even the most basic of cooking techniques feel laden with innuendo – her understanding of food and the way she describes it in print has always been accessible.'[56]

Conclusion

British Jewish cookery as a distinctive branch of British cuisine was first codified in themed-1800s with Judith Montefiore's *The Jewish Manual*, and for the next century was confined largely to the tastes and dietary preferences of Jewish audiences, as epitomised by the early twentieth century career of Florence Greenberg. It was not until after the Second World War that Jewish food writers such as Evelyn Rose began to bring Jewish food to the wider British public, paving the way for Nigella Lawson to emerge as a global food personality, bringing a Jewish sensibility about preparing, eating and enjoying food to the world of cooking. These four women shared some similarities in background, and though their paths to becoming cookery authors and journalists varied greatly, they each in succession fused Jewish and British cookery, eventually bringing the foods of Sephardi and Ashkenazi Jews to wider British audiences.

It is perhaps not surprising that all four of the women discussed in this chapter came from middle or upper middle-class backgrounds, but it is notable that most of their families were not recent Eastern European immigrants, but had lived in Britain for generations, and included both central European Ashkenazi and Sephardi branches. For Montefiore, Greenberg and Rose, these origins bore significantly on the cuisines and recipes they developed for cookbooks and other publications and appearances. Since they were catering to largely Jewish audiences, their own religious heritage did not pose any issues for them, though it is significant that Montefiore's recipes were judged insufficiently Jewish by later critics and Greenberg's cookery advice for a general wartime audiences in lectures and on the radio was mute on her Jewishness, despite having already established herself as a leading Jewish cookbook author and food expert. It was not until Evelyn Rose openly promoted Jewish cooking to non-Jewish audiences after the war that specifically Jewish cookery entered the mainstream. With no religious upbringing, Nigella Lawson never promoted herself as a Jewish cook, but incorporated certain Jewish cultural and culinary elements in her philosophy and approach to meal preparation and the enjoyment of food.

None of these four women set out to become authors and purveyors of Jewish or British cuisine. Montefiore, as a member of upper-class society felt the need to blend certain Jewish traditions with the sensibilities of mid-nineteenth century fine dining and entertaining, glassing recipes of Yiddish origin with French names and Continental flair. Greenberg approached her career as a food writer from her background as a nurse in the First World War, and her emphasis on nutrition and healthy eating meant omitting some traditional Jewish dishes. She, too, dropped the Yiddish names for many of her recipes. Evelyn Rose, who was on a path to study psychology at university, changed course after being exposed to home economics in wartime America, where she had been evacuated in 1940. She was the first to reintroduce traditional Yiddish names to her dishes, and uniquely blended both Ashkenazi and Mediterranean inspired Sephardi dishes with modern techniques and newly available ingredients. Nigella came to prominence as a food personality after studying languages at Oxford and embarking on a career as a literary editor and restaurant critic. Her literary sensibilities and talents infused her food writing with a revolutionary new voice that dramatically changed the way many in Britain and across the globe understood cooking and the enjoyment of food. Together these four women helped bring Jewish cuisine and Jewish cultural approaches to meals and the sharing of food to wider audiences in Britain and beyond.

Conclusion

Though the creative arts and leisure pursuits that are the focus of this volume generally posed fewer obstacles to entry and success than careers in medicine, law and science, the Jewish women whose lives are detailed herein faced many of the same gender and ethnic/religious prejudices as their counterparts in the professions. By the beginning of the twentieth century, women were well represented in the fields of acting, writing, singing, and cookery—only art and sport remained stubbornly male dominated, and in the case of the latter, also markedly antisemitic. Jewishness, whether it was perceived in appearance as for the actors, or in subject matter for the novelists and cookbook writers, sometimes acted as a constraint to women's full participation in their chosen fields and limited their range and audiences. And while many of the women in these creative fields share a common immigrant background, it was challenging to pursue a career in art or sport without the means to acquire the necessary training and equipment, making the women featured in this book a varied group by class, social milieu, economics, education, and connection to a Jewish identity.

Acting has long been a career open to women, and to British Jewish women in particular especially since the advent of Yiddish Theatre in the nineteenth century. The actresses in this volume all share an immigrant heritage and for many, the respectability conferred by the early East End actresses and the security achieved by the third generation and the support of their families freed many of them to pursue careers in the arts rather than the professions. Although generationally they faced different challenges, these were more a reflection of trends in the acting world rather than obstacles imposed by their gender or background. However, in a field driven as much by appearance as talent, their Jewishness affected their acting careers in significant ways, limiting their range of both Jewish and non-Jewish roles. For many of the earlier generations of actors, being Jewish prevented them from achieving all their artistic aspirations in classic roles or on the West End stages, but the younger actresses have been more emboldened to demand the right to take on roles that highlight their background and heritage.

Like acting, writing has been historically available as a career for women and British Jewish women writers have been well represented in the field as novelists since the late nineteenth century. Coming from a range of religious and social backgrounds, the Jewish women writers profiled in this book wrote in a variety of genres, featuring both Jewish and non-Jewish characters, plots and settings. Yet notably their works focus on themes of belonging tied to their common identities as Jewish women who were born to immigrant or refugee families in Britain, and grew up as outsiders trying to fit in. These women writers often explored themes of family conflict and alienation, born of background, gender, and alternate sexualities, but their Jewishness and upbringing in explicitly Jewish milieus remained their fundamental identities. Significantly, the Jewish women writers featured here converted their estrangements and marginalities into award-winning and critically successful writing.

Perhaps more than any other creative field, embarking on a career in the musical arts, especially as a popular artist, presented fewer obstacles for women, and being Jewish was largely incidental to success for most of the women pop singers presented in this book. A few were urged to downplay their Jewish heritage by changing their appearance or name, and some endured antisemitism on social media but most were untroubled by their Jewishness in their professional lives and many embraced it fully in their private lives and charitable activities. The British Jewish women whose pop careers are explored here all experienced at least a fleeting pinnacle of fame, and their music, while spanning many decades and styles, was often at the cutting edge of emerging genres and in some cases, such as Amy Winehouse, became icons of their age. Like many pop stars, these women's careers were often troubled by personal demons and professional challenges, but as a group their success in popular culture represents the independence and acceptance that was possible for the second, third and fourth generation descendants of Jewish immigrants in post-Second World War Britain.

Female classical musicians faced greater challenges to professional recognition than did their contemporaries in the pop world, but British Jewish women were at the forefront of this effort and found that musicianship and determination helped them to surmount social and ethnic barriers on the way to productive professional careers. Encouraged by families, some of whom had to make considerable sacrifices in order to provide their talented daughters the training necessary to become classical musicians, these women all acknowledged the influence of their Jewishness on their creativity and drive. Interestingly, the Second World War and the

Holocaust had a profound effect on the lives and career directions of all three classical musicians profiled in this volume, as did the changing social structures of the twentieth century, which made it possible for women to have a family and pursue a professional career as a classical musician, and to perform, compose and teach.

Even more than the world of classical music, the art world remains male-dominated and has presented multiple challenges to women who wish to gain recognition as professional artists. Jewish women have faced the same gender-based obstacles as other women artists and remain underrepresented in the contemporary art scene. Still, the British Jewish women artists represented in this book demonstrate the possibilities open to them with the rise of revolutionary new art movements in the nineteenth century and the expansion of opportunities in the twentieth and twenty-first centuries. In the world of art, it has been gender, much more than religion, ethnicity or heritage that has limited the careers of British Jewish women.

In the world of sport, however, both gender and religion have challenged those women who have tried to break in to male-dominated fields such as golf, tennis and motor sports. The British Jewish women whose sporting careers are explored in this book all came from backgrounds that enabled them to get the training and equipment necessary to complete at the highest levels, but faced antisemitic exclusionary rules in sporting clubs and outsider status as both Jews and women. In all their sporting endeavours, these women battled misogyny and stereotypes about women focused on appearance and traditional ideas about domestic roles, and it is a testament to the grit and determination to the three women profiled here that each succeeded beyond expectations in her chosen field.

If the sporting world was an almost exclusively male domain, the world of cookery and food writing was a woman's world and British Jewish women have featured prominently in the field since the nineteenth century. Emerging from a tradition that was almost entirely aimed at the Jewish cook, Jewish women cookbook authors and cookery journalists expanded their reach in the twentieth century to first bring Jewish food to a larger British audience and then to fuse Jewish sensibilities about food and cooking with contemporary global cuisine. Alone among the women whose lives are chronicled in this book, the cookery writers did not emerge from immigrant backgrounds, but came from long-established British Jewish families, both Ashkenazi and Sephardic, and none set out to become a doyen of either British or Jewish cuisine. Backgrounds as varied as health and nutrition and literature and languages informed these women's careers and enriched their food writing for the wider British public, enhancing its understanding of cooking and the enjoyment of food.

For all the notable and outstanding women whose careers in creative, sporting and leisure endeavours chronicled in this book, both gender and Jewishness were intrinsic to the challenges they faced and the successes they achieved. With varying backgrounds and hailing from different eras and social milieus, as British women in the creative arts, they share in common the experience of being Jewish, which for some was limiting, for others liberating, but for all, something that enriched and enhanced their drive and creativity.

–––––

Endnotes

INTRODUCTION

1 Redefining the Diva, www.vam.ac.uk

2 Sarah Bernhardt, daughter of a Jewish courtesan, was known for her melodrama, using extravagant gesture to express emotion. She took on powerful stage roles both male and female, from Hamlet to Joan of Arc.

3 Michael Galchinsky, *The Origin of the Modern Jewish Woman Writer. Romance and Reform in Victorian England* (Detroit: Wayne State University Press, 1996), pp. 10-11.

4 Nadia Valman, *The Jewess in Nineteenth-Century British Literary Culture* (Cambridge: Cambridge University Press, 2007).

5 Deborah Epstein Nord, *Victorian Studies*, vol. 50 (3), Spring 2008 (Indiana: Indiana University Press), pp. 503-504.

6 Rebecca is the courageous, virtuous daughter of Isaac of York, a Jewish moneylender in twelfth century England. She is a devout Jew and a practicing healer who tends to the knight Ivanhoe after he is wounded in a tournament and falls in love with him. As it is impossible for a Jew and Christian to be together she suppresses her feelings. Her empathy, compassion and tolerance make her a true nineteenth century heroine.

7 Heidi Kaufman, *Victorian Review*, Vol. 35 (1), 2009, p. 263.

8 *Leah, the Forsaken* is about a Hungarian Jewish refugee woman who falls in love with an Austrian but is prohibited from staying in his village because of her religion.

9 A romance about a Christian girl from Prague who falls in love with a Jewish merchant.

10 Nadia Valman, *The Jewess in Nineteenth-Century British Literary Culture*, p. 16.

11 Heidi Kaufman, *Victorian Review*, Vol. 35 (1) 2009, p. 263.

12 Nadia Valman, *The Jewess in Nineteenth Century British Literary Culture*, pp. 52-53.

13 Ibid., p. 12.

14 Food from eastern-central Europe.

15 An assortment of cooking traditions that developed among the Jews of Spain, the Mediterranean, Turkey and Arab countries.

1. THEATRE

1   Rachel (Eliza Rachel Felix) 1821-1858 is often credited with reviving the classical French tragedies of Racine and Corneille in the era of Romanticism. Rachel was born near the Swiss town of Mumpf to itinerant Jewish peddlers who sold second hand clothes from a wagon they used as both home and warehouse. In 1931 the family settled in Marais, the Jewish neighbourhood in Paris. Throughout her life she remained faithful to her family and Judaism and had numerous well publicized love affairs including one with Louis Napoleon (Emperor Napoleon III).

2   *Times of Israel*, 1 October 2019.

3   Robert Gottlieb, *Sarah* (New Haven and London: Yale University Press, 2010), p. 154.

4   Ibid.

5   *Haaretz*, 22 October 2013.

6   Robert Gottlieb, *Sarah*, p. 154.

7   *Times of Israel*, 1 October 2019.

8   Abraham Goldfaden (1840-1908) was a Russian-born Jewish poet, playwright, stage director and actor and author of some 40 plays. He is considered the father of modern Jewish theatre.

9   Nahum Meir Schaikewitz (1849-1905), also known by his pseudonym Shomer, was a Russian-born Yiddish Hebrew novelist and playwright.

10 David Mazower, *Yiddish Theatre in London* (London: Museum of the Jewish East End, 1987), pp. 9-18.

11 David Mazower, 'Women in East End Yiddish Theatre'. Talk given at Tower Hamlets Library, 23 March 2017.

12 Vivi Lachs, *Whitechapel Noise* (Detroit, Michigan: Wayne State University Press, 2018), p. 50.

13 Alice Malin, 'Yiddish Theatre: Genre Blurring, Feminist, Forgotten?' *Exeunt*, 21 October 2015.

14 David Mazower, *Yiddish Theatre in London*, p. 22.

15 Maggie B. Gale, 'British Actresses, 1900-1950: Professional Transformations', in *The Palgrave Handbook of Women on the Stage*, ed. by Jan Sewell and Clare Snout (Basingstoke: Palgrave Macmillan, 2020).

16 Maggie B. Gale and John Stokes (eds.), *The Cambridge Companion to the Actress* (Cambridge: Cambridge University Press, 2007), pp. 95, 108.

17 *Jewish Chronicle*, 10 February 1956, p. 17.

18 *Guardian*, 3 June 2011.

19 Miriam Karlin, *Some Sort Of A Life* (London: Oberon, 2007), pp. ix-x.

20 Ibid., p. 32.

21 A woman's wig, worn for religious purposes as a form of head-covering. Married Jewish women are expected to cover their hair when in the presence of men other than husband or close family members.

22   *Jewish Chronicle*, 22 September 1989, p. S10.

23   *Jewish Chronicle*, 17 December 1982, p. 12.

24   *Jewish Chronicle*, 15 December 2006, p. S28.

25   *The Stage and Television Today*, 10 July 1958, p. 12.

26   *The Stage and Television Today*, 24 December 1947, p. 5.

27   *The Stage and Television Today*, 30 September 1948.

28   *Sunday Empire News*, 5 March 1950.

29   *Jewish Chronicle*, 13 January 1950, p. 5.

30   *The Stage and Television Today*, 19 February 1955, p. 16.

31   *The Stage and Television Today*, 16 June 1954, p. 59.

32   *The Stage and Television Today*, 6 January 1955, p. 9.

33   *The Stage and Television Today*, 26 June 1958, p. 8.

34   *Telegraph*, 3 June 2011.

35   *Guardian*, 23 April 2018.

36   *The Scotsman*, 5 June 2011.

37   *Jewish Chronicle*, 16 March 2012, 0. 28.

38   Miriam Karlin, *Some Sort Of A Life*, p. 100.

39   *The Daily Express*, 12 September 1977, p. 19.

40   *The Stage and Television Today*, 4 August 1949, p. 7.

41   *The Stage and Television Today*, 4 December 1952, p. 9.

42   *The Stage and Television Today*, 24 September 1953, p. 12.

43   *The Stage and Television Today*, 13 January 1955, p. 9.

44   *Jewish Chronicle*, 9 November 1956, p. 26.

45   *The Stage and Television Today*, 5 December 1956; 6 December 1956, p. 9.

46   *The Stage and Television Today*, 2 June 1966, p. 13.

47   *Variety*, 21 March 1962, p. 66.

48   *Jewish Chronicle*, 24 February 1967, p. 27.

49   *Jewish Chronicle*, 17 March 1967, p. 27.

50   *Jewish Chronicle*, 21 February 1992.

51   Laurence Marks and Maurice Gran have been one of the most successful writing partnerships since they co-wrote the popular sitcom *Holding the Fort* in 1980. Other works included *The New Statesman*, *Birds of a Feather* and *Goodnight Sweetheart*.

52   Ibid.

53   *The Stage and Television Today*, 21 November 1985, p. 14.

54   *Jewish Chronicle*, 11 March 1955, p. 13.

55   Miriam Karlin, *Some Sort Of A Life*, p. 60.

56   Ibid., p. 68.

57   *Jewish Chronicle*, 22 September 1989, p. 10.

58   Miriam Karlin, *Some Sort Of A Life*, p. 45.

59   *The Stage and Television Today*, 24 October 1951, p. 71.

60   *The Stage and Television Today*, 26 June 1952, p. 10.

61   *The Stage and Television Today*, 12 February 1953, p. 9.

62   *The Stage and Television Today,* 26 September 1957, p. 9.
63   *The Stage and Television Today,* 18 February 1960, p. 17.
64   *The Stage and Television Today,* 8 July 1954, p.10.
65   *The Stage and Television Today,* 7 May 1970, p. 14.
66   *The Stage and Television Today,* 30 January 1975, p. 11.
67   *The Stage and Television Today,* 1 October 1981, p. 13.
68   *The Stage and Television Today,* 9 June 1983, p. 11.
69   *The Stage and Television Today,* 11 October 1983, p. 23.
70   *The Stage and Television Today,* 7 January 1954, p. 8.
71   *Jewish Chronicle,* 21 February 1992, p. 21.
72   *Jewish Chronicle,* 26 November 1993, p. 56.
73   The Anti-Nazi League was an organisation set up in 1977 on the initiative of
     the Socialist Workers Party with sponsorship from some trade unions and the
     endorsement of a list of prominent people to oppose the rise of the far-right
     groups in the United Kingdom. It was wound down in 1981. It was relaunched
     in 1992 but merged into Unite Against Fascism in 2003.
74   *Jewish Chronicle,* 6 March 1981, p. 4.
75   *Jewish Chronicle,* 21 February 1992.
76   *Jewish Chronicle,* 23 July 1973.
77   Miriam Karlin, *Some Sort Of A Life,* pp. 108-109.
78   Leader of the Labour Party and Leader of the Opposition 1983-1992.
79   Miriam Karlin, *Some Sort Of A Life,* pp. 192-197.
80   *Jewish Chronicle,* 16 June 2008, p. 38.
81   Ibid., p. 211.
82   *Guardian,* 3 June 2011.
83   Ibid.
84   Miriam Karlin, *Some Sort Of A Life,* pp. 7-8.
85   Ibid., p. 223.
86   *Jewish Chronicle,* 28 October 1960, p. 12.
87   *Jewish Chronicle,* 2 May 1969, p. 19; 11 May 1973, p. 14.
88   Miriam Karlin, *Some Sort of A Life,* p. 90.
89   Ibid., pp. 88, 90, 120.
90   *Jewish Chronicle,* 16 June 2008, p. 38.
91   Miriam Karlin, *Some Sort of a Life,* p. 3.
92   *Guardian,* 3 June 2011.
93   Sydney Tafler was an English Jewish actor remembered for numerous films
     and TV appearances from the 1940s-1970s. These included *The Spy Who
     Loved Me* (1977), *The Birthday Party* (1968) and *It Always Rains on Sunday*
     (1947).
94   *Jewish Chronicle,* 16 December 1977, p. 8.
95   Miriam Karlin, *Some Sort Of A Life,* p. 69.
96   *Telegraph,* 3 June 2011.
97   *Jewish Chronicle,* 1 December 2017, p. 30.

98 Baron Basil Feldman was a very successful businessman and Conservative member of the House of Lords (1996-2017).

99 Fenella Fielding and Simon McKay, *Do You Mind if I Smoke?* (London: Peter Owen Publishers, 2017).

100 Interview with Gita Feldman, 24 May 2019, London.

101 Fenella Fielding and Simon McKay, *Do You Mind if I Smoke?*

102 Interview with Gita Feldman, 24 May 2019, London.

103 *Jewish Chronicle*, 21 December 1962, p. 25.

104 *Jewish Chronicle*, 30 November 1962, Supplement p. 11.

105 Fenella Fielding and Simon McKay, *Do You Mind if I Smoke?*

106 *The Stage*, 8 October 1953, p. 10.

107 Fenella Fielding and Simon McKay, *Do You Mind If I Smoke?*

108 Jeffrey Bernard was an English journalist best known for his weekly column 'Low Life' in the *Spectator* magazine. He became associated with the bohemian atmosphere that existed in London's Soho district.

109 Andrew Ross, *Carry on Actors* (Clacton on Sea: Apex Publishing Limited, 2011), p. xii.

110 Sally Hibbin, *What A Carry On* (London: Hamlyn, 1988), p. 96.

111 *The Sun*, 12 September 2018.

112 *Jewish Chronicle*, 27 September 1963, p. 47.

113 *Jewish Chronicle*, 3 July 1964, p. 30.

114 *Jewish Chronicle*, 11 September 1964, p. 35.

115 *Jewish Chronicle*, 17 June 1966, p. 33.

116 *Jewish Chronicle*, 3 November 1967, p. 33.

117 *Jewish Chronicle*, 12 January 1968, p. 30.

118 *Jewish Chronicle*, 31 May 1985, p. 3.

119 *Jewish Chronicle*, 3 January 1997, p. 24.

120 Interview with Gita Feldman, 24 May 2019, London.

121 Ibid.

122 *Jewish Chronicle*, 1 December 2017, p. 30.

123 Interview with Gita Feldman, 24 May 2019, London.

124 *Jewish Chronicle*, 1 December 2017, p. 30.

125 *Jewish Chronicle*, 14 September 2018, p. 2.

126 Funeral programme for Order of Service, 17 October 2018.

127 *Daily Telegraph*, 28 May 2019, p. 26.

128 *Jewish Chronicle*, 14 September 2018, p. 2.

129 *Telegraph*, 18 March 2002.

130 Jewish Women's Archive, www.jwa.org.

131 Claire Bloom, *Leaving a Doll's House* (London: Virago Press, 1996), pp. 1, 8.

132 Jewish Women's Archive.

133 *Jewish Chronicle*, 6 January 2017, p. 32.

134 Tony Earshaw in conversation with Claire Bloom, Widescreen Weekend, Bradford, March 2011.

135 Claire Bloom, *Limelight and After: The Education of an Actress* (Harper & Row, 1982), p. 36.
136 *Telegraph*, 18 March 2002.
137 Jewish Women's Archive.
138 *Guardian*, 23 December 2016.
139 *Huffington Post*, 4 October 2012.
140 *Jewish Chronicle*, 7 May 2004, p. 23.
141 *Jewish Chronicle*, 17 October 1952, p. 24.
142 *New York Times*, 24 October 1952.
143 Tom Earshaw in conversation with Claire Bloom, Widescreen Weekend, Bradford, March 2011.
144 *Wall Street Journal*, 25 May 2011.
145 Mailonline, 13 May 2009.
146 *Jewish Chronicle*, 6 January 2017, p. 31.
147 The BBC six-part drama follows Russian born Jewish inventor Samuel Petrukin who specialises in developing hearing aids and who is approached by MI5 to use his technological expertise to spy on an aristocratic family, Kathleen and Richard Shaw. Bloom plays the aunt of Kathleen Shaw.
148 *Guardian,* 23 December 2016.
149 Interview with George McGhee, JW3, London, 31 March 2019.
150 Ibid.
151 *Jewish Chronicle*, 25 June 1982, p. 48.
152 *Guardian*, 23 December 2016.
153 MailOnline, 13 May 2009.
154 Jewish Women's Archive
155 MailOnline, 13 May 2009.
156 *Jewish Chronicle*, 6 January 2017, p. 33.
157 MailOnline, 13 May 2009.
158 *People*, 46 (18), 1996.
159 Mary Grew appeared on the West End stage. Her performances included roles in *Welded* by Eugene O'Neill at the Gate Theatre Studio where she played a prostitute 'and gave the finest piece of acting in the play' (*Jewish Chronicle*, 14 June 1929, p. 30); *Forty-Seven* at the Prince of Wales Theatre, a drama of the Black and Tan period in Ireland. Grew played the lover of a British spy masquerading as an Irish liberator. Her performance was 'a deeply sincere and intelligent reading of the part' (*Jewish Chronicle*, 24 April 1930, p. 32). She also appeared in Ibsen's *Ghost* at the Everyman alongside Sybil Thorndike (*Jewish Chronicle*, 25 April 1930, p. 32).
160 *Jewish Chronicle*, 25 June 1982, p. 48.
161 *Jewish Chronicle*, 7 May 2004, p. 23.
162 Claire Bloom, *Limelight and After*, p. 5.
163 The Zebulun Palestine Seafaring Society was set up in the early 1920s and dedicated to the revival of Jewish seafaring and the development of Jewish Merchant Marine in Palestine.

164 *Jewish Chronicle*, 24 October 1952, p. 6.

165 *Jewish Chronicle*, 25 June 1982, p. 48.

166 *Jewish Chronicle*, 7 March 1997.

167 Bloom, *Leaving a Doll's House*, p. 27.

168 *Jewish Chronicle*, 10 January 1997, p. 28.

169 Ibid.

170 Tom Earshaw in conversation with Claire Bloom.

171 *Jewish Chronicle*, 21 June 2013, p. 8.

172 Tom Earshaw in conversation with Claire Bloom.

173 *Jewish Chronicle*, 21 June 2013, p. 8.

174 *Sunday Times*, 27 May 2010.

175 *Guardian*, 23 November 2015.

176 *Independent*, 6 July 1993.

177 *Desert Island Discs*, 24 June 1968, www.bbc.co.uk

178 *Independent*, 6 July 1993.

179 *Jewish Chronicle*, 29 April 1966, p. 9.

180 *Guardian*, 23 November 2015.

181 *New York Times*, 4 November 1979.

182 *Jewish Chronicle*, 14 June 1996, p. 28.

183 www.varsity.co.uk

184 *Guardian*, 26 October 2019.

185 Harry Thompson, *Peter Cook: A Biography* (London: Hodder & Stoughton, 1997).

186 Tara Taghizadeh, *A Great Silly Grin: The British Satire Boom of the 1960s*, www.popmatters.com, 16 July 2002.

187 *Guardian*, 23 November 2015.

188 Tara Taghizadeh, *A Great Silly Grin*.

189 *Guardian*, 23 November 2015.

190 *Desert Island Discs*, 24 June 1968.

191 Eleanor Bron, *The Pillow Book of Eleanor Bron* (London: Metheun, 1987), p. xi.

192 *Independent*, 6 July 1993.

193 www.varsity.co.uk

194 *Independent*, 20 August 1992.

195 *Independent*, 6 July 1993.

196 *Birmingham Daily Post*, 14 November 1978, p. 6.

197 *Jewish Chronicle*, 25 December 1964, p. 19.

198 *Jewish Chronicle*, 6 November 1998.

199 *Desert Island Discs*, 24 June 1968

200 *Guardian*, 23 November 2015.

201 *Jewish Chronicle*, 8 January 2016, p. 24.

202 *Guardian*, 23 November 2015.

203 *Jewish Chronicle*, 6 May 1988, p. 21.

204 *Jewish Chronicle*, 4 October 1991, p. 5.

205 *Jewish Chronicle*, 6 November 1998.

206 Ibid.

207 www.bbc.co.uk, 25 July 2014.

208 *Jewish Chronicle*, 25 December 1964, p. 19.

209 www.screenonline.org.uk

210 *Jewish Chronicle*, 6 November 1998.

211 www.screenonline.org.uk

212 Miriam Margolyes, *This Much Is True* (London: John Murray 2021), pp. 5, 8, 13-14.

213 Jewish service organisation.

214 *Jewish Renaissance*, January 2007, p. 6.

215 *Telegraph*, 21 February 2015.

216 *Desert Island Discs*, 28 September 2008.

217 *Telegraph*, 21 February 2015.

218 *Daily Record*, 2 November 2011.

219 *Jewish Renaissance*, January 2007, p. 6.

220 *Guardian*, 25 September 2021, p. 69.

221 *Jewish Renaissance*, January 2007, p. 6.

222 *Scotsman*, 6 August 2012.

223 *Desert Island Discs*, 28 September 2008.

224 *Guardian*, 22 June 2012.

225 Miriam Margolyes, *This Much Is True*, pp. 7, 91, 367.

226 A prayer sung in Jewish synagogues at the beginning of the service on the eve of the Day of Atonement.

227 *Desert Island Discs*, 28 September 2008.

228 Miriam Margolyes, *This Much is True*, p. 368

229 Ibid., p. 367

230 *Jewish Renaissance*, January 2007.

231 *Telegraph*, 21 February 2015.

232 *Jewish Renaissance*, January 2007.

233 Ibid.

234 *Times*, 13 July 2020.

235 *Jewish Renaissance*, January 2007.

236 *Telegraph*, 21 February 2015.

237 Guardian, 7 February 2021.

238 *Mirror*, 14 November 2019.

239 *Guardian*, 7 February 2021.

240 Ibid.

241 *Telegraph*, 21 February 2019.

242 *Jewish Renaissance*, January 2007.

243 *Scotsman*, 8 August 2012.

244 *Guardian*, 25 September 2021, p. 69.

245 Dame Joan Plowright (1929 -) is one of the most distinguished actors of her generation. She has had a distinguished career on stage and screen spanning six decades and was a member of the National Theatre.

246 *Desert Island Discs*, 28 September 2008.

247 *Telegraph,* 21 February 2015.

248 *The Scotsman,* 6 August 2012.

249 *Telegraph,* 21 February 2015.

250 Tourette syndrome is a neurological disorder characterized by repetitive, stereotyped, involuntary movements and vocalisations called tics.

251 *Desert Island Discs,* 28 September 2008.

252 *Desert Island Discs,* 24 January 1986, interviewed by Michael Parkinson.

253 *Jewish Quarterly,* Winter 2006/2007, no. 204.

254 *Jewish Renaissance,* July 2005, p. 10.

255 *Jewish Quarterly,* Winter 2006/7.

256 *Jewish Chronicle,* 19 April 1968, p. 9.

257 *Desert Island Discs,* 24 January 1986.

258 *Telegraph,* 4 April 2014.

259 *Jewish Quarterly,* Winter 2006/7.

260 *Jewish Renaissance,* July 2005, p. 10.

261 Jack Rosenthal (1931-2004) was an English playwright who wrote 129 early episodes of the ITV soap *Coronation Street* and over 150 screenplays, including original TV plays, feature films and adaptations.

262 *Jewish Renaissance,* July 2005, p. 10.

263 *Jewish Chronicle,* 10 March 2017, p. 21.

264 Joyce Grenfell (1910-1979) was a British comedienne who was the queen of the comic monologue and was an acclaimed comedy performer on stage, radio and television.

265 *Guardian,* 26 January 2001.

266 *Jewish Chronicle,* 25 July, 2016.

267 *The Guardian,* 30 May 2002.

268 *The Oldie,* 13 September 2018.

269 *The Wee Review,* 10 August 2018.

270 *Independent,* 19 July 2006.

271 *Jewish Chronicle,* 15 July 2015, p. 9.

272 Maureen Lipman, *Something to Fall Back On* (London: Robson Books, 1987).

273 Yiddish word for person of integrity.

274 *Daily Telegraph,* 29 October 2014.

275 *Daily Telegraph,* 27 January 2015.

276 *Jewish Chronicle,* 27 April 2018, p. 49.

277 *Times,* 9 April 2018.

278 *Independent,* 8 April 2018.

279 *Daily Express,* 22 November 2019.

280 *Desert Island Discs,* 24 January 1986.

281 *Daily Telegraph,* 11 October 2011.

282   OfficialLondonTheatre.com, 17 October 2007.

283   *Daily Telegraph*, 17 June 2006.

284   Digitalspy, 23 July 2009.

285   OfficialLondonTheatre.com, 18 April 2008/

286   *Daily Telegraph*, 17 June 2006.

287   Ibid.

288   Ibid.

289   www.digitalspy.com, 27 October 2005.

290   www.mihigh.fandom.com

291   British Theatre Guide, 2003.

292   *Evening Standard*, 22 October 2003.

293   *Daily Telegraph*, 11 October 2011.

294   *Jewish Chronicle*, 11 January 2019, p. 45.

295   Londontheatre.co.uk, 2 January 2019.

296   *Jewish Chronicle*, 27 January 2017, p. 42.

297   *Daily Express*, 30 July 2017.

298   *Goodness Gracious Me* is a BBC2 comedy show (1998-2001) that explored British Asian culture and the conflict and integration between traditional South Asian culture and modern British life.

299   *Inews*, 9 August 2021.

300   *Jewish Chronicle,* 26 June 2009, p. 28.

301   *Jewish Chronicle,* 22 April, 2016, p. 11.

302   *Jewish Chronicle,* 19 April 2012.

303   *Jewish Chronicle,* 14 July 2017 p. 36.

304   *Guardian*, 1 July 2017.

305   *Jewish Chronicle,* 14 July 2007 p. 36.

306   *Guardian*, 13 March 2019.

307   *Jewish Chronicle*, 24 June 2016, p. 40.

308   OfficialLondonTheatre.com, 17 April 2007.

309   *Independent*, 1 February 2008.

310   *Guardian*, 30 January 2008.

311   *Times Saturday Review*, 3 February 2024, p. 6.

312   *Guardian*, 9 March 2019

313   *Times Saturday Review*, 3 February 2024, p. 6.

314   *Jewish Chronicle*, 7 April 2017, p. 4.

315   BritishTheatre.com, 12 March 2020.

316   *Guardian*, 21 February 2019.

317   *Inews*, 9 August 2021.

318   *Jewish Chronicle,* 30 November 2018, p. 004.

319   Podtail.com.trolled

320   Londontheatre.co.uk, 2 January 2019.

321   *Jewish Chronicle*, 8 October 2021, p. 27.

322   'Sophie Okonedo Wins a Tony Award for *Raisin in the Sun*', 8 June 2014, Jewish Women's Archive, jwa.com.

323 *Jewish Chronicle*, 9 May 2008, p. 21.

324 *Daily Mail*, 28 January 2005.

325 Sophie Okonedo, Jewish Women's Archive.

326 *Jewish Chronicle*, 25 June 1999, p. 40.

327 *Jewish Chronicle*, 11 December 1998, p. 38.

328 *Evening Standard*, 6 December 2018.

329 Hanif Kureishi is an actor and writer who was born in London to Pakistani and English parents.. His 1985 screenplay *My Beautiful Laundrette*, a play about a gay British Pakistani youth in 1980s London was nominated for an Oscar after being made into an award winning film by Stephen Frears. His debut novel *The Buddha of Suburbia* won the 1990 Whitbread First Novel Award.

330 Sophie Okonedo, encyclopedia.com

331 *Jewish Journal*, 21 October 2009.

332 *Guardian*, 16 July 2009.

333 *Guardian*, 10 April 2014.

334 'Ratched: Sophie Okonedo Masterfully Plays Five Unique Characters', 29 September 2020, cbr.com.

335 'Sophie Okonedo Wins a Tony Award for *Raisin in the Sun*, 8 June 2014, Jewish Women's Archive.

336 *Evening Standard*, 6 December 2018.

337 *Jewish Chronicle*, 11 December 1998, p. 38.

338 Sophie Okenodo, Jewish Women's Archive.

339 *Jewish Chronicle*, 7 October 2016.

340 *Evening Standard*, 6 December 2018.

341 *Express*, 6 May, 2016.

342 *Times*, 8 December 2017.

343 'Sophie Okonedo: On Her Way From Wembley', *Jewish Chronicle*, 7 October 2016.

344 Miriam Margolyes, *This Much is True* (London: John Murray, 2021), p. 14.

345 James Agate, *Ego 6* (London: George G Harlan & Co. Ltd, 1944), pp. 89-90. James Agate (1877-1947) was an English diarist and theatre critic in the inter-war period, working for *The Saturday Review*, *The Sunday Times* and the BBC.

346 Samantha Spiro (1968 -) is best known for portraying Barbara Windsor (famous for her roles in the *Carry On* films and the soap opera *EastEnders)* on stage and screen.

347 *Inews*, 9 August 2021.

348 *Jewish Chronicle*, 31 December 2021, p. 3.

2. WRITERS

1 Michael Galchinsky, *The Origin of the Modern Jewish Woman Writer. Romance and Reform in Victorian England* (Detroit: Wayne State University Press, 1996, pp. 10-11.

2   Ibid., pp. 191-192.

3   Ibid.

4   Marion Hartog (1821-1907) and her sister Celia Moss (1819-1973) wrote and published their first book of poems *Early Efforts* (1839) before publishing a collection of historical romances entitled *The Romance of Jewish History*. This book and its sequel *Tales of Jewish History* are among the first works of fiction ever published by Jewish women anywhere in the world; they promoted reform of English Jews' gender and religious practices and an early version of political Zionism. In 1855 Hartog published *The Jewish Sabbath Journal*, the first Jewish women's periodical in history that intended to provide mothers with material with which to further their children's education.

5   Cecil Bloom, 'People of the Book: Grace Aguilar and Amy Levy',*Jewish Currents*, 30 January 2013.

6   Michael Galchinsky, Grace Aguilar, jwa.org.

7   *Jewish Chronicle*, 28 January 2011, p. 31.

8 ' A New Woman at Cambridge', *Jewish Currents*, 10 November 2014.

9   Cecil Bloom, 'People of the Book: Grace Aguilar and Amy Levy', *Jewish Currents*, 30 January 2013.

10 *Jewish Renaissance*, April 2007, pp. 37-38.

11 Julia Neuberger, 'The Short Brilliant Life of Amy Levy', *Jewish Renaissance*, Autumn 2021, p. 32.

12 Jewish Lives Project, www.jewishlivesproject.com

13 Paul Bailey, *Three Queer Lives* (London: Hamish Hamilton, 2001). pp. 71-76.

14 Ibid.

15 A scroll containing a handwritten copy of the Torah, the five books of Moses.

16 *Jewish Chronicle*, 12 January 1934, p. 13.

17   Paul Bailey, *Three Queer Lives*, pp. 77-79.

18 Remembering Naomi Jacob, womenshistorynetwork.org, 27 August 2014.

19 Paul Bailey, *Three Queer Lives*, p. 69.

20 Claire Tylee, *In the Open. Jewish Women Writers and British Culture* (Newark: University of Delaware Press, 2006), p. 31.

21 Paul Bailey, *Three Queer Lives*, pp. 155-56.

22 *Jewish Chronicle*, 21 November 2014, p. 50.

23 Claire Tylee, *In the Open*, p. 31

24 *Jewish Chronicle*, 7 August 1992, p. VI.

25 Claire Tylee, *In the Open*, pp. 30-32.

26 Ibid.

27 Ibid.

28 Ibid.

29 *Jewish Chronicle*, 13 November 1936, p. 26.

30 *Jewish Chronicle*, 13 March 1953, p. 22.

31 *Jewish Chronicle*, 12 June 1936, p. 15.

32 *Jewish Chronicle*, 2 June 1939, p. 16.

33   Claire Tylee, *In the Open*, p. 31.

34 Paul Bailey, *Three Queer Lives,* p. 69.

35 Ibid., p. 237.

36 Claire Tylee, *In the Open,* p. 32.

37 Ibid., pp. 16, 19.

38 *Jewish Renaissance*, January 2019, p. 45.

39 *Jewish Renaissance*, July 2007, p. 45.

40 Anglo-Jewish writers: Twentieth Century, www.jwa.org

41 Glenda Abramson (ed.), *The Encyclopedia of Modern Jewish Culture* (London: Routledge, 2004).

42 *Jewish Chronicle*, 15 November 1996, p. 23.

43 *Guardian*, 27 May 1971, p. 11.

44 *Coventry Evening Telegraph*, 14 May 1959, p. 9.

45 *Jewish Chronicle*, 15 November 1996, p. 23.

46 www.jewishlivesproject.com

47 *Jewish Chronicle*, 6 December 1996, p. 29.

48 *Times Literary Supplement*, 10 June 1960, p. 365.

49 *Jewish Chronicle,* 10 June 1960, p. 20.

50 Ibid.

51 *Jewish Chronicle*, 28 November 1975, p. 56.

52 *Jewish Chronicle,* 3 February 1989.

53 *Birmingham Daily Post*, 7 June 1960, p. 3.

54 *Guardian*, 15 November 1996, p. 18.

55 The James Tait Prize is awarded annually. Previous winners include C P Snow, Evelyn Waugh, Angus Wilson and Ivy Compton-Burnett.

56 *Guardian*, 15 November 1996, p. 18.

57 *Jewish Chronicle*, 10 May 1963, p. 26.

58 *Times Literary Supplement*, 17 May 1963, p. 353.

59 *Times Literary Supplement*, 25 May 1967, p. 471.

60 *Jewish Chronicle*, 22 October 1971, p. 7.

61 *Jewish Chronicle,* 16 April 1971, p. 26.

62 *Jewish Chronicle*, 13 September 1963, p. 37.

63 *Jewish Chronicle*, 26 April 1968, p. 28.

64 *Jewish Chronicle*, 7 April 1961, p. 10.

65 *Jewish Chronicle*, 1 January 1962.

66 *Jewish Chronicle*, 31 January 1964, p. 8.

67 *Jewish Chronicle*, 27 September 1968, p. 24.

68 *Guardian*, 27 May 1971, p. 11.

69 Ibid.

70 *Jewish Chronicle*, 6 December 1996, p. 29.

71 *Jewish Chronicle*, 15 November 1996, p. 23.

72 *Jewish Renaissance*, October 2007, p. 47.

73 Bernice Rubens, *When I Grow Up* (London: Little Brown, 2005), p. 1.

74 www.roathlocalhistorysociety.org, 4 June 2020.

75 *Desert Island Discs*, BBC Radio Four, 8 December 1991.

76 *Independent,* 15 October 2004.

77 *Jewish Renaissance,* Winter 2002, p. 6.

78 *Desert Island Discs,* BBC Radio Four, 8 December 1991.

79 *Jewish Renaissance,* October 2007, p. 47.

80 Jewish Women's Archive.

81 *Independent,* 15 October 2004.

82 Jewish Women's Archive.

83 Sorrell Kerbel (ed.), *Jewish Writers of the Twentieth Century* (London: Fitzroy Dearborn, 2003), p. 477.

84 Ibid.

85 *Guardian,* 14 October 2004.

86 Sorrel Kerbel (ed.), *Jewish Writers of the Twentieth Century.*

87 Yiddish expression for 'pride'.

88 Sorrell Kerbel (ed.,) *Jewish Writers of the Twentieth Century*

89 *Guardian,* 14 October 2004

90 *Jewish Renaissance,* October 2007, p. 47.

91 Sorrel Kerbel (ed.), *Jewish Writers of the Twentieth Century.*

92 Desert Island Discs, 8 September 1991.

93 *Guardian,* 14 October 2004.

94 Sorrel Kerbel (ed.), *Jewish Writers of the Twentieth Century.*

95 Ibid.

96 Jewish Women's Archive.

97 *Guardian,* 14 October 2004.

98 *Jewish Renaissance,* Winter 2002, p. 6.

99 *Guardian,* 14 October 2004.

100 Sorrel Kerbel (ed.). *Jewish Writers of the Twentieth Century.*

101 *Jewish Renaissance,* Winter 2004, p. 42.

102 *Guardian,* 17 October 2003.

103 *Jewish Renaissance,* Winter 2004, p. 42.

104 *Guardian,* 14 October 2004.

105 *Jewish Chronicle,* 21 October 2016, p. 28.

106 www.Jewishlivesproject.com

107 Cheryl Alexander Malcolm, *Understanding Anita Brookner* (Columbia: University of South Carolina Press, 2002), p.4.

108 *Guardian,* 15 March 2016.

109 John Haffenden, *Novelists in Interview* (London: Metheun, 1985), p. 60.

110 Cheryl Alexander Malcolm, *Understanding Anita Brookner,* p.1.

111 John Haffenden, *Novelists in Interview,* pp. 60-61.

112 Cheryl Alexander Malcolm, *Understanding Anita Brookner,* p.1.

113 John Haffenden, *Novelists in Interview,* pp. 61, 68.

114 *Jewish Chronicle,* 17 March 1995, p. 25.

115 *Jewish Renaissance,* January 2008, p. 47.

116 Clare Hanson, *Hysterical Fictions. The Woman's Novel in the Twentieth Century* (London: Macmillan Press, 2000), p. 147.

117 Olya Kenyon, *Women Novelists Today* (Brighton: Harvester Press, 1988), p. 12.

118 *Jewish Chronicle*, 26 October 1984, p. 24.

119 John Haffenden, *Novelists in Interview*, p. 75.

120 *Jewish Renaissance*, January 2008, p. 47.

121 Cheryl Alexander Malcolm, *Understanding Anita Brookner*, pp. 112-117.

122 Adrienne Baker, *The Jewish Woman in Contemporary Society: Transitions and Traditions* (London: Macmillan, 1993), pp. 17-20.

123 Jill Swale, 'Feminism and the Jewish Novel', *Jewish Quarterly*, 39 (3), Autumn 1992, p. 49.

124 Claire M. Tylee (ed.), *In The Open: Jewish Women Writers and British Culture* (Newark: University of Delaware Press, 2006), pp. 110-111.

125 *Jewish Renaissance*, January 2008, p. 47.

126 This is a Jewish mourning rite. Jews will tear a piece of their clothing and this torn garment is worn for the seven days of mourning following the funeral.

127 *Jewish Renaissance*, January 2008, p. 47.

128 *Jewish Chronicle*, 27 September 1985, p. 8.

129 *Jewish Renaissance*, January 2008, p. 47.

130 The Kindertransport was the informal name of a series of rescue efforts which brought thousands of Jewish children to Britain from Germany and parts of Europe controlled by the Nazis prior to the Second World War.

131 *Jewish Chronicle*, 9 August 2002, p. 26.

132 Olga Kenyon, *Women Novelists Today*, pp. 104-5.

133 Cheryl Alexander Malcolm, *Understanding Anita Brookner*, p. 2.

134 Ibid., p. 3.

135 *Jewish Chronicle*, 18 March 2016, p. 49.

136 Emanuel Litvinoff (1915-2011). Poet and writer who chronicled his Jewish East End upbringing.

137 Cheryl Alexander Malcolm, *Understanding Anita Brookner*, pp. 11-12.

138 Sorrel Kerbel (ed.), *Jewish Writers of the Twentieth Century* (London: Fitzroy Dearborn, 2003), p. 104.

139 *Jewish Chronicle*, 26 August 1994, p. 8.

140 BBC News, 15 March 2016.

141 *Jewish Chronicle*, 18 March 2016, p. 49.

142 John Haffenden, *Novelists in Interview*, p. 75.

143 *Jewish Renaissance*, January 2008, p. 47.

144 *Jewish Renaissance*, July 2006, p. 6.

145 *Jewish Renaissance,* January 2008, p. 19.

146 *Jewish Renaissance*, July 2006, p. 6.

147 Linda Grant, *Remind Me Who I Am Again* (London: Granta, 2011), pp. 71-72.

148 Ruth Gilbert, *Writing Jewish. Contemporary British-Jewish Literature* (Basingstoke: Palgrave Macmillan, 2013), pp. 6-7.

149 *Guardian*, 17 January 2011.

150 'Unsettling Women: Contemporary Women's Writing and Diaspora' conference, University of Leicester, 2008; University of Leicester archive, accessed 2 February 2020.

151 *Jewish Chronicle*, 12 July 1996, p. 27.

152 Ibid.

153 Unsettling Women: Contemporary Women's Writing and Diaspora.

154 Ibid.

155 *Jewish Chronicle*, 16 September 1994, p. 21.

156 Linda Grant, *Remind Me Who I Am Again*, pp. 34-35.

157 Ibid., pp. 49, 77.

158 *Jewish Renaissance*, July 2006, pp. 6-7.

159 Linda Grant, *Cast Iron Shore* (London: Granta, 1996), p. 2.

160 Ruth Gilbert, *Writing Jewish*, pp. 64-66.

161 *Jewish Chronicle*, 2 June 2017, p. 31.

162 *Jewish Renaissance*, July 2006, p. 6.

163 Ruth Gilbert, *Writing Jewish*, pp. 82-83.

164 Linda Grant, *The People on the Street: A Writer's View of Israel* (London: Virago, 2006), p. 17.

165 Ruth Gilbert, *Writing Jewish*, p. 84

166 *Jewish Renaissance*, April 2006, p. 40.

167 *Jewish Renaissance*, July 2006, p. 6.

168 Linda Grant, *Remind Me Who I Am Again*, p. 33.

169 Ruth Gilbert, *Writing Jewish*, pp. 38-39; 54.

170 *Guardian*, 6 November 2015.

171 Ruth Gilbert, *Writing Jewish*, p. 133.

172 *Jewish Renaissance*, July 2014, p. 50.

173 Ruth Gilbert, *Writing Jewish*, pp. 38-39.

174 *Jewish Chronicle*, 23 June 2006, p. 29.

175 *Jewish Chronicle*, 29 June 2017, p. 39.

176 *Guardian*, 28 October 2016.

177 Ibid.

178 *Independent*, 26 October 2016.

179 It is forbidden for Orthodox Jews to carry on the Sabbath.

180 *Guardian*, 28 October 2016.

181 Nadia Valman (ed.), *Jewish Women Writers in Britain* (Detroit: Wayne State University Press, 2014), p.7.

182 *Jewish Chronicle*, 3 March 2006, p. 43.

183 *Jewish Renaissance*, January 2006, p. 43.

184 *Jewish Chronicle*, 3 March 2006, p. 43.

185 *Telegraph*, 2 July 2006.

186 *Scotsman*, 10 April 2010.

187 Nadia Valman, *Jewish Women Writers in Britain*, p. 8.

188 *Scotsman*, 10 April 2010.

189 *Jewish Chronicle*, 16 June 2006, p. 33.

190 *Jewish Chronicle*, 1 March 2013, p. 12.

191 *Jewish Chronicle*, 3 May 2019, p. 44.

192 *Guardian*, 28 October 2016.

193 *Jewish Chronicle*, 5 October 2012, p. A035.

194 *Jewish Chronicle*, 7 May 2010, p. 31.

195 *Scotsman*, 10 April 2010.

196 Ibid.

197 *Guardian*, 28 October 2010.

198 *Jewish Chronicle*, 12 May 2017, p. 44.

199 *Jewish Renaissance*, July 2017.

200 Ruth Gilbert, *Writing Jewish*, pp. 38-39.

201 Ibid., pp. 133-134.

202 *Guardian*, 8 May 2007.

203 Ibid.

205 *Jewish Chronicle*, 27 April 2007, p31

206 *Guardian*, 8 May 2007.

207 *Jewish Chronicle*, 4 May 2001, p. 33.

208 *Guardian*, 8 May 2007.

209 Splashmags.com, 20 June 2021.

210 *Guardian*, 8 May 2007.

211 *Jewish Chronicle*, 28 February 2003, p. 40.

212 *Jewish Chronicle*, 16 August 2012, p. 29.

213 *Jewish Chronicle*, 2 August 2013, p. 27.

214 *Jewish Renaissance*, Spring 2022, p. 48.

215 *Jewish Quarterly*, 60, 2013, pp. 146-147.

216 *Jewish Renaissance*, July 2007, p. 45.

217 *Jewish Chronicle*, 27 April 2007, p. 51.

218 *Jewish Renaissance*, July 2014, p. 50.

219 *Jewish Chronicle*, 27 April 2007, p. 31.

220 *Jewish Chronicle*, 8 April 2022, p. 50.

221 *Jewish Renaissance*, Spring 2022, p. 48.

222 *Open Book*, BBC Radio 4, 14 March 2019.

223 Splashmag.com, 20 June 2021.

224 *Jewish Quarterly*, 206 (2007), pp. 39-42.

225 *Jewish Chronicle*, 27 April 2007, p. 5.

226 *Jewish Renaissance*, July 2007, p. 45.

227 Ruth Gilbert, *Writing Jewish*, pp. 139-140.

3. POPULAR SINGERS

1 Bob Stanley, *Yeah! Yeah! Yeah! The Story of Pop Music from Bill Haley to Beyonce* (London: Norton, 2015), p. xvii.

2　Lucy O'Brien, *She POP II. The Definitive History of Women in Rock, Pop and Soul* (London: Continium, 2002), pp. 4, 39, 41, 45.

3　Bob Stanley, *Yeah! Yeah!*, p. xvii.

4　Lucy O'Brien, *She POP II*, p. 46.

5　*Daily Mail*, 7 November 2006.

6　*Jewish Chronicle*, 23 December 1994, p. 26.

7　Sandra Caron, *Alma Cogan: A Memoir* (London: Bloomsbury, 1991), pp. 8-10.

8　Ibid., pp. 11-14.

9　Ibid., pp. 16-28.

10　A comical or nonsensical song performed for its comic effect.

11　Sandra Caron, *Alma Cogan*, pp. 39-54.

12　Ibid., pp. 65, 77.

13　*Jewish Chronicle*, 19 June 1959, p. 24.

14　*Jewish Chronicle*, 14 August 1959, p. 10.

15　*Jewish Chronicle*, 28 October 1966, p. 20.

16　Sandra Caron, *Alma Cogan*, pp. 103, 180.

17　*Jewish Chronicle*, 2 August 2002, p. 9.

18　Sandra Caron, *Alma Cogan*, p. 8.

19　Ibid., p. 119.

20　*Daily Mail*, 7 May 2006.

21　*Jewish Chronicle*, 13 September 1991, p. 8.

22　Deborah Geller, *The Brian Epstein Story* (London: Faber and Faber, 2000), p. 60.

23　Sandra Caron, *Alma Cogan*, p. 152.

24　Ray Coleman, *Brian Epstein: The Man Who Made the Beatles* (London: Penguin, 1990), pp. 373-374.

25　*Daily Mail*, 7 May 2006.

26　Lucy O'Brien, *She POP II*, p. 46.

27　*Girl with a Giggle in Her Voice*, BBC documentary 1991.

28　*Daily Express*, 20 October 2016.

29　*Jewish Chronicle*, 29 November 1991, p. 31.

30　Colin Cripps, *Popular Music in the 20th Century* (Cambridge: Cambridge University Press, 1988), p. 42.

31　Simon Napier-Bell, *Black Vinyl White Powder* (London: Ebury Press, 2002), p. 41.

32　John S. Jansen, *Helen Shapiro – Pop Princess* (London: The New English Library Ltd, 1963), pp. 10-11.

33　Helen Shapiro, *Walking Back To Happiness* (London: Harper Collins, 1992), pp. 1-9.

34　*Jewish Chronicle*, 1 January 1961, p. 37.

35　*Jewish Chronicle*, 13 June 2003, p. 43.

36　*Jewish Chronicle*, 30 September 1977, p. 35.

37   *Jewish Chronicle*, 27 May 2011, p. 26.
38   *Jewish Chronicle*, 18 May 1962, p. 32.
39   *Jewish Chronicle*, 28 September 1962, p. 33.
40   *Helen Shapiro – The Kids are Alright. Story of Child Pop Stars*, youtube.
41   *Jewish Chronicle*, 9 May 1969, p. 42.
42   Colin Larkin (ed.), *The Virgin Encyclopedia of Popular Music* (London: Virgin, 1997).
43   *Jewish Chronicle*, 18 August 1967, p. 8.
44   *Jewish Chronicle*, 22 December 1972.
45   Helen Shapiro, *Walking Back to Happiness*, p. 123.
46   *Jewish Chronicle*, 11 January 1963, p. 29.
47   *Jewish Chronicle* 2 November 1979, p. 18.
48   Helen Shapiro, *Walking Back to Happiness*, pp. 180-183.
49   *Church Times*, 14 August 2000.
50   www.jewishtestimonies.com
51   *Jewish Chronicle*, 9 June 1989, p. 31.
52   *Jewish Chronicle* 23 June 1989, p. 5.
53   Helen Shapiro, *Walking Back to Happiness,* p. 188.
54   *Jewish Chronicle*, 16 October 2009, p. 3.
55   Colin Cripps, *Popular Music in the 20th Century* (Cambridge: Cambridge University Press, 1988), p. 67.
56   'The Story of Vinegar Joe', www.loudersound.com, 6 April 2019.
57   Colin Larkin (ed.), *Encyclopedia of Popular Music* (London: Omnibus Press, 2007), p. 221.
58   *Jewish Chronicle*, 10 August 2012, p. 29.
59   www.allmusic.com
60   Elkie Brooks, *Finding My Voice* (London: The Robson Press, 2012), pp. 1-6.
61   *Northern Life Magazine*, 22 February 2017.
62   Elkie Brooks, *Finding My Voice*, pp. 31, 41-42.
63   *Northen Life Magazine*, 22 February 2017.
64   Elkie Brooks, *Finding My Voice*, p. 45.
65   Brenda Lee is an American performer and top charting solo female vocalist of the 1960s. She sang rockabilly, pop and country music and had 47 US chart hits in the 1960s. She is known for her 1960 hit 'I'm sorry' and 1958's 'Rocking around the Christmas tree' which has become a Christmas standard.
66   Elkie Brooks, *Finding My Voice*, p. 54.
67   www. readysteadygirls.eu
68   Elkie Brooks, *Finding My Voice*, pp. 98-99.
69   www.readysteadygirls.eu
70   *Melody Maker*, 30 December 1972, p. 1.
71   Elkie Brooks, *Finding My Voice,* pp. 10-11, 16.
72   Ibid., pp. 18-25.
73   Soup dumplings and triangular noodles filled with chopped meat.

74   *Jewish Chronicle*, 11 February 2005, p. 41.

75   Elkie Brooks, *Finding My Voice*, p. 205.

76   Ibid., p. 275.

77   *Jewish Chronicle,* 14 July 2017, p. 38.

78   Colin Cripps, *Popular Music in the 20th Century*, p. 70.

79   *Jewish Chronicle*, 12 August 2011, p. 16.

80   Pauline Black, *Black By Design* (London: Serpent's Tail, 2012), p. 330.

81   Ibid., p. 35.

82   *Scotsman*, 21 August 2011.

83   Pauline Black, *Black by Design*, pp. 8, 12, 38.

84   *Scotsman*, 21 August 2011. Ready Steady Go was a pop television show broadcast every Friday night (ITV, 1963-1966).

85   *Coventry Telegraph*, 4 August 2011.

86   *Coventry Telegraph*, 3 August 2004.

87   A youth subculture characterized by aggressively masculine hair and dress styles, including shaved heads and heavy boots. Often extreme right-wing nationalists or neo-fascists who espoused racist views.

88   Mods were usually teens from white working-class families who were trying to transcend the mundane, traditional customs of the 1950s and adopt a more exciting, expensive, fashionable and social lifestyle. They used their disposable income to buy tailor-made suits and Italian scooters. They enjoyed a heavy social and party life. They were the first postwar generation not to undergo National Service or austerity.

89   Tonic suits had a shiny texture, usually consisting of a mohair blend fabric, often resulting in a two tone texture that changed appearance according to the light.

90   *National Geographic*, 22 August 2020.

91   *Guardian*, 26 May 2021.

92   *National Geographic*, 22 August 2020.

93   *Coventry Telegraph*, 3 August 2004.

94   The term 'rude boy' arose from the poorer sections of Kingston, Jamaica and was associated with discontented youths. It was Jamaica's first youth culture, borne from dissatisfaction, poverty and rising unemployment following Jamaica's independence in 1962. They listened to ska and favoured sharp suits, thin ties and pork pie or Trilby hats.

95   A female member of the subculture associated with ska. The term rude boy was adopted predominantly – but not exclusively – by black teenagers who dressed in sweatshirt fabrics and took pride in having the latest Nikes. There was an attitude and swagger, as opposed to race and gender, that qualified a Rude boy or Rude girl.

96   *Guardian*, 21 April 2015.

97   *Scotsman*, 21 August 2011.

98   Ibid.

99 Pauline Black, *Black By Design*, p. 312.

100 *Jewish Chronicle*, 12 August 2011, p. 16.

101 Pauline Black, *Black By Design,* p. 324.

102 Ibid., pp. 369, 374.

103 *Jewish Chronicle*, 12 August 2011, p. 16.

104 Black British Jewish Lives, *Jewish Renaissance* zoom recording, 13 June 2021.

105 Ibid.

106 *Jewish Chronicle*, 12 August 2011, p. 16.

107 'Pauline Black on Bringing Diverse Two-Tone Music since 1979', 25 September 2015, www.vice.com

108 *Guardian*, 26 May 2021.

109 *Scotsman*, 21 August 2011.

110 2 September 2011, www.kentonline.co.uk.

111 *Guardian*, 22 July 2012.

112 *Times Magazine*, 12 June 2021, p. 18.

113 www.classicfm.com, 24 July 2019.

114 *Jewish Chronicle*, 29 July 2011, p. 20.

115 Elizabeth Selby, *Amy Winehouse: A Family Portrait* (London: Jewish Museum, 2014), p. 77.

116 The British Phonographic Industry's annual popular music awards.

117 *Jewish Chronicle*, 29 July 2011, p. 20.

118 Ibid.

119 *Jewish Chronicle*, 23 January 2004, p. 35.

120 Elizabeth Selby, *Amy Winehouse*, pp. 23-27, 31.

121 Mitch Winehouse, *Amy My Daughter* (London: Harper Collins, 2012), p. 7.

122 Janis Winehouse, *Loving Amy: A Mother's story* (London: Bantam Press, 2014), p. 7.

123 www.totallyJewish.com

124 *The Times of Israel*, 3 July 2013.

125 *Huff Post*, 23 July 2015.

126 *Jewish Chronicle*, 4 January 2008, p. 17.

127 *Jewish Chronicle*, 15 February 2008, p. 29.

128 *Australia Sunday Times*, 2007.

129 *Jewish Chronicle*, 1 October 2010, p. 27.

130 *Jewish Chronicle*, 11 March 2011, p. 30.

131 Elizabeth Selby, *Amy Winehouse: A Family Portrait*, pp. 3, 6.

132 *Jewish Chronicle*, 11 May 2007, p. 29.

133 *Lilith*, 24 January 2008.

134 *Guardian*, 22 May 2004.

135 *Toronto Star*, 12 May 2007.

136 *Rolling Stone*, May 2007.

137 *Washington Post*, 13 March 2007.

138 *Jewish Chronicle*, 5 August 2011, p. 20.

139	*Jewish Chronicle*, 29 July 2011, p. 3.

140	*Jewish Chronicle*, 22 January 2010, p. 31.

141	Ibid., p. 25.

142	*Jewish Chronicle*, 24 August 2007, p. 19.

143	Janis Winehouse, *Loving Amy.*

144	Nick Johnstone, *Amy Amy Amy – The Amy Winehouse Story* (London: Omnibus Press, 2011), pp. 159-160.

145	*Jewish Chronicle*, 29 July 2011, p. 3.

146	Nick Johnstone, *Amy Amy Amy*, pp. 228-229.

147	*The Observer*, 23 June 2013.

148	Chas Newkey-Burden, *Amy Winehouse: The Biography* (London: John Blake Publishing Ltd, 2011), pp. vii-viii.

149	*Independent,* 22 June 2020.

150	John Ware was a reporter on BBC programme *Panorama* (1986-2012). He investigated Labour Party antisemitism for *Panorama* in 2019.

151	*Guardian*, 19 May 2019.

152	*Guardian*, 15 February 2020.

153	*Guardian*, 27 February 2021.

154	Felix White is a founding member of the indie rock band The Maccabees.

155	Jack Penate is a singer-songwriter and musician whose music incorporates rockabilly, indie rock and soul.

156	*Jewish Chronicle*, 24 August 2014, p. 3.

157	*Independent*, 29 August 2012.

158	Indie is a genre of rock music that originated in the 1970s. Originally used to describe independent record labels, the term became associated with the music they produced and was initially used interchangeably with alternative rock or 'guitar pop rock'.

159	*Independent*, 22 June 2020.

160	*Jewish Chronicle*, 24 August 2014, p. 3.

161	*Time Out*, 19 December 2012.

162	The BRIT awards are the British Phonographic Industry's annual popular music awards.

163	*Jewish Chronicle*, 19 September 2014, p. 75.

164	*New York Times*, 30 June 2020.

165	*AP News*, 27 October 2017.

166	*New York Times*, 30 June 2020.

167	*NME*, 24 June 2020.

168	*Jewish Chronicle*, 24 August 2014, p. 3.

169	Jewishlivesproject.com.

170	*Jewish Chronicle*, 26 July 2013, p. 30.

171	The ceremony typically held on the Sabbath before the wedding where the groom is called up in the synagogue to recite a blessing.

172	*Jewish Chronicle*, 19 September 2014, p. 76.

173 *Jewish Chronicle*, 5 October 2018, p. 20.

174 *Jewish Chronicle*, 31 August 2012, p. 5.

175 *Sunday Post*, 8 April 2020.

176 *Guardian*, 19 May 2019.

177 *Guardian*, 15 February 2020.

178 *New York Times*, 30 June 2020.

179 *Guardian*, 15 February 2020.

180 *Table Manners,* Series 4, Episode 1, 10 October 2018.

181 A potato pancake that is eaten on the Jewish festival of Hannukah.

182 *Friday Night Dinner* (2011) was a Channel 4 sitcom set in suburban north London that focused on the Friday night dinner experience of the British Jewish Goodman family.

183 Youtube, 21 August 2013.

184 Lucy O'Brien, *She POP II*, p. 215.

185 Udiscovermusic.com. 17 April 2020.

186 'The Legacy of Amy Winehouse', umusic.co.nz.

4. CLASSICAL MUSICIANS

1 Lise Karin Merling, 'The Lady at the Piano: From Innocent Pastime to Intimate Discourse', musicandpractice.org

2 J. Flanders, *Consuming Passions* (London: Harper Press, 2006).

3 C. Ehrlich, *The Piano. A History* (Oxford: Clarendon Press, 1976), p. 97.

4 D. Hildebrant, *Piano Forte. A Social History of the Piano* (London: Hutchison, 1988).

5 D. Rohr, 'Women and the Music Profession in Victorian England: The Royal Society of Female Musicians 1839-1866', *Journal of Musicological Research*, 18 (4), pp. 307-346.

6 D. J. Golby, *Instrumental Teaching in Nineteenth Century Britain* (Aldershot: Ashgate, 2004), p. 8.

7 C. Ehrlich, *The Piano. A History* (Oxford: Clarendon Press, 1976).

8 Sophie Fuller, 'The Society of Women Musicians', www.bl.uk.

9 Cynthia Collins, 'Contribution of Women Musicians to Symphony Orchestras', www.cmuse.org, 9 March 2015.

10 Marian C. McKenna, *Marion Hess* (London: Hamish Hamilton, 1976), p. 49.

11 *Jewish Chronicle,* 14 March 2004, p. 20.

12 Ruth Rosenfelder, 'Dame Myra Hess', Jewish Women's Archive, jwa.org.

13 Marian C. McKenna, *Marion Hess*, p. 4.

14 Tobias Matthay (1858-1945), one of Britain's foremost piano teachers, was Professor of Advanced Piano Playing at the Royal Academy of Music. He had a great reputation for his approach to learning which laid stress on arm movement and muscular relaxation.

15 Marion C. McKenna, *Marion Hess,* p. 54.

16   Ibid.

17   Robertgreenbergmusic.com, 25 February 2019.

18   *The Musical Times,* Vol. 107, No. 1475 (January 1966), p. 59.

19   Holocaustmusic.ort.org.

20   International Music Foundation, imfchicago.org.

21   Nationalgallery.org.uk.

22   Holocaustmusic.ort.org.

23   Nationalgallery.org.uk.

24   Ibid.

25   Ibid.

26   Robertgreenbergmusic.com

27   *Jewish Chronicle,* 3 December 1965, p. 11.

28   *Listen to Britain,* bfi.org.uk

29   Holocaustmusic.ort.org.

30   Ruth Rosenfelder, Jewish Women's Archive.

31   Robergreenbergmusic.com, 25 February 2019.

32   Marian C. McKenna, *Marian Hess,* pp. 2, 8-9, 49.

33   Ruth Rosenfelder, Jewish Women's Archive.

34   *Jewish Chronicle,* 4 September 1942, p. 5.

35   *Jewish Chronicle,* 3 June 1955, p. 6.

36   *Jewish Chronicle,* 7 October 1927, p. 13.

37   *Jewish Chronicle,* 14 January 1977.

38   www.tumblr.com.

39   *Jewish Chronicle,* 18 November 1966, p. 33.

40   *Jewish Chronicle,* 3 December 1965, p. 37.

41   www.thepianofiles.com.

42   *Jewish Chronicle,* 2 March 2018, p. 38.

43   *Jewish Chronicle,* 23 January 1942, p. 22.

44   Marian C. McKenna, *Marion Hess,* p. 36.

45   *Jewish Chronicle,* 1 January 2021, p. 46.

46   Murray Freedman, 'Leeds Jewish Community – The Early Years', *Shemot,* vol.
     1 (2), Spring 1993, pp. 11-12.

47   *Desert Island Discs,* 4 July 2010.

48   *Jewish Chronicle,* 29 August 2003, p. 25.

49   Fanny Waterman, A Lifetime in Music, BBC youtube.

50   Ibid.

51   Tobias Matthay (1858-1945) was an English pianist, teacher and composer
     noted for his detailed examination of the problems of piano technique, the
     interpretation of music and the psychology of teaching.

52   Fanny Waterman, *My Life in Music,* (London: Faber Music Ltd, 2015), p. 16.

53   *Desert Island Discs,* 4 July 2010.

54   *Jewish Chronicle,* 29 August 2003, p. 25.

55   Fanny Waterman, A Lifetime in Music.

56   *Jewish Chronicle,* 25 March 1960, p. 32.

57   Fanny Waterman, A Lifetime in Music.
58   *Jewish Chronicle*, 29 August 2003, p. 25.
59   Ibid.
60   *Jewish Renaissance*, January 2012, pp. 20-21.
61   Ibid.
62   *Jewish Chronicle*, 29 August 2003, p. 25.
63   *Independent,* 13 March 2014.
64   *Jewish Chronicle*, 7 June 2018, p. 13.
65   *New York Times*, 26 December 2020.
66   *Jewish Chronicle*, 29 August 2003, p. 25.
67   Ibid.
68   *Jewish Chronicle*, 1 January 2021, p. 46.
69   *New York Times*, 26 December 2020.
70   www.greatbritishlife.co.uk, 9 December 2014.
71   *Jewish Chronicle*, 1 January 2021, p. 46.
72   *Jewish Chronicle*, 12 March 2004, p. 20.
73   *Jewish Renaissance*, January 2012, pp. 20-21.
74   Jewish Chronicle, 12 March 2004, p. 20.
75   *Desert Island Discs*, 4 July 2010.
76   Fanny Waterman, *A Lifetime in Music.*
77   BBC News, 21 December 2020.
78   Cambridge.org.uk, 14 November 2016.
79   *Irish Times*, 2 June 2009.
80   *Jewish Chronicle*, 5 July 2019, p. 23.
81   www.jewishtelegraph.com.
82   *Sunday Times*, 20 January 2008.
83   Natalie Clein in Cello Unwrapped, youtube.
84   *Guardian*, 27 April 2009.
85   *Sunday Times*, 20 January 2008.
86   *Dorset Magazine*, 1 September 2014.
87   www.jewishtelegraph.com.
88   Louisa Clein made her television debut in 2001 the BBC legal drama *Judge
      John Deed.* Her television appearances include *Holby City* and *Emmerdale.*
89   *Jewish Chronicle*, 5 July 2019, p. 23.
90   *Jewish Chronicle*, 15 November 2002, p. 51.
91   Bloch/Bruch: *Schelomo, Kol Nidrei* & other works with the BBC Scottish
      Symphony Orchestra, Hyperion 2012.
92   Ernest Bloch (1880-1959) was born in Switzerland and his music reflected
      Jewish cultural and liturgical themes as well as European post-Romantic
      traditions.
93   *Jewish Chronicle*, 27 August 2010, p. 28.
94   Max Bruch (1834-1920) was a German romantic composer and conductor
      who wrote over 200 works. He wrote three violin concertos, the first of which,
      in G Minor has become a staple of the violin repertoire.

95 *Ham & High*, 9 August 2012.

96 *Jewish Chronicle*, 10 September 2010, p. SO8.

97 Julia Pascal is a theatre director and playwright. She was the first woman director at the National Theatre in 1978 with her adaptation of Dorothy Parker's writings *Men Seldom Make Passses*. Her theatre scripts include *Theresa, A Dead Woman on Holiday* and the *Dybbuk* (collected as *The Holocaust Trilogy*) and *The Yiddish Queen Lear*.

98 *Jewish Chronicle*, 25 January 2002, p. 39.

99 *My Family, the Holocaust and Me, BBC1*, Series 1, episode 1.

100 Stolpersteine (stumbling stones) are blocks which are laid into the pavement in front of the last voluntarily chosen place of residence of Holocaust victims. Their names and fate are engraved into a 10cm brass square plate on the top of each Stolpersteine.

101 *Jewish Chronicle*, 21 September 2012, p. 39.

102 Guardian, 27 April 2009.

103 Culturebuzz Israel, youtube.

104 *The Strad*, July 2019.

105 *Jewish Chronicle*, 27 August 2010, p. 28.

106 *Dorset Magazine*, 1 September 2014.

107 *BBC Music Magazine*.

108 Fanny Waterman, *My Life in Music*, p. 132.

109 Ibid., p. 36.

5. ARTISTS

1 www.society-women-artists.org.uk

2 'British women artists emerge', Artlyst.com, 10 February 2021.

3 Julia Weiner, 'Artists in Britain: 1700-1940', jwa.org.

4 *Jewish Chronicle*, 24 May 2024, JC2, p. 2.

5 Abraham (1823-1862) was a popular painter of Victorian narrative scenes and Simeon (1840-1905) was part of the Pre-Raphaelite circle. He initially had a very successful career and became well known for his paintings of Jewish subjects. His career came to a halt when he was arrested in a public urinal off Oxford Street, London and charged with attempting to commit sodomy with a stableman. He was arrested again a year later in Paris and was sentenced to three months in prison.

6 www.jwa.org.

7 Press release, 8 June 2023, www.tate.org.uk.

8 Rebecca Solomon: Success and Prejudice in the Victorian World, www.dailyartmagazine.com.

9 John Singer Sargent (1856-1925) was an American expatriate artist considered the leading portrait painter of his generation. His elegant portraits provide an enduring image of Edwardian Age society.

10   Julia Weiner, 'Artists in Britain 1700-1940', jwa.org.

11   *Jewish Chronicle*, 20 January 1989, p. 15.

12   *Jewish Renaissance*, July 2017, p. 32.

13   *Jewish Chronicle*, 20 January 1989, p. 15.

14   *Jewish Chronicle*, 3 January 2003, p. 19.

16   Amongst Jewish people the anniversary of the death of a parent or close relative is marked by the burning of a memorial candle.

17   *Jewish Chronicle*, 4 June 1999, p. 42.

18   Ibid.

19   *Jewish Chronicle*, 4 June 1999, p. 42.

20   Jewisheastendmemorymap.org

21   *Jewish Chronicle*, 3 April 2020, p. 45.

6. SPORT

1   Harold Abrahams (1899-1978) won gold in the 100 metres sprint in the 1924 Paris Olympics.

2   Jews and Sports, myjewishlearning.com.

3   Daniel Mendoza (1764-1836), bareknuckle pugilist, 16th in the succession of English heavyweight champions and the first Jewish champion.

4   David Dee, *Sport and British Jewry. Integration, Ethnicity and Anti-semitism 1890-1970* (Manchester: Manchester University Press, 2013), pp. 1-9.

5   Andrew Hosken, *Nothing Like A Dame. The Scandals of Shirley Porter* (London: Granta Publications, 2006), pp. 18-19.

6   David Dee, *Sport and Jewish Jewry*, pp. 174-5.

7   Robert J. Lake, *A Social History of Tennis in Britain* (London: Routledge, 2015), p. 244.

8   David Dee, *The 'Estranged' Generation? Social and Generational Change in Interwar British Jewry* (London: Palgrave Macmillan, 2017), p. 215.

9   Ibid., pp. 311-313.

10   S.C.H. Davis, *Atalanta* (London: G T Foulis & Co. Ltd, 1957), p. 31.

11   John Bullock, *Fast Women* (London: Robson Books, 2002), p. xi.

12   *Jewish Chronicle*, 18 March 1910, p. 27.

13   David B. Green, 'Sephardi Jew becomes first English woman to win automobile race', 3 October 2014, Haaretz.com

14   S.C.H. Davis, *Atalanta*, p. 32.

15   Dorothy Levitt, *The Woman and the Car* (London: Hugh Evelyn Ltd, 1970), p. 6.

16   French celebrity Camille Du Gast (1858-1942) was a wealthy flamboyant socialite who became the first woman to race consistently at international level.

17   John Bullock, *Fast Women*, p. 15.

18   David B. Green, 'Sephardi Jew becomes first English woman to win automobile race', 3 October 2014, Haaretz.com

19   Ibid.

20   Ibid.

21   John Bullock, *Fast Women*, p. 20.

22   Jasper Carrott, Driven to Distraction, 1981, youtube.

23   Georgina Clarsen, *Eat My Dust, Early Women Motorists* (Baltimore: John Hopkins University Press, 2008), pp. 2, 161.

24   S. C. H. Davis, *Atalanta*, p. 185.

25   Sheila Van Damm, British Pathe 1956, youtube.

26   *Jewish Chronicle*, 24 July 1908, p. 32.

27   Sir Joseph Nathaniel Lyons was the chairman of J. Lyons and Co, a restaurant chain, food manufacturing and hotel conglomerate created in 1884 that dominated British mass catering in the first half of the twentieth century.

28   Sheila van Damm, *No Excuses* (London: Oldhams Press Ltd, 1958), pp. 11-13.

29   Theatre censorship had existed since the sixteenth century and a 1737 Act appointed the Lord Chamberlain, the most senior officer of the Royal Household, as official licenser of plays and regulated restrictions on drama. Theatre censorship was finally abolished in 1968.

30   Rachel Cooke, *Her Brilliant Career: Ten Extraordinary Women of the Fifties* (London: Virago, 2013).

31   *Leicester Chronicle*, 13 October 1967, p. 13.

32   Rachel Cooke, *Her Brilliant Career.*

33   Sheila van Damm, Windmill Theatre, 1970, youtube.

34   *Daily Mirror*, 2 October 1964, p. 16.

35   *Jewish Chronicle*, 10 March 1961, p. 31.

36   *The Stage*, 30 September 2004, p. 18.

37   Barry Cryer OBE, writer, comedian and actor, has written for many noted performers including Dave Allen, Tommy Cooper, Dick Emery, Spike Milligan and Morecombe and Wise.

38   *The Stage,* 30 September 2004, p. 18.

39   *Worthing Gazette*, 20 August 1958, p. 5.

40   *The Stage*, 30 September 2004, p. 18.

41   *The Stage*, 8 October 1964, p. 3.

42   Sir Stirling Moss was born in London in 1929. His grandfather was Jewish and the family had changed their name from Moses to Moss. His father was a dentist and part-time racing driver. *Jewish Chronicle*, 12 April 2020.

43   www.historicracing.com

44   Ibid.

45   *Tatler*, 8 June 1955, p. 34.

46   *Newcastle Evening Chronicle*, 25 March 1959, p. 21.

47   Max Mosley, one of the driving forces behind the global success of Formula One, was the son of Oswald Mosley, the founder of the British Union of Fascists. Whilst a student at Oxford he had called for 'Free Speech for Fascists'.

Bernie Ecclestone, former chief executive of Formula One, declared his admiration for Hitler. The inter-war history of the sport was bound up with the rise of the far-right and appealed to those supporting these policies. Hitler's determination to see Germany triumph on the world stage of motor racing led him to push the auto industry to new heights of engineering and sporting perfection, led by teams from Mercedes Benz and Auto Union. 'Why Formula One is still so in thrall to the Nazis', Mailonline. 7 July 2009.

48 *Western Mail*, 27 October 1955, p. 10.
49 *Coventry Evening Telegraph*, 27 October 1955, p. 14.
50 *Jewish Chronicle*, 28 July 1905, p. 3.
51 *Jewish Chronicle*, 23 December 1960, p. 26.
52 *Jewish Chronicle*, 28 August 1987, p. 22.
53 Sheila van Damm, *No Excuses*.
54 *Port Talbot Guardian*, 3 November 1961, p. 4.
55 Rachel Cooke, *Her Brilliant Career*.
56 *Western Mail*, 2 July 1957, p. 5.
57 *Miami Herald*, 18 August 2020
58 *Daily Telegraph*, 17 August 2020.
59 *Jewish Chronicle*, September 11, 2020, p. 63.
60 Bruce Schoenfeld, *The Match. Althea Gibson and a Portrait of a Friendship* (New York: Harper Collins, 2004), Chapter 2.
61 Sandy Harwitt, *The Greatest Jewish Tennis Players of All Time* (New York: New Chapter Press, 2014), p. 73.
62 Ibid., p. 74.
63 Bruce Schoenfeld, *The Match*, Chapter 2.
64 Ibid.
65 Sandy Harwitt, *The Greatest Jewish Tennis Players of All Time*, p. 78.
66 *New York Times*, 27 August 2020.
67 Bruce Schoenfeld, *The Match*, Chapter 2.
68 *Times of Israel*, 9 September 2014.
69 *New York Times*, 28 August 2020.
70 *Jewish Chronicle*, 10 December 1999, p. 24.
71 Interview with Rebecca Silk, London. 23 September 2020.
72 *New York Times*, 27 August 2020.
73 *Times of Israel*, 9 September 2014.
74 *Guardian*, 8 July 2001.
75 Ibid.
76 Bruce Schoenfeld, *The Match*, Chapter 8.
77 *Guardian*, 8 July 2001.
78 *The Times*, 18 August 2020.
79 *Guardian*, 8 July 2001.
80 Robert Lake, *A Social History of Tennis in Britain*, (London: Routledge, 2014) pp. 244-245.

81   *Times of Israel*, 9 September 2014.

82   *Jewish Chronicle*, 25 June 2004.

83   *Sun*, 18 August 2020.

84   Interview with Rebecca Silk, London. 23 September 2020.

85   Ibid.

86   *Jewish Chronicle*, 7 November 2003.

87   *Jewish Chronicle*, 4 September 1959, p. 28.

88   *Jewish Chronicle*, 24 September 2004, p. 24.

89   Interview with Rebecca Silk, London. 23 September 2020.

90   Jean-Francois Bouzanquet, *Fast Ladies. Female Racing Drivers 1888-1970* (Dorchester: Veloce Publishing Ltd, 2009), Introduction.

91   Robert Lake, *A Social History of Tennis in Britain*, p. 246, 248.

7. COOKERY AND THE WORLD OF FOOD

1   Laura Mason, *Food Culture in Great Britain* (Westport, Conn.: Greenwood Press, 2002) p. ix.

2   Ibid., pp. 113-115.

3   Jane Gerson, 'From Bola D'amour to the Ultimate Cheesecake: 150 Years of Anglo-Jewish Cookery Writing', in: Hannah Ewence and Tony Kushner (eds.), *Whatever Happened to British Jewish Studies* (London: Vallentine Mitchell, 2012), p. 308.

4   *Jewish Chronicle*, September 1998, p. 39.

5   Pudding made from egg noodles or potato.

6   Jane Gerson, pp. 310-312.

7   *Aunt Sarah's Cookery Book for a Jewish Kitchen* (Liverpool: Yates and Hess, 1872); May Henry and Edith B. Cohen, *The Economical Cook: A Modern Jewish Recipe Book for Housekeepers* (London: Werthheimer, Lea and Co., 1889).

8   *Financial Times*, 15 August 2014.

9   *Ha'aretz*, 13 April 2017.

10   Isabella Beeton (1836-1865) was one of the most recognised names in the British history of cookery book writers and was known around the world as Mrs Beeton. She was the author of *Mrs Beeton's Book of Household Management*.

11   *Jewish Chronicle*, Supplement, 21 March 1980, p. 28.

12   Jane Gerson, p. 314.

13   Ibid., p. 314.

14   Ibid., pp. 314-315.

15   Ibid., p. 317.

16   Ibid.

17   Ibid., pp. 318-319.

18   Ibid., p. 320.

19   *Guardian*, 24 May 2003.

20   *Independent*, 24 May 2003.

21   *Guardian*, 24 May 2003.

22   Jane Gerson, p. 321.

23   *Jewish Chronicle*, 15 June, 2018, p. 42; 9 March 2018, p. 44.

24   Jane Gerson, p. 322.

25   'The icing on our cake', *Jewish Chronicle*, 23 May 2003, p. 25.

26   Jane Gerson, p. 323.

27   Ibid., pp. 324-325.

28   Claudia Roden grew up in Cairo, living a charmed existence in a tight knit Jewish community. Her family were Syrian and Turkish Jews who left Egypt after the Suez crisis. Her *Book of Middle Eastern Food* (1968) brought colour, spice and a raft of new flavours to many a bland English kitchen and kicked off a love affair with the food of the Middle East. *Jewish Chronicle,* 1 April 2011, p. 46.

29   *Jewish Chronicle*, 15 December 2006, p. S24.

30   *Jewish Chronicle*, 10 February 2006, p. 27.

31   Charlotte Druckman, *Women on Food* (New York: Abrams Press, 2019), p. 273.

32   *Irish Times*, 20 February 2019.

33   'Kitchen Revolution: How Nigella Lawson Changed Food Writing', *Guardian*, 6 October 2013.

34   *Jewish Chronicle*, 29 September 2006, p. 56.

35   'Who Do You Think You Are?', BBC 26 September 2006.

36   Gilly Smith, *Nigella Lawson* (London: Andre Deutsch, 2005), pp. 6-9.

37   Ibid., p. 4.

38   Ibid., pp. 56, 68, 70.

39   *Guardian*, 10 October 2020.

40   *Guardian*, 3 March 2001.

41   Guardian, 10 October 2020.

42   Charlotte Druckman, *Women on Food*, pp. 274-276.

43   'An Angel at our Table', *Observer*, 17 December 2012.

44   *Irish Times*, 20 February 2019.

45   Gilly Smith, *Nigella Lawson*, pp. 115, 117.

46   Elizabeth David (1913-1922) was an influential British cookery writer who brought the cuisines of provincial France and Italy to Britain.

47   *Guardian*, 6 October 2018.

48   *Jewish Chronicle*, 28 November 2014, p. 29.

49   *Jewish Chronicle*, 25 August 2000, p. 25.

50   A dumpling made of matzah meal and beaten eggs usually served in chicken broth.

51   *Jewish Chronicle*, 27 July 2001, p. 33.

52   *Jewish Chronicle*, 26 December 2003, p. 21.

53   *Jewish Chronicle*, 23 June 2001, p. 28.
54   *Jewish Chronicle*, 15 October 2004, p. 42.
55   Gilly Smith, *Nigella Lawson*, pp. 203-204.
56   *Vogue*, 30 April 2021.

Bibliography and Sources

ARCHIVAL MATERIAL
University of Bristol
Theatre Collection

University of Leicester
Conference on 'Unsettling Women: Contemporary Women's Writing and Diaspora',
    University of Leicester 2008.

INTERVIEWS WITH THE AUTHOR
Gita Feldman, 24 May 2019, London.
Rebecca Silk, 23 September 2020, London.

NEWSPAPERS AND PERIODICALS
Australia Sunday Times
BBC Music Magazine
Birmingham Daily Post
British Theatre Guide
Church Times
Coventry Telegraph
Daily Express
Daily Mail
Daily Mirror
Daily Record
Daily Telegraph
Dorset Magazine
Evening Standard
Financial Times
Guardian
Ha'aretz
Ham & High
Huffington Post
Independent
Irish Times
Jewish Chronicle

Jewish Currents
Jewish Journal
Jerusalem Post
Jewish Quarterly
Jewish Renaissance
Leicester Chronicle
Lilith
Melody Maker
Miami Herald
Mirror
National Geographic
New York Times
Newcastle Evening Chronicle
NME
Northern Life Magazine
Observer
People
Port Talbot Guardian
Rolling Stone
Shemot
Sunday Empire News
Sunday Post
Sunday Times
Tatler
The Musical Times
The Oldie
The Scotsman
The Stage
The Stage and Television Today
The Strad
The Sun
The Wee Review
Time Out
Times Literary Supplement
Times of Israel
Toronto Star
Variety
Vogue
Wall Street Journal
Washington Post
Western Mail
Worthing Gazette

AUTOBIOGRAPHIES

Pauline Black, *Black by Design* (London: Serpent's Tail, 2012).

Claire Bloom, *Limelight and After: The Education of an Actress* (Harper & Row, 1982).

Claire Bloom, *Leaving a Doll's House* (London: Virago Press, 1996).

Eleanor Bron, *The Pillow Book of Eleanor Bron* (London: Metheun, 1987).

Elkie Brooks, *Finding My Voice* (London: The Robson Press, 2012).

Fenella Fielding and Simon McKay, *Do You Mind if I Smoke?* (London: Peter Owen Publishers, 2017).

Linda Grant, *Remind Me Who I Am Again* (London: Grants, 2011).

Miriam Karlin, *Some Sort of Life* (London: Oberon, 2007).

Maureen Lipman, *Something To Fall Back On* (London: Robson Books, 1987).

Miriam Margolyes, *This Much Is True* (London: John Murray, 2021).

Bernice Rubens, *When I Grow Up* (London: Little Brown, 2005).

Helen Shapiro, *Walking Back to Happiness* (London: Harper Collins, 1992).

TALKS

Tony Earnshaw in conversation with Claire Bloom, Widescreen Weekend, Bradford, March 2011.

George McGhee in conversation with Claire Bloom, JW3, London, 31 March 2019.

David Mazower, 'Women in East End Yiddish Theatre'. Tower Hamlets Library, 23 March 2017.

INTERNET

Freddy Alva, 'Pauline Black on Bringing Diverse Two-Tone Music Since 1979', 25 September 2015, www.vice.com

Geoff Barton, 'The Story of Vinegar Joe', 8 April 2019, www.loudersound.com

BBC One, 'Who Do You Think You Are', 26 September 2006.

Apeksha Bagchi, 'Ratched: Sophie Okonedo Masterfully Plays Five Unique Characters', 29 September 2020, www.cbr.com.

'British women artists emerge: An Overlooked Phenomenon', 10 February 2021, Artlyst.com.

Cynthia Collins, 'Contribution of Women Musicians to Symphony Orchestras', www.cmuse.org.

Sophie Fuller, 'The Society of Women Musicians', www.bl.uk.

David B. Green, 'Sephardi Jew becomes first English woman to win automobile race', 3 October 2014, Ha'aretz.com.

Lisa Karin Merling, 'The Lady at the Piano: From Innocent Pastime to Intimate Discourse', musicandpractice.org.

Ruth Rosenfelder, 'Dame Myra Hess', jwa.org.

Tara Taghizadeh, 'A Great Silly Grin: The British Satire Boom of the 1960s', 16 July 2002, www.popmatters.com.

Julia Weiner, 'Artists in Britain: 1700-1940', jwa.org.

PODCAST
Podtail.com.trolled
Tablemannerspodcast.com

Youtube
Jasper Carrott, Driven to Distraction, 1981.
Natalie Clein in Cello Unwrapped, 14 June, 2017
Culturebuzz Converses: with Natalie Clein, Culturebuzz Israel
Sheila van Damm, British Pathe 1956.
Sheila van Damm, Windmill Theatre, 1970.
Fanny Waterman, A Lifetime in Music, 7 November 2012.

WEBSITES
www.allmusic.com
www.bbc.co.uk
www.bfi.org.uk
www.bl.uk
www.cambridge.org.uk
www.classicalmusicchicago.org
www.classicfm.com
www.cmuse.org
www.dailymail.co.uk
www.digitalspy.com
www.greatbritishlife.co.uk
www.historicracing.com
www.holocaustmusic.ort.org
www.huffpost.com
www.iNews.co.uk
www.jewisheastendmemorymap.org
www.jewishlivesproject.com
www.jewishtelegraph.com
www.jewishtestimonies.com
www.jwa.org
www.kentonline.co.uk
www.loudersound.com
www.mihigh.fandom.com
www.musicandpractice.org
www.myjewishlearning.com
www.nationalgallery.org.uk
www.OfficialLondonTheatre.com
www.popmatters.com
www.readysteadygirls.eu

www.roathlocalhistorysociety.org
www.robertgreenbergmusic.com
www.screenonline.org.uk
www.society-women-artists.org.uk
www.splashmags.com
www.tate.org.uk
www.thepianofiles.com
www.tumblr.com
www.totallyJewish.com
www.tumblr.com
www.udiscovermusic.com
www.umusic.co.nz
www.vam.ac.uk
www.varsity.co.uk
www.vice.com

RADIO
Desert Island Discs, BBC Radio 4, 24 June 1968.
Desert Island Discs, BBC Radio 4, 24 January 1986.
Desert Island Discs, BBC Radio 4, 8 December 1991.
Desert Island Discs, BBC Radio 4, 28 September 2008.
Desert Island Discs, BBC Radio 4, 4 July 2010.
Open Book, BBC Radio 4, 14 March 2019.

TELEVISION
Girl with a Giggle in her Voice, BBC 2, 1991.
My Family, the Holocaust and Me, BBC1, Series 1, Episode 1, 9 November 2020.

SECONDARY SOURCES
Glenda Abramson (ed.), *The Encyclopedia of Modern Jewish Culture* (London: Routledge, 2004).
James Agate, *Ego 6* (London: George G Harlan & Co. Ltd, 1944).
Paul Bailey, *Three Queer Lives* (London: Hamish Hamilton, 2001).
Adrienne Baker, *The Jewish Woman in Contemporary Society: Transitions and Traditions* (London: Macmillan, 1993).
Cecil Bloom, 'People of the Book: Grace Aguilar and Amy Levy', *Jewish Currents*, 30 January 2013.
Jean-Francois Bouzanquet, *Fast Ladies: Female Racing Drivers 1888-1970* (Dorchester: Veloce Publishing Ltd, 2009).
John Bullock, *Fast Women* (London: Robson Books, 2002).
Sandra Caron, *Alma Cogan: A Memoir* (London: Bloomsbury, 1991).
Georgina Clarsen, *Eat My Dust, Early Women Motorists* (Baltimore: John Hopkins University Press, 2008).

Ray Coleman, *Brian Epstein: The Man Who Made the Beatles* (London: Penguin, 1990).

Rachel Cooke, *Her Brilliant Career: Ten Extraordinary Women of the Fifties* (London: Virago, 2013).

Colin Cripps, *Popular Music in the 20ᵗʰ Century* (Cambridge: Cambridge University Press, 1988).

S.C.H. Davis, *Atlanta* (London: G T Foulis & Co. Ltd, 1957).

David Dee, *Sport and British Jewry. Integration, Ethnicity and Anti-Semitism 1890-1970* (Manchester: Manchester University Press, 2013.

David Dee, *The 'Estranged Generation? Social and Generational Change in Interwar British Jewry* (London: Palgrave Macmillan, 2017).

Charlotte Druckman, *Women On Food* (New York, Abrams Press, 2019).

Deborah Epstein Nord, *Victorian Studies,* Vol. 50 (3), Spring 2008 (Indiana: Indiana University Press).

C. Ehrlich, *The Piano. A History* (Oxford: Clarendon Press, 1976).

J. Flanders, *Consuming Passions* (London: Harper Press, 2006).

Murray Freedman, 'Leeds Jewish Community – The Early Years', *Shemot*, vol.1 (2), Spring 1993.

Michael Galchinsky, *The Origin of the Modern Jewish Woman Writer. Romance and Reform in Victorian England* (Detroit: Wayne State University Press, 1996).

Maggie B. Gale and John Stokes (eds.), *The Cambridge Companion to the Actress* (Cambridge: Cambridge University Press, 2007).

Maggie B. Gale, 'British Actresses 1900-1950: Professional Transformations', in *The Palgrave Handbook of Women on Stage,* ed. By Jan Sewell and Clare Snout (Basingstoke: Palgrave Macmillan, 2020).

Deborah Geller, *The Brian Epstein Story* (London: Faber and Faber, 2000).

Jane Gerson, 'From Bola D'Amour to the Ultimate Cheesecake: 150 Years of Anglo-Jewish Cookery Writing', in: Hannah Ewence and Tony Kushner (eds.), *Whatever Happened to Jewish British Studies* (London: Vallentine Mitchell, 2012).

Ruth Gilbert, *Writing Jewish. Contemporary British-Jewish Literature* (Basingstoke: Palgrave Macmillan, 2013).

D. J. Golby, *Instrumental Teaching in Nineteenth Century Britain* (Aldershot: Ashgate, 2004).

Robert Gottlieb, *Sarah* (New Haven and London: Yale University Press, 2010).

Linda Grant, *Cast Iron Shore* (London: Granta, 1996).

Linda Grant, *The People on the Street: A Writer's View of Israel* (London: Virago, 2006).

John Haffenden, *Novelists in Interview* (London: Metheun, 1985).

Clare Hanson, *Hysterical Fictions. The Woman's Novel in the Twentieth Century* (London: Macmillan Press, 2000).

Sandy Harwitt, *The Greatest Jewish Tennis Players Of All Time* (New York: New Chapter Press, 2014).

May Henry and Edith B. Cohen, *The Economical Cook: A Modern Jewish Recipe Book for Housekeepers* (London: Werthheimer, Lea and Co., 1889).

Sally Hibbon, *What A Carry On* (London: Hamlyn, 1988).

D. Hildebrant, *Piano Forte. A Social History of the Piano* (London: Hutchison, 1988).

Andrew Hosken, *Nothing Like A Dame: The Scandals of Shirley Porter* (London: Granta Publications, 2006).

John S. Jansen, *Helen Shapiro – Pop Princess* (London: The New English Library Ltd, 1983).

Nick Johnstone, *Amy Amy Amy – The Amy Winehouse Story* (London: John Blake Publishing Ltd, 2011).

Heidi Kaufman, *Victorian Review*, Vol. 35 (1), 2009.

Olga Kenyon, *Women Novelists Today* (Brighton: Harvester Press, 1998).

Sorrel Kerbel (ed.), *Jewish Writers of the Twentieth Century* (London: Fitzroy Dearborn, 2003).

Vivi Lachs, *Whitechapel Noise* (Detroit, Michigan: Wayne State University Press, 2018).

Robert J. Lake, *A Social History of Tennis in Britain* (London: Routledge, 2015).

Colin Larkin (ed.), *The Virgin Encyclopedia of Popular Music* (London: Virgin, 1997).

Dorothy Levitt, *The Woman and the Car* (London: Hugh Evelyn Ltd, 1970).

Cheryl Alexander Malcolm, *Understanding Anita Brookner* (Columbia: University of South Carolina Press, 2002).

Alice Malin, 'Yiddish Theatre: Genre Blurring, Feminist Forgotten?' *Exeunt*, 21 October 2015.

Laura Mason, *Food Culture in Great Britain* (Westport, Conn: Greenwood Press, 2002).

David Mazower, *Yiddish Theatre in London* (London: Museum of the Jewish East End, 1987).

Marian C. McKenna, *Marion Hess* (London: Hamish Hamilton, 1976).

Simon Napier-Bell, *Black Vinyl White Powder* (London: Ebury Press, 2002).

Julia Neuberger, 'The Short Brilliant Life of Amy Levy', *Jewish Renaissance*, Autumn 2021, p. 32.

Chas Newkey-Burden, *Amy Winehouse: The Biography* (London: John Blake Publishing Ltd, 2011).

Lucy O'Brien, *She POP II. The Definitive History of Women in Rock, Pop and Soul* (London: Continium, 2002).

D. Rohr, 'Women and the Music Profession in Victorian England: The Royal Society of Female Musicians 1839-1866', *Journal of Musicological Research*, 18 (4), pp. 307-346.

Andrew Ross, *Carry on Actors* (Clacton on Sea: Apex Publishing Limited, 2011).

Sarah, *Aunt Sarah's Book for a Jewish Kitchen* (Liverpool: Yates and Hess, 1872).

Bruce Schoenfeld, *The Match. Althea Gibson and a Portrait of a Friendship* (New York: Harper Collins, 2004).

Elizabeth Selby, *Amy Winehouse: A Family Portrait* (London: Jewish Museum, 2014).

Gilly Smith, *Nigella Lawson* (London: Andre Deutsch, 2005).

Bob Stanley, *Yeah! Yeah! The Story of Pop Music from Bill Hayley to Beyonce* (London: Norton, 2015).

Jill Swale, 'Feminism and the Jewish Novel', *Jewish Quarterly*, 39 (3), Autumn 1992.

Claire Tylee, *In the Open. Jewish Women Writers and British Culture* (Newark: University of Delaware Press, 2006).

Harry Thompson, *Peter Cook: A Biography* (London: Hodder & Stoughton, 1997).

Nadia Valman, *The Jewess in Nineteenth Century British Literary Culture* (Cambridge: Cambridge University Press, 2007).

Nadia Valman (ed.), *Jewish Women Writers in Britain* (Detroit: Wayne State University Press, 2014).

Sheila van Damm, *No Excuses* (London: Oldhams Press Ltd, 1958).

Fanny Waterman, *My Life in Music* (London: Faber Music Ltd, 2015).

Bee Wilson, 'Kitchen Revolution: How Nigella Lawson Changed Food Writing', *Guardian*, 6 October 2013.

Mitch Winehouse, *Amy My Daughter* (London: Harper Collins, 2012).

Janis Winehouse, *Loving Amy: A Mother's Story* (London: Bantam Press, 2014).

Index

Note: The index covers people and places. References to notes are indicated by 'n' after the page number (225n51).

www.ingramcontent.com/pod-product-compliance
Ingram Content Group UK Ltd.
Pitfield, Milton Keynes, MK11 3LW, UK
UKHW030958260625
460105UK00001B/63